The Line of Beauty

The Line of Beauty

BRITISH DRAWINGS AND

WATERCOLORS OF THE

EIGHTEENTH

CENTURY

Scott Wilcox

Gillian Forrester

Morna O'Neill

Kim Sloan

YALE CENTER FOR BRITISH ART ∾ 2001

CONTRIBUTORS
The authors of the catalogue entries and biographies of
artists are identified by their initials:

GF   Gillian Forrester
RO   Rachel Oberter
MO   Morna O'Neill
ES   Eric Stryker
SW   Scott Wilcox

Published on the occasion of the exhibition
The Line of Beauty: British Drawings and Watercolors of the Eighteenth Century

Yale Center for British Art
New Haven, Connecticut
May 17 – September 2, 2001

ISBN 0-930606-95-7
Library of Congress Catalog Card Number 2001088718

Photography by Richard Caspole
Design by Lyn Bell Rose
Printed by Thames Printing Company, Norwich, Connecticut

front cover:
Thomas Rowlandson (1756-1827), *Georgiana, Duchess of Devonshire,
her sister Harriet, Viscountess Duncannon, and a Musician*, 1790 (detail, cat. 7)

below:
William Hogarth (1697-1764), *The Analysis of Beauty*, 1753,
(detail of title page; see fig. 4, p. 192), Paul Mellon Collection

 CONTENTS

The Yale Center for British Art's collection of drawings, watercolors, and prints is so comprehensive and attains such a high level of aesthetic and historical significance that it rivals the national collections held in Britain. Access to the collection can be easily obtained by any member of the University or the general public during the working week in one of the most beautiful and congenial study rooms in any museum. Sound and established conservation practices, however, dictate that the collection can be shown only in temporary exhibitions. To give some account of the richness and pleasure of the collection, the Center is embarking on a series of major exhibitions of which *The Line of Beauty* is the first. We deliberately chose Yale's Tercentennial Year to launch the series and to remind the University and the wider community of this exceptional aspect of Paul Mellon's activity as the greatest collector of British art in the second half of the twentieth century and the founder of the Yale Center for British Art. A preference for the immediately and freshly realized sketch was central to his taste, as was his penchant for the small-scale and the intimate in works of art. The fact that watercolor as a medium for important works of art is a distinctively British contribution no doubt played a part in Paul Mellon's enthusiastic and omnivorous collecting.

Although some fine and important watercolors were produced earlier, the eighteenth century saw the medium come into its own. The expansion of themes and subjects for art is particularly striking in eighteenth-century drawings and watercolors, with *The Line of Beauty* providing a vivid picture of eighteenth-century life and enlightenment attitudes. The clear sense of the eighteenth century as a rapidly expanding universe is here demonstrated comprehensively and luminously. Science and nature in many different guises and forms; the built environment including both ancient monuments and modern cityscapes; travel within the British Isles and on the continent of Europe, and beyond – all these and more become subjects for art and have shaped the thematic presentation of our exhibition.

The practice of art similarly expanded in eighteenth-century Britain, specifically with regard to watercolors and drawings. It became the province of the talented amateur as well as the trained professional. Sketching in watercolor and other media became an attribute of gentility and cultivation. The rise of the amateur equally signaled the proliferation of the artist's manual. These books of instruction, so richly represented in the Center's collection of rare books, gave to the art of drawing a social as well as an artistic dimension.

These and other themes diversify and enrich our view of eighteenth-century British watercolors and drawings. Aesthetic delight will always play a significant part in the appreciation of these arresting sheets. But delight, reinforced by knowledge of the artistic and social context, can only deepen into a new understanding. Such, we hope, will be the effect of this exhibition and its catalogue.

I wish to acknowledge the exceptional effort made by Scott Wilcox and Gillian Forrester, respectively Curator and Assistant Curator of Prints and Drawings at the Yale Center for British Art, in the creation of this exhibition and catalogue. The contributions of the department's three Curatorial Assistants, Adrianna Bates, Martha Buck, and Alice Steinhardt, were equally critical in the preparation of the exhibition. Elisabeth Fairman, Curator of Rare Books, played a central role in the selection of artists' manuals, and we are most grateful to Kim Sloan, Curator of British Drawings and Watercolours in the Department of Prints and Drawings at the British Museum, for her distinguished contribution to the catalogue.

Our Duncan Robinson Fellow, Katherine Roach, made an important contribution to this exhibition in the summer of 2000. Morna O'Neill, Paul Mellon Centre doctoral student and Curatorial Intern in the Department of Prints and Drawings, was a key player in the creation of the exhibition and catalogue. Two other graduate students, Rachel Oberter and Eric Stryker, wrote artists' biographies. We are grateful to all these Yale students for their participation. The authors would also like to thank Christy Anderson, Elizabeth Barker, Charles Beddington, Judy Egerton, John Ingamells, Anne Lyles, and Jill Springall for providing information and assistance.

The Yale Center for British Art is delighted to offer *The Line of Beauty: British Drawings and Watercolors of the Eighteenth Century* as one of its chief offerings in the celebration of Yale's Tercentennial.

PATRICK McCAUGHEY

Thomas Lawrence,
William Lock II of Norbury Park, Surrey,
c. 1800 (cat. 13)

 *"Emanations of Genius"*

William Hogarth's *The Analysis of Beauty. Written with a View of Fixing the Fluctuating Ideas of Taste* (1753) was part of a lifelong campaign to wrest control of art from the connoisseurs and the picture dealers and return it to his fellow artists. His little treatise attempted to show that the aesthetic means by which the Old Masters had achieved greatness were not an arcane mystery but simple commonsense principles discoverable in everyday nature as well as in the rarefied precincts of high art. Empowered by this knowledge, the modern artist was ready to take his place alongside the masters of the past.

At the heart of Hogarth's *Analysis* was the S-shaped "line of beauty," which he reproduced on his title page. Though Hogarth did not discuss drawing as such in the *Analysis*, his characterization of this fundamental "line of beauty" makes clear that its power is associated with the art of drawing. For Hogarth, the line "being composed of two curves contrasted, becomes still more ornamental and pleasing, insomuch that the hand takes a lively movement in making it with pen or pencil." That the evidence of the movement of the artist's hand is in itself a source of pleasure lies behind the appeal of the drawing as a work of art.

The response to *The Analysis of Beauty* was mixed. Predictably, those who sought to uphold the preeminence of the Old Masters and an academic approach to art dismissed and ridiculed it. Charles Rogers, a connoisseur and collector of Old Master drawings, wrote of Hogarth's book: "The Unlearned confess they are not instructed, and the Learned declare they are not improved by it." *The Analysis of Beauty* was, nevertheless, symptomatic of the changing role of art and the artist in a society that was itself undergoing far-reaching changes. In the transformation of the artist from "mechanic" to creative genius, drawing played a key role. It was at the heart of an artist's training (whether that training was purely practical and utilitarian or part of a liberal academic education), it was central to his practice, and, as the status of the artist increased, it was valued increasingly as the purest expression of the artist's genius.

Joshua Reynolds ended his first *Discourse*, delivered as President of the Royal Academy at the institution's opening in 1769, with an encomium on drawing, that is, drawing as the preparation for painting or as a means of study. Citing the practice of "the most eminent Painters," he observed that "when they conceived a subject, they first made a variety of sketches; then a finished drawing of the whole; after that a more correct drawing of every part, – heads, hands, feet, and pieces of drapery." Speaking to the students who would be following the academic discipline of a course of drawing first from casts of the antique and then from the living figure, Reynolds remarked: "He who endeavours to copy nicely the figure before him not only acquires a habit of exactness and precision, but is continually advancing in his knowledge of the human figure." There is nothing in the first *Discourse* about the beauty or the value of drawings as works of art in themselves. Reynolds himself was not a particularly accomplished draftsman, though he did assemble a significant collection of Old Master drawings. In his second *Discourse*, given to the Royal Academy students at the distribution of prizes at the end of 1769, he returned to the subject of the importance of drawing yet qualified it: "But while I mention the porte-crayon as the student's constant companion, he must still remember, that the pencil [meaning, in its eighteenth-century sense, paintbrush] is the instrument by which he must hope to obtain eminence."

In the *Discourses* Reynolds treated drawing as a crucial tool for the artist but ignored the drawing as an aesthetic object. Yet the collecting of Old Master drawings was avidly pursued both by artists, who could benefit from the lessons about composition and modeling these drawings could impart, and by connoisseurs, who prized their direct evidence of a master's hand. In addition to Joshua Reynolds, many of the artists represented in this exhibition – Jonathan Richardson, Paul Sandby, Richard Cosway, and Thomas Lawrence – had distinguished collections of drawings by the Old Masters. Richardson in *An Essay on the Theory of Painting* (1715) suggested that to the man of taste the drawing might speak more directly and eloquently of an artist's true genius than would an oil painting. Writing of preliminary drawings by the Old Masters, he noted:

> These are exceedingly priz'd by all who understand, and can see their Beauty; for they are the very Spirit, and Quintessence of the Art; there we see the Steps the Master took, the Materials with which he made his finish'd Paintings, which are little other than Copies of these, and frequently (at least in part) by some other Hand; but these are undoubtedly altogether his Own, and true, and proper Originals.

In *An Essay on the Whole Art of Criticism as It Relates to Painting*, one of the *Two Discourses* that Richardson published in 1719, he reiterated the idea that drawings give access to the creative process in a way that paintings, further removed either from the artist's direct observation or from his original inspiration, could not:

> Drawings (generally speaking) are Preferrable to Paintings, as having those Qualities which are most Excellent in a Higher Degree than Paintings generally have, or can possibly have, and the Others (excepting only Colouring) Equally with them. There is a Grace, a Delicacy, a Spirit in Drawings which when the Master attempts to give in Colours is commonly much diminish'd both as being a sort of Coppying from those First Thoughts, and because the Nature of the Thing admits of no better.

When Charles Rogers published *A Collection of Prints in Imitation of Drawings* in 1778, he could write of the centrality of drawing as a critical commonplace:

> As the best Writers on Painting, Sculpture, &c. have been lavish in their Panegyrics on Drawings, it would be superfluous for me to expatiate on their Merits and Service: for it must be unquestionably allowed that Drawing is the Fountain from which all the imitative Arts have issued; and that none of his Branches can appear with any beauty, without their being generously supported by this Head of a very numerous Progeny.

The drawings that Rogers reproduced were by the Old Masters. (Michael Rysbrack is the only draftsman in this exhibition whom Rogers included in his compilation.) As the efforts of both academically minded artist/polemicists such as Richardson and Reynolds and staunch anti-academicians such as Hogarth bore fruit in the advancing status of British artists, the same arguments that Richardson had made for the value of Old Master drawings could be seen to apply to drawings by modern British artists. Thus Paul Sandby could collect drawings by his contemporaries William Taverner and Richard Wilson, and artists such as Wilson, in his series of drawings for the Earl of Dartmouth (see cat. 98), or Richard Cosway, in his mythological and religious drawings (see cat. 40), could quite self-consciously follow the tradition of the Old Master presentation drawing. For, as Richardson pointed out,

> In Drawings one finds a great Variety, from their being First Thoughts, (which often are very Slight, but Spirituous Scrabbles) or more Advanced, or Finish'd. So some are done one Way, some Another; a Pen, Chalks, Washes of all Colours; heightened with White, Wet, or Dry, or not Heightened.

This variety of function, finish, and media gave the artist tremendous scope and a certain freedom. As British artists reshaped traditional genres and pioneered new ones, drawing allowed a degree of experimentation that might be suspect in the more circumscribed realm of painting. For Thomas Gainsborough, the drawings that he made for his own pleasure allowed him to indulge fully a taste for landscape and an adventurous use of materials and techniques that would have been deemed inappropriate in his oil paintings. The distinction between what was acceptable in drawings and in paintings is clear in the comment on Gainsborough's landscape drawings by his friend William Jackson:

> No man ever possessed methods so various in producing effect, and all excellent – his washy, hatching style, was here in its proper element. The subject which is scarce enough, for a picture, is sufficient for a drawing, and the hasty loose handling, which in painting is poor, is rich in a transparent wash of bistre and Indian ink.

Because the drawing was less of an investment in time and effort than a painting, was more personal, and was generally – with the exception of presentation drawings – less public, an artist was free to take greater liberties. That is not to say that drawings were inconsequential. Following Richardson's line, they could be the finest expression of an artistic spirit. Henry Angelo, another friend of the artist, gave his own account of Gainsborough's drawing methods:

He had all the kitchen saucers in requisition; these were filled with warm and cold tints, and, dipping the sponges in these, he mopped away on cartridge paper, thus preparing the masses, or general contours and effects; and drying them by the fire (for he was as impatient as a spoiled child waiting for a new toy), he touched them into character, with black, red, and white chalks.

Some of these moppings, and grubbings, and hatchings, wherein he had taken unusual pains, are such emanations of genius and picturesque feeling, as no artist perhaps ever conceived, and certainly such as no one ever surpassed.

Like Gainsborough, Thomas Lawrence was a portrait painter known for the bravura and elegance of his portraits in oils, who also enjoyed a reputation as a spirited and sensitive draftsman. Lawrence's charcoal-on-canvas portrait of William Lock (cat. 13) celebrates the brilliance of Lawrence's draftsmanship, as something not to be relegated to the portfolio but framed and hung on the wall as the equivalent of a painted portrait.

D rawing was an integral part of the concept of the artist as a creative genius and was therefore associated with the rising esteem and social standing of artists through the century. Drawing also retained less serious and humbler associations: as the polite accomplishment of gentlemen and gentlewomen of taste, as a useful practical skill to be acquired by mechanics and tradesmen, and as the means of documenting an expanding world through the efforts of topographical draftsmen. These areas too had their own trajectories of advancement.

Amateur drawing, long ignored as a subject for serious study, has been admirably covered in two recent publications: Ann Bermingham's *Learning to Draw: Studies in the Cultural History of a Polite and Useful Art* (2000) and Kim Sloan's *"A Noble Art": Amateur Artists and Drawing Masters, c. 1600-1800* (2000). Drawing as a fashionable pastime for gentlemen and, increasingly as the century progressed, gentlewomen, generated a small industry in drawing masters, the production of drawing manuals and drawing materials. This flourishing amateur activity promoted and was a part of a culture of drawing that embraced professional practice as well. Indeed, the line between amateur and professional could be blurred, as in the case of the lawyer William Taverner, whose work was admired by professional artists and whose signifi-

cance in the development of landscape art was widely acknowledged.

Descending from the polite to the practical, one finds the architect John Gwynn publishing an *Essay on Design* in 1749 in which he proposed an academy "for Educating the British Youth in Drawing," asserting that "there is scarce any Mechanic, let his Employment be ever so simple, who may not receive advantage" from being able to draw. Five years later the artist William Shipley founded the Society for the Encouragement of Arts, Manufactures and Commerce, which in its early years shared premises in the Strand with Shipley's drawing school. The Society offered premiums for practical and commercial inventions and improvements but also offered, as the minutes of its first meeting recorded, "Rewards for the Encouragement of Boys and Girls in the Art of Drawing ... it being the opinion of all present that the Art of Drawing is absolutely necessary in many Employments, Trades, and Manufactures, and that the Encouragement thereof may prove of great Utility to the Public." In advertising his drawing school, Shipley undertook "to introduce Boys and Girls of Genius to Masters and Mistresses in such Manufactures as require Fancy and Ornament, and for which the Knowledge of Drawing is absolutely necessary."

Not all of Shipley's pupils went into the trades and manufacturing. Richard Cosway and William Pars both studied with Shipley, and Thomas Jones came up to Shipley's school from Wales in 1761, after the running of the establishment had been taken over by William Pars and his elder brother Henry Pars. Within a few years William Pars would accompany Richard Chandler as topographical draftsman on his expedition to record the classical antiquities of Asia Minor, and in 1775, as the recipient of a scholarship from the Society of Dilettanti, he would go to Rome to study. Jones would go on to join the studio of Richard Wilson and make his way to Italy in 1776.

The watercolors that Pars made of Asia Minor and that he and Jones made together in Italy in the 1770s belong to a tradition of topographical drawing with roots extending back through the seventeenth century. Working for the military, for antiquaries, for noblemen, recording their travels abroad or their possessions at home, topographical draftsmen provided valuable practical records of cities and country, monuments and natural curiosities.

As vehicles for conveying information, their drawings needed to be clear and precise. The combination of pen outlines with monochrome ink washes or pale washes of watercolor, known at the time as "stained" or "tinted" drawings, was ideally suited to the informational requirements of the genre. When the naturalist Gilbert White employed Samuel Hieronymous Grimm to produce illustrations for his *Natural History and Antiquities of Selborne*, White described Grimm's working method, which followed this standard practice:

> He first of all sketches his scapes with a lead pencil; then he pens them all over, as he calls it, with Indian ink, rubbing out the superfluous pencil strokes; then he gives a charming shading with a brush dipped in Indian ink; and last he throws a light tinge of water-colours over the whole. The scapes, many of them at least, looked so lovely in their Indian-ink shading that it was with difficulty the artist could prevail on me to permit him to tinge them.

Though White thought the addition of watercolor unnecessary, it was in that very use of color that the topographical drawing was developing and would eventually break free of the bounds of the "stained" drawing. In the hands of topographical draftsmen such as William Pars and his contemporaries John "Warwick" Smith, John Robert Cozens, Thomas Hearne, and Michael "Angelo" Rooker, the underlying gray wash modeling began to be replaced by modeling directly in color, and the pen outline receded before the more atmospheric touches of the watercolor brush. The shift from drawing in watercolors to painting in watercolors was underway, and the practitioners were shedding their lowly status as topographical draftsmen to become landscape painters in watercolors.

From 1760, when the Society of Artists inaugurated annual public exhibitions (to be followed by the exhibitions of the Free Society and the Royal Academy), watercolors appeared on the walls of the galleries along with oils. This public display helped the watercolorists, most of whom were essentially topographers, to demonstrate that watercolor painting could have the richness and visual heft of oil painting. Their efforts culminated in the establishment in the early nineteenth century of the watercolor societies. That they should, in naming the organization they founded in 1804 the Society of Painters in Water-Colours, call themselves painters rather than draftsmen was both a bid for status and a recognition that the nature of the practice of watercolor

had changed. Of course, the changes were not simply limited to matters of technique; the watercolor painting, even if it had as its subject the appearance of a particular place, could be as poetic and as expressive of genius as an Old Master painting – or drawing.

It is not surprising that the development of landscape painting in watercolors should be represented with force and depth in the collections with which Paul Mellon endowed the Yale Center for British Art. Mr. Mellon acknowledged that his collecting of British art had roots in a love of the English countryside formed in childhood. Yet the acquisition of drawings and watercolors came relatively late in his collecting. In the 1930s and 1940s he purchased paintings and illustrated books in, as he put it, "a desultory way." His more serious collecting of British art began with his meeting of Basil Taylor in 1959. According to Mr. Mellon: "It was he who opened up my eyes to the beauty and freshness of English drawings and water-colors, their immediacy and sureness of technique, their comprehensiveness of subject matter, their vital qualities, their Englishness."

In 1961 Basil Taylor recommended that Mr. Mellon purchase Martin Hardie's collection of British watercolors. Hardie, who had been Keeper of Prints and Drawings at the Victoria and Albert Museum, was one of the key figures in a generation of collector/scholars who pioneered the study of British draftsmanship and watercolor painting. In addition to acquiring his collection, Mr. Mellon also underwrote the editing and publication between 1966 and 1968 of Hardie's magnum opus, *Watercolour Painting in Britain*, left unfinished at his death. It remains an important reference on the subject. Acquisitions of large important groups of drawings and watercolors from collections put together by others of that pioneering generation followed. Between the early 1960s and 1973, Mr. Mellon purchased drawings from the collection of Leonard G. Duke. In 1964 he added drawings from the collection of Iolo Williams, whose 1952 book *Early English Watercolours* had helped to define the field. After Mr. Mellon made the decision to give his British collections to Yale and to establish a center for their display and study, he acquired in 1970 drawings from Thomas Girtin, the descendant of the artist, who had added significantly to the collection of drawings that had passed down in his family. The scholarly and collecting interests of Girtin, Williams, and Hardie certainly contributed to the concentration on the landscape watercolor in the Mellon collection. The acquisition in 1963 of drawings from the collection of the artist Thomas Edmond Lowinsky, rich in figural subjects, helped to give the collection balance.

It would be misleading to suggest that the Mellon collection is simply the aggregate of the distinguished collections that he purchased. With the advice and assistance of Dudley Snelgrove, John Baskett, and (in the area of architectural drawing) John Harris, Mr. Mellon enriched, expanded, and personalized the collection, with an eye to the scholarly institutional requirement that it be as representative and comprehensive as possible and, at the same time, with a decided taste and keen enjoyment guiding his purchases. The outstanding collections he amassed of works by William Blake and Thomas Rowlandson testify to his eclecticism as well as his personal enthusiasm for these two very different artists. Three other significant purchases – of the archive of the Scottish explorer James Bruce, including the botanical and natural-history drawings by his draftsman Luigi Balugani (see cats. 60-3), of archaeological drawings of Giovanni Battista Borra (cats. 59, 97, and 118), and of the comparative anatomical studies by one of Mr. Mellon's favorites, George Stubbs (cats. 64-8) – give a sense of the range of Mr. Mellon's interests and his intellectual curiosity.

This exhibition is a celebration of the richness and variety of the Mellon collection of works on paper and a tribute to the perspicacity and vision of Paul Mellon, his advisers, and those enthusiasts for British drawings on whose work – as both collectors and scholars – this collection was built. The collection is not static. Since the opening of the Center in 1977, the curators have made a number of important acquisitions (with funds generously provided by Paul Mellon). These include the Rowlandson *Place des Victoires* (cat. 86), the Lawrence *William Lock II of Norbury Park* (cat. 13), and most recently the Loutherbourg *Figures by a Stream with Cattle Watering* (cat. 50). Perhaps even more significantly the collection has been the beneficiary of a number of gifts. In 1962 Mr. and Mrs. J. Richardson Dilworth gave their extraordinary collection of 685 drawings by George Romney to Yale; they were transferred from the University Art Gallery to the Center in 1979. Over the past fourteen years Ann and Kenneth Rapoport have added substantially to the holdings of eighteenth-century miniatures. And in 2000 Paul Walter, with his gift of 176 working drawings by Thomas and William Daniell from their travels in India, immeasurably enriched the already strong representation of work by eighteenth-century British topographical artists abroad. To all our generous donors, this exhibition is gratefully dedicated.

SCOTT WILCOX

"A True and Legible Representation of the Mind"
THE PORTRAIT DRAWING

I N 1755 ANDRÉ ROUQUET, a French enamellist working in London, marveled at "how fond the English are of having their portraits drawn," noting that "peoples fortunes are more upon a level in England than any other country." Increased prosperity, the evolution of a middle class, and the introduction of public exhibition spaces all contributed to the expansion of the market for portraits; the demand for portrait drawings, which were less costly than paintings and more appropriate in scale for bourgeois homes, was correspondingly high. Versatile portrait draftsmen worked within a wide range of genres, including the new forms of the conversation piece and theatrical portrait, and used diverse media, such as graphite, watercolor, gouache, and pastel, often combining these materials with innovative eclecticism.

Portraiture occupied a lowly position in the accepted hierarchy of the visual arts, and its practitioners (many of whom aspired to be history or landscape painters, but were forced into their field by financial necessity) were constantly seeking to improve the status of their genre. One of their most pervasive strategies was to argue that portraiture was a kind of history painting, the visual equivalent of biography. The portrait painter Jonathan Richardson was one of the most eloquent and influential proponents of this view. In his seminal *Essay on the Theory of Painting* (1715) Richardson argued that the "great business" of painting was "to relate a history or fable as the best historians or poets have done ... to do justice to a portrait and reveal the mind as well as the visual appearance," and claimed that "to sit for one's Picture, is to have an Abstract of one's Life written, and published, and ourselves thus consign'd over to Honour, or Infamy."

Despite their attempts to elevate the genre, portraitists invariably found themselves working under considerable aesthetic constraints and intense commercial pressures. Running a successful portrait practice demanded a range of skills in addition to the obvious requirement of being able to make a good (or at least flattering) likeness of a sitter, including business acumen, social connections, tact, and diplomacy. Sir Thomas Lawrence's lament that "I begin to be really uneasy at finding myself so harnessed and shackled into this dry mill-horse business" was commonplace among his fellow "phiz-mongers."

Portrait drawings of this period often have a freshness and informality lacking in large-scale painted portraits, and these qualities can be found in Lawrence's own vivid and economical drawing of William Lock (cat. 13). Portrait painters seldom made preparatory studies of their sitters (Allan Ramsay is a rare exception; see cat. 3), but they often drew for recreation and pleasure. Several of the drawings included in this catalogue – such as Jonathan Richardson's penetrating self-portrait and portrait of his friend Sir Hans Sloane (cats. 1-2), and George Dance's delicate profile of an unknown sitter (cat. 14) – clearly belong to this category and provide insights into the private lives of eighteenth-century artists.

GILLIAN FORRESTER

1

JONATHAN RICHARDSON
THE ELDER (1665-1745)

I

Sir Hans Sloane, 1740

Graphite on vellum;
5 15/16 x 4 5/16 in. (15.1 x 11.0 cm)

Inscribed, lower right, with stamp of
Jonathan Richardson the Younger
(Lugt 2170); in graphite, on verso: *Sr Hans
Sloane | 10 Sep 1740*; with stamp of artist,
on verso (Lugt 2184)

PROVENANCE: The artist; by descent
to Jonathan Richardson the Younger,
Queen's Square, Bloomsbury, London;
...; E. A. Heather, Esq.; sold Christie's,
4 June 1974 (22), bt Paul Mellon
through John Baskett

SELECTED EXHIBITIONS: YCBA, *English
Portrait Drawings*, 1979-80, no. 33

SELECTED LITERATURE: Gibson-Wood,
1994, p. 214; Gibson-Wood, 2000,
pp. 123-4

Paul Mellon Collection
B1977.14.4206

2

Self-Portrait, c. 1733

Black, red and white chalk on blue
paper; 18 5/16 x 12 1/2 in. (46.5 x 31.8 cm)

Inscribed in red chalk, lower right:
Quod adest componere; in pen and brown
ink, lower left: *EP*; in pen and brown
ink, upper left: *E1740*; artist's stamp,
center right (Lugt 2184); stamp of
Edward Peart, bottom left (Lugt 891);
in an 18th-century hand in pen and
brown ink, verso: *Jon. Richardson Jun |
by himself*; in graphite, verso: *116-/5*

PROVENANCE: The artist; Daniel
Daulby; sold Vernon, Liverpool, 12
August 1799 (116); Dr. Edward Peart,
sold Christie's, 22 April 1822 (probably
in 136), bt Lyall; Hon. Sir Albert Napier;
Mrs. Philip English, sold Christie's,
5 March 1974 (86), bt Paul Mellon
through John Baskett

SELECTED EXHIBITIONS: YCBA, *English
Portrait Drawings*, 1979-80, no. 31

Paul Mellon Collection
B1977.14.4333

JONATHAN RICHARDSON was a
highly successful portrait painter,
collector, and art theorist, whose
pioneering writings were extremely
influential throughout Europe,
inspiring artists as diverse as
Reynolds and Delacroix. Richardson
was a keen if not obsessive draftsman, and, having amassed a considerable fortune, he devoted much of
the last fifteen years of his life to
drawing portraits of himself, his
family, and his friends. Generally
executed in graphite on vellum or
blue paper, these finished drawings
have a vivacity and sensitivity often
lacking in Richardson's painted portraits. (Horace Walpole remarked,

not without justification, that the artist "drew nothing well below the head and was void of imagination.") More than five hundred of these portrait drawings remained in the family's possession until the death of Richardson's eldest son, Jonathan, in 1771, and it seems likely that the artist made them exclusively for personal, commemorative purposes.

In his *Essay on the Theory of Painting* (1715), Richardson argued that "a Portrait is a sort of General History of the Life of the Person it represents, not only to Him who is acquainted with it, but to Many Others." The artist's creation of a private gallery of self-portraits (which depict Richardson at different stages in his life) and portraits of those close to him could be read as a process of constructing a personal history, or visual autobiography. A drawing by Richardson of his beloved son Jonathan in the Center's collection shares the same provenance with cat. 2 back to the eighteenth century, and the two drawings may have been conceived as companion pieces commemorating the affectionate relationship between father and son. All the sitters Richardson drew had personal significance to him, including his friend Sir Hans Sloane (1660-1753), the physician and natural historian whose extraordinary collection of books, manuscripts, prints, and coins formed the basis of the British Museum. GF

2

3

ALLAN RAMSAY (1713-84)

Head of a Young Woman

Black and white chalk on blue laid paper; 12⁷⁄₁₆ x 10⁷⁄₁₆ in. (31.6 x 26.5 cm)

Collector's stamp of Thomas Lowinsky (Lugt 2420a), below left

PROVENANCE: ...; Thomas Lowinsky (1892-1947); Justin Lowinsky, 1963, from whom bt Paul Mellon

SELECTED EXHIBITIONS: PML, *English Drawings*, 1972, no. 24

Paul Mellon Collection
B1977.14.6046

THE SCOTTISH PAINTER and writer Allan Ramsay grew up in Edinburgh and attended the Academy of St. Luke, where his teachers included the engraver Richard Cooper (see cat. 5). After further studies in London and Rome Ramsay set up as a portrait painter in London in 1738; within a year he became "the most imployed in ye portrait way of any" and was particularly favored by the Scottish nobility. Ramsay was praised from early in his career for his "delicate and Genteel" portrayals of women. In his theoretical essay *A Dialogue on Taste* (1755) Ramsay identified "naturalness" as a highly desirable quality in art, and his adoption in the mid-1750s of the more "natural" and refined style which he admired in the French pastellist Maurice-Quentin de la Tour brought him further renown as a painter of women. As Horace Walpole noted in 1759, "Mr Reynolds seldom succeeds in women: Mr Ramsay is formed to paint them."

Ramsay drew extensively, unusually for a British portrait painter of this period; a large number of preparatory studies for paintings survive (see cat. 153), and he also produced some highly-finished and exquisite portrait drawings. Cat. 3 is one of a group of drawings by Ramsay on blue paper in the Center's collection which formerly belonged to the British collector Thomas Lowinsky (1892-1947). It is not known to be related to a painting, and the sitter has not been identified, but the features are similar to those of Ramsay's second wife, Margaret Lindsay, whom he painted and drew on several occasions. The informality of this delicate sketch and the directness of the sitter's gaze imply that the sitter was someone close to Ramsay, if not Margaret Lindsay herself.

G F

4

Attributed to PRINCE HOARE
THE YOUNGER (1755-1834)

Head of a Young Girl, c. 1780

Graphite, red and black chalk on laid
paper; 6⅞ x 4¼ in. (17.5 x 10.8 cm)

Inscribed in graphite, lower left:
Prince Hoare, fect

PROVENANCE: ...; Leonard G. Duke;
sold to Spencer, March 1935; ...;
Colnaghi, from whom bt Paul Mellon,
1961

Paul Mellon Collection
B1977.14.5050

THIS DELICATE STUDY was attributed
to Prince Hoare the Younger by its
former owner, Leonard G. Duke, the
distinguished collector of British
drawings. The son of the portrait
painter and pastellist William Hoare
(1707-92), and nephew of his name-
sake, the sculptor Prince Hoare
the Elder (c. 1711-69), the younger
Prince Hoare is best known for the
neoclassical figure drawings he produced during his association with
the Fuseli circle in the 1770s. Hoare
showed an aptitude for drawing
from an early age and entered the
Royal Academy Schools in 1773.
He traveled to Italy in 1776, visiting
first Florence and then settling in
Rome, where he was to spend the
next three years. On his return to
England in 1780, Hoare exhibited
portraits and history paintings at
the Royal Academy, but he abandoned painting in 1785, avowedly
for reasons of "delicacy of health."
Hoare confided in his friend Joseph
Farington that "he acquitted the
profession because he could not

succeed in that practice as he
wished," but his surviving works
nonetheless indicate that Hoare was
an accomplished draftsman and
portrait painter.

The subject has never been identified, nor has the drawing been
securely dated. The cap worn by the
young woman indicates a date of
the late 1770s, and Hoare may have
made the drawing in Italy. During

his stay in Rome Hoare fell in love
with the talented and attractive
painter Maria Hadfield, who later
married Richard Cosway (see cats.
19-20 and 40). The features of the
sitter resemble Maria's, and it is
tempting to speculate that this study
commemorates this romantic
episode. G F

19

form of drawing was capable of considerable refinement and tonal subtlety in the hands of a skilled practitioner. Jonathan Richardson's portrait of Sir Hans Sloane (cat. 1) is another example of this genre, though the drawing is less highly finished than Donaldson's.

The little-known miniaturist John Donaldson was born in Edinburgh; he showed early promise and, after being awarded premiums by the Edinburgh Society of Arts in 1757 and 1758, moved to London to develop his career. Donaldson exhibited portrait miniatures of Richard Cooper in London at the Free Society and the Society of Artists in 1762 and 1764, and cat. 5 may have been exhibited on one or both occasions. The drawing presumably was made in Edinburgh before Donaldson's departure for London. Cooper, who studied art in Italy in his youth and was an accomplished draftsman, is depicted, pencil in hand, pausing in the act of making a figure study rather than in his professional capacity as an engraver. GF

5

JOHN DONALDSON (1737-1801)

Richard Cooper the Elder

Graphite on vellum; 10¼ x 8½ in. (26.0 x 21.0 cm)

PROVENANCE: ...; Colnaghi, from whom bt Paul Mellon, 1987

SELECTED EXHIBITIONS: Possibly Free Society, London, 1762, no. 148; possibly Society of Artists, London, 1764, no. 32

Paul Mellon Fund
B1987.4

JOHN DONALDSON's portrait of the Edinburgh engraver Richard Cooper (d. 1764) is of the kind of monochrome miniature drawing first introduced in England from the Continent in the seventeenth century. The graphite drawing on vellum, or plumbago, as it became known, was developed as a cheaper alternative to the miniature and could also be used readily as a model for engraving. The plumbago was popular throughout the first half of the eighteenth century, and as Donaldson's miniature shows, this rather austere

6

Attributed to
FRANÇOIS-XAVIER VISPRÉ
(fl. 1730-90)

Louis-François Roubiliac,
c. 1760

Pastel on paper laid onto canvas;
24½ x 21½ in. (62.2 x 54.6 cm)

PROVENANCE: Louis-François
Roubiliac; by descent to his great-great-
grandson, François Roubiliac Conder,
1870; his daughter, 1928; ...; anon. sale,
Christie's, 20 March 1953 (53 as by
Maurice-Quentin De la Tour); ...; David
Drey, London, 1976; Cyril Humphris,
from whom bt Paul Mellon, November
1976

SELECTED EXHIBITIONS: Possibly
Society of Artists, London, 1760, no. 63;
YCBA, *English Portrait Drawings*, 1979-
80, no. 51

SELECTED LITERATURE: *The Art
Journal*, 1870, p. 259; Esdaile, 1928,
pp. 180-90; Johnson, 1976, no. 82;
Kerslake, 1977, vol. I, p. 238; vol. II,
fig. 697; Murdoch, 1983, p. 42, pl. VI

Paul Mellon Collection
B1977.14.132

THE FRENCH-BORN HUGUENOT
sculptor Louis-François Roubiliac
(1702-62) settled in London around
1730. Roubiliac "met with small
encouragement at first," but his celebrated statue of George Frideric
Handel for Vauxhall Gardens established his reputation as the foremost sculptor of the English rococo
movement. Renowned for his vivid
portrait busts and theatrical large-
scale funerary monuments,
Roubiliac eclipsed his contemporaries, and only his older rival

Michael Rysbrack (see cat. 152)
enjoyed such high public estimation.
One of his best-known and most
influential sitters, Lord Chesterfield,
opined: "Roubiliac only was a statuary, the rest stone-cutters."

In this eloquent portrait drawing
Roubiliac is depicted with his sculptor's calipers in hand, deep in con-
templation or awaiting inspiration.
The terra-cotta sculpture on which
Roubiliac thoughtfully leans bears
some resemblance to the head of the
Britannia figure in the sculptor's 1753
monument to Admiral Sir Peter
Warren in Westminster Abbey; it was
also described as a head of Medusa
by a nineteenth-century reviewer –
an appropriate emblem for a portrait
of a sculptor, whose occupation is to
transform living features into stone.

The portrait has been attributed
recently to François-Xavier Vispré,
a fellow-Huguenot and close friend
and neighbor of Roubiliac. Although
stylistic comparison with known
works by Vispré has not been conclusive, circumstantial detail makes the
attribution seem very likely. Vispré
exhibited a pastel of Roubiliac at the
Society of Artists in London in 1760,
and this may have been cat. 6. The
exhibited portrait made a powerful
impression on the reviewer of the
*Imperial Magazine, or Complete
Monthly Intelligencer,* whose en-
thralled account suggests at least
affinities with the Center's drawing:
"the man himself alive, breathing
and just going to speak; most
admirable! and himself never in
marble cut a better." GF

7

THOMAS ROWLANDSON
(1756-1827)

Georgiana, Duchess of Devonshire, her sister Harriet, Viscountess Duncannon (later the Countess of Bessborough) and a Musician, 1790

Pen and ink and watercolor over graphite on wove paper; 19⅝ x 16⅞ in. (49.9 x 42.9 cm)

Signed and dated, lower left: *Rowlandson – 1790*

PROVENANCE: George, 5th Duke of Gordon (1770-1836); by descent to William Brodie of Brodie; with Agnew, London, from whom purchased by Paul Mellon, 1963

SELECTED EXHIBITIONS: YCBA, *Pursuit of Happiness,* 1977, no. 66; YCBA, *Rowlandson Drawings,* 1977-8, no. 23; Frick, *Rowlandson,* 1990, no. 47

SELECTED LITERATURE: Hayes, 1972, pp. 138-9, pl. 175; Sutton, 1977, pp. 282-3, fig. 18; Baskett and Snelgrove, 1977, p. 65, no. 260; Ribeiro, 1984, no. 138, p. 125

Paul Mellon Collection
B1975.3.141

THOMAS ROWLANDSON'S popular reputation as a perceptive and gently mocking – if rarely overtly satirical – commentator on eighteenth-century social life has tended to detract from our appreciation of his extraordinary talents as a draftsman and colorist. Rowlandson's lively portrait of the two celebrated socialites, Georgiana, Duchess of Devonshire (1757-1806), and her sister Harriet (1761-1821), demonstrates the refinement and facility characteristic of his drawing style, qualities which are all the more remarkable given his prodigious output (the Center alone owns more than four hundred watercolors by Rowlandson).

Georgiana, Duchess of Devonshire, epitomized the extravagant *modus operandi* of the aristocracy in late eighteenth-century England. Married at the age of seventeen to William, 5th Duke of Devonshire, she became a celebrated society hostess, renowned for her cutting-edge sartorial sense and notorious for her love-affairs and unregenerate addiction to gaming. Georgiana also played an influential role in political life with her active promotion of the Whig cause. Her mother once remarked caustically: "Without being handsome or having a single feature in her face [she is] one of the most showy girls I ever saw," but like her sister Harriet, Georgiana was considered a great beauty, and the two women's legendary vivacity and charm are vividly conveyed in Rowlandson's drawing. Georgiana, who is depicted holding a sheet of music, seems to have been a talented musician; she played the harp, and in 1799 the song she wrote for Richard Brinsley Sheridan's tragedy *Pizarro* became a success in its own right. The sisters also appear prominently in Rowlandson's evocation of fashionable life, *Vauxhall Gardens* (cat. 87). GF

8

JOHN DOWNMAN (1750-1824)

John Edwin and Mrs. Mary Wells, as Lingo and Cowslip in "The Agreeable Surprise," 1787

Watercolor, gouache and black chalk with stump on thin laid paper; 16¼ x 12⅝ in. (41.3 x 32.1 cm), irregular edges

Signed and dated in black chalk, lower right: *J. Downman | 1787*; in pen and brown ink, on a paper label attached to the back of the original frame: *For this Drawing | Georgiana the celebrated and beautiful | Dutchess of Devonshire | offered one hundred Guineas. | It is the only Picture for which Edwin | ever sat and such was his reluctance | that it was with difficulty he was persuaded | to give Mr Downman the Painter, three | sittings in the course of two years. | The resemblance is perfect. | 29th December 18[1]0 – J.S. [?].*

PROVENANCE: Mary Montgomerie, Lady Currie; Christie's, 30 June 1906 (8), bt Hodgkins; E. M. Hodgkins, Christie's, 29 June 1917 (29), bt Agnew, London; sold to M. Knoedler & Co., London, 1918; possibly Mrs. P. Daingerfield (not listed in her sale, American Art Association Galleries, 15 May 1937); Mortimer Brandt, New York, from whom bt Paul Mellon, 1966

SELECTED EXHIBITIONS: RA, London, 1788, no. 452; YCBA, *English Portrait Drawings*, 1979-80, no. 70

SELECTED LITERATURE: Williamson, 1907, pp. xx, xlii, xliii, xlvii, pl. 33; Friedman, 1976, p. 192, fig. 172

Paul Mellon Collection
B1977.14.6154

THEATER-GOING was an immensely popular and fashionable leisure activity in eighteenth-century Britain, and from the 1760s this passionate engagement with the dramatic arts was reflected in the enormous output of theatrical portraits, which were widely disseminated through engravings. The multi-talented actor-manager and theater proprietor David Garrick astutely recognized the value of portraits for promoting individual actors and productions, and he played a leading role in the development of the theatrical conversation piece.

John Downman's drawing portrays John Edwin and Mary Wells in their roles of Lingo and Cowslip in John O'Keeffe's three-act comedy, *The Agreeable Surprise*. The play was immensely successful, and between its opening at the Haymarket Theatre, London, in 1781 and 1800 it was performed more than two hundred times. The comic actor John Edwin (1749-90) made his first professional appearance in 1775 and was most famous for his role as Lingo. Edwin was as celebrated for his singing as his acting; according to the manager-playwright, George Colman, "While he sung in a style which produced roars of laughter, there was a melody in some of the upper tones of his voice that was beautiful." The inscription on the original frame is somewhat misleading, since at least eighteen engraved portraits of Edwin after various artists are known. Mary Wells, née Davies (c. 1759-before 1826), was born in Birmingham and performed in regional theaters before making her London acting debut in 1781. Constantly in debt and involved in amorous intrigue, the raffish actress conformed to the popular notion of her profession as dissolute and unrespectable, an image which the many portraits of Garrick – who assiduously cultivated himself as a model of social propriety – strove to contradict. GF

9

DANIEL GARDNER (1750-1805)

Mrs. Justinian Casamajor and Eight of her Children, 1779

Gouache, pastel and (?)oil on laid paper laid onto linen; 31½ x 38 in. (80.0 x 96.5 cm)

Inscribed in brush and blue gouache, lower left: 1779

PROVENANCE: Mrs. Justinian Casamajor; the sitter's son-in-law, J. Proctor Anderson, Farley Hall, Berkshire; his daughter, Mrs. Campbell Robertson; her nephew, Mr. Alexander Anderdon-Weston, Holme Grange, Wokingham, 1889; his widow, after 1921; Mrs. Isabella Frances Weston; Mortimer Brandt, New York, from whom bt Paul Mellon, 1965

SELECTED EXHIBITIONS: Grosvenor Gallery Winter Exhibition, London, 1889, no. 201; Kenwood, Gardner, 1972, no. 32; YCBA, English Portrait Drawings, 1979-80, no. 80; YCBA, Devis, 1980, no. 64

SELECTED LITERATURE: Williamson, 1921, pp. 16, 67, 70-1, 132-3; Steegman, 1958, p. 256, fig. 1; Praz, 1971, p. 152, fig. 114

Paul Mellon Collection
B1981.25.307

10

JOHANN HEINRICH RAMBERG (1763-1840)

The St. Aubyn Family, 1787

Pen and brush and black ink, graphite, watercolor, and gouache; 22 x 33½ in. (55.9 x 85.1 cm)

Signed and dated in pen and black ink, lower left: "[Ra]mberg | 1787"

PROVENANCE: By descent from Lady Dorothy Barrett-Lennard (d. 1831), née St. Aubyn, to Sir Thomas Barrett-Lennard (1853-1923), 3rd Bart., Belhus, Aveley, Essex; sold Sevill and Sons, Belhus, 15 May 1923 (999); McKenzie; Nina Drummond, from whom bt Paul Mellon, 1974

SELECTED EXHIBITIONS: YCBA, English Portrait Drawings, 1979-80, no. 74

Paul Mellon Collection
B1977.14.6249

THE GENRE of the family conversation piece (or "family piece" as it was termed) flourished in the later eighteenth century. The development of a more informal and intimate form of portraiture reflected contemporary notions of family life developed by the influential philosopher Jean-Jacques Rousseau, who advocated the adoption of more "natural" relationships within families and recommended that parents participate actively in child-rearing and education. Despite its apparent modernity of conception, the "family piece" of the period nonetheless retained the portrait's traditional functions as a statement of dynastic rights and social status, and a memorial for future generations. Formerly associated with the aris-

tocracy, this genre became popular with the middle classes who often favored large-scale drawings, which were less costly and faster to execute than oil paintings, and more appropriate in scale for relatively modest homes.

Daniel Gardner had a successful portrait practice catering to an aristocratic and middle-class clientele. Although primarily known as a pastellist and watercolorist, Gardner also worked from the mid-1770s in an unorthodox combination of oil media, gouache, and pastel. This technique, which he used for cat. 9, presumably was intended to replicate the textures and density of oil painting, while retaining the brilliancy of color associated with pastel. Gardner's brief period as an assistant in Joshua Reynolds's studio clearly had a lasting influence; demonstrating Reynolds's conception of historical portraiture, Gardner's work uses poses and compositional patterns derived from antique sources and the works of Old Masters. The portrait of Mrs. Justinian Casamajor with eight of her children is a fine example of Gardner's small-scale Grand Manner portraiture. In this ambitious drawing the mother is depicted as an allegorical figure of Charity, presumably in allusion to her astonishing fecundity (the Casamajors, a landed Hertfordshire family, reportedly had no fewer than twenty-two children); the group of children with a ram on the left is suggestive of a bacchanalian procession, rather incongruously, and probably derives from a Renaissance or antique model.

Though presumably commissioned as a dynastic portrait, not all the sitters in Johann Heinrich Ramberg's drawing of the Aubyn family have been identified conclusively. It seems likely, however, that it depicts Lady Elizabeth St. Aubyn (d. 1796) and her second husband John Baker sitting on the right with one of her four daughters. The portrait may have been commissioned to celebrate the marriage of her daughter Dorothy to Sir Thomas Barrett-Lennard, 1st Bart. of Belhus in 1787, the year the drawing was executed, and the figures on the left may be Dorothy and her fiancé or husband, or her brother, Sir John St. Aubyn, 5th Bart. of Clowance and St. Michael's Mount, Cornwall. The drawing belonged to Dorothy, and it remained in the Barrett-Lennard family until 1923.

Johann Heinrich Ramberg was born in Germany; he studied in London with Benjamin West from 1781 to 1788 but does not seem to have pursued his career as a history painter very seriously. Best known as a caricaturist, theater designer, and illustrator, Ramberg was influenced by the graphic work of Hogarth and Rowlandson (see cats. 7, 86-9, 148, 154), and the latter's drawing style is evident in the Aubyn family portrait. G F

9

10

II

HUGH DOUGLAS HAMILTON
(c. 1740-1808)

Portrait of a Divine

Pastel, black and white chalk, and graphite on laid paper; 10½ x 8½ in. (26.7 x 21.5 cm), oval

PROVENANCE: ...; Sutch, 1949; Leonard G. Duke, 1949-61; Colnaghi, from whom bt Paul Mellon, 1961

SELECTED EXHIBITIONS: YCBA, *English Portrait Drawings*, 1979-80, no. 66

Paul Mellon Collection
B1977.14.6184

THE IRISH ARTIST Hugh Douglas Hamilton trained at the Dublin Society Drawing School, where he showed considerable talent as a draftsman. By 1757 he was practicing successfully as a portraitist in crayons, producing attractive pastels in a hallmark oval format. According to his friend Thomas Mulvany, Hamilton's drawings were "laid in with very few colours, the prevailing tone of which was grey, and then finished with red and black chalk. They were marked with great skill and truth, the features, particularly the eyes, were expressed with great feeling; but ... they had all the appearance of having been hurried rather than neglected." As Mulvany observed, Hamilton's early pastels often seem unfinished and indicate that the artist was already working under great pressures to fulfill the demands of his large clientele.

In 1764 Hamilton moved to London, where he enlarged his repertoire to include large full-length pastel portraits rivaling those of Daniel Gardner (see cat. 9). His portrait practice was so successful that "he could scarcely execute all the orders that came in upon him," but like many of his contemporaries, Hamilton resented the drudgery of portraiture, and in 1779 he went to Rome to pursue his cherished ambition of becoming a history painter. He remained there for thirteen years, but economic necessity forced him to return reluctantly to Dublin ("exile for one who truly loves art," Hamilton observed bitterly) and resume his portrait practice. Hamilton abandoned pastels in 1793. The ecclesiastical subject of cat. 11 has not been identified, nor has the drawing been securely dated, but in execution it is similar to portraits known to have been produced in London in the 1770s. G F

12

JOSEPH WRIGHT OF DERBY
(1734-97)

Portrait of a Man, c. 1768

Black, white and brown chalk and
charcoal on laid paper; 14¼ x 11¼ in.
(36.2 x 28.5 cm)

PROVENANCE: ...; Mortimer Brandt,
New York, from whom bt Paul Mellon,
1965

SELECTED EXHIBITIONS: NGA, *Wright
of Derby*, 1969-70, no. 1 (as *Self-portrait*);
YCBA, *English Portrait Drawings*, 1979-
80, no. 72

SELECTED LITERATURE: Nicolson,
1968(2), vol. I, p. 38, n. 1, p. 229, no.
166; vol. II, pl. 69

Paul Mellon Collection
B1977.14.6320

THIS STRIKING DRAWING is one
of a group of monochrome chalk
portraits executed by Joseph Wright
in the late 1760s and early 1770s.
The early provenance for cat. 12 is
not known, and it is undated, but,
according to the scholar Benedict
Nicolson, the original backboard
was inscribed in another hand with
the date of 1768, and the style
seems consistent with Wright's
work of this period. It has been suggested convincingly that Wright's
chalk studies may have been influenced by a group of drawings and
related mezzotint engravings of life-
size heads by Thomas Frye (1710-
62), but, in any case, these essays in
monochrome are congruent with
Wright's lifelong preoccupation
with exploring the relationship
between light and dark. The rich
texture of the chalk medium resembles mezzotint, and Wright also
may have been inspired by the
appearance in May 1768 of William
Pether's mezzotint after his celebrated nocturnal painting, *The
Philosopher Giving a Lecture on the
Orrery*, which was the first print
after his work to be published.

Nicholson identified cat. 12 as a
self-portrait, but it does not resemble any authenticated self-portraits
or portraits of Wright. The directness of the man's gaze suggests a
close relationship between sitter
and artist, and the features are very
similar to those of the artist's friend
Peter Perez Burdett. Wright painted
a double portrait of Burdett and his
wife in 1765, and Burdett almost
certainly was the model for figures
in Wright's *Orrery* and *Three Persons
Viewing the Gladiator by Candle-light*,
which were first exhibited in the
mid-1760s. The sitter wears a tur-
ban and Van Dyck collar reminis-
cent of masquerade dress, which
was popular in the mid-eighteenth
century; similar fancy costume
appears in a number of Wright's
works of the period, including the
Center's *Academy by Lamplight*.
GF

13

THOMAS LAWRENCE (1769-1830)

William Lock II of Norbury Park, Surrey, c. 1800

Oiled charcoal on prepared canvas; 26 x 19 in. (66.0 x 48.3 cm), oval

PROVENANCE: William Lock; by descent to The Lord Wallscourt; The Hon. Mrs. Leycester Storr; ...; anon. sale, Christie's, 17 November 1992 (28); Hazlitt, Gooden and Fox, from whom bt, 1994

SELECTED EXHIBITIONS: RA, *Lawrence*, 1961, no. 71

SELECTED LITERATURE: Garlick, 1964, p. 235, no. 2; Garlick, 1968, p. 670. fig. 31

Paul Mellon Fund and Friends of British Art Fund
B1994.11

THE VIRTUOSO PORTRAIT PAINTER Sir Thomas Lawrence was an extremely talented draftsman, despite his lack of formal training, and he frequently drew for pleasure as an antidote to the pressures and tedium of his professional life. It has been suggested that Lawrence's sensitive portrait of the younger

William Lock may be a study for an untraced portrait of the sitter exhibited at the Royal Academy in 1791. Lock's attire and hairstyle indicate a later dating, however, and Lawrence did not usually make preliminary drawings for his paintings, preferring to prepare them by drawing directly on the canvas with chalk.

This technique clearly fascinated his sitters. Joseph Farington recorded in his diary for 7 May 1794: "This morning I sat to Lawrence when He drew in my portrait with black chalk on the Canvass, which employed him near 2 hours. He did not use colour today. – This is his mode of beginning," and Lady Elizabeth Leveson-Gower recalled: "what struck me most ... was the perfection of the drawing of his portraits before any colour was put on." Lawrence also made a number of chalk portraits on canvas which he seems to have regarded as drawings in their own right, and no. 13 almost certainly falls into this category. Moreover, the portrait was owned by Lock, which implies that Lawrence would have considered it a finished work.

The sitter was the son of the connoisseur William Lock (1732-1810), who was one of Lawrence's first sitters and a close friend of the artist. The younger Lock (1767-1847) was a keen patron of the arts and an aspiring artist, but after visiting Rome he lost faith in his talent and gave up painting, though he continued to draw. GF

14

GEORGE DANCE (1741-1825)

Portrait of a Boy, 1793

Graphite and watercolor on wove paper; 9 9/16 x 7 9/16 in. (24.5 x 19.3 cm)

Signed and dated in graphite, lower right: *Geo. Dance*; lower left: *Aug^st 3^d 1793.*

PROVENANCE: ...; Colnaghi, from whom bt Paul Mellon, 1961

SELECTED EXHIBITIONS: NGA, *English Drawings*, 1962, no. 28; VMFA, *Painting in England*, 1963, no. 406; Colnaghi-Yale, *English Drawings*, 1964-5, no. 8; PML, *English Drawings*, 1972, no. 47; YCBA, *English Portrait Drawings*, 1979-80, no. 86

SELECTED LITERATURE: Hardie, 1967-8, vol. I, pl. 122

Paul Mellon Collection
B1986.29.359

THE DISTINGUISHED ARCHITECT George Dance the Younger was a prolific draftsman. Dance particularly enjoyed making portrait drawings, and on weekends, released temporarily from his onerous duties as the Clerk of Works of the City of London, he drew "profiles," as he termed them, of his family and friends. Dance regarded this activity as "a great relaxation from the severed studies and more laborious employment of my professional life," but these distinctive drawings nonetheless betray their author's occupational concerns. His chosen formula of a pencil or chalk outline, occasionally tinted with watercolor, is close to the technique used for architectural drawings of the period, and the profile view he adopted habitually for the portraits suggests analogies with an orthographic elevation. Dance also may have been influenced by the contemporary taste for silhouettes, which were often referred to as "profiles."

Dance's portraits were admired by his contemporaries, and in 1793 he embarked on a project to draw likenesses of his fellow Royal Academicians, with a view to having them engraved and published. Seventy-two of Dance's portraits, including his "Academical Heads," were etched in soft-ground by William Daniell and eventually published in two volumes (1808-14), with a dedication to the connoisseur and amateur artist Sir George Beaumont. The Center owns twenty-three of Daniell's preliminary pencil and chalk drawings for the project. The sitter of cat. 14 has not been identified. GF

15

John Russell (1745-1806)

John Collins of Devizes, 1799

Pastel on (?)blue paper; 30 x 25¼ in.
(76.2 x 64.1 cm)

Signed and dated, in red crayon, lower
right: *J. Russell RA | pinxt 1799.*

provenance: Artist's sale, Christie's,
14 February 1807 (63), bt Spackman;
...; The Baptist Manse, Broughton,
Hampshire, 1894; ...; Harland Peck,
sold Christie's, 16 June 1900 (121); ...;
Fine Art Society, 1969, from whom bt
Paul Mellon

selected exhibitions: RA, 1799,
no. 362; YCBA, *English Portrait Drawings*,
1979-80, no. 79

selected literature: Williamson,
1894, pp. 121, 138

Paul Mellon Collection
B1977.14.6261

THE SUCCESSFUL AND PROLIFIC
portraitist John Russell was best
known for his work in pastels (often
referred to as "crayons"). Apprenticed
to the portrait painter Francis Cotes,
Russell set up his own practice in
1767 and was appointed Crayon
Painter to George III and to George,
Prince of Wales, in 1788. Russell
evolved a distinctive and effective
technique, which he elucidated in
his popular manual, *Elements of
Painting with Crayons* (1772). After
tracing the sitter's outline in chalk
on blue paper and laying in the col-
ors, Russell smudged the outlines
using his fingers and crayon; the
resulting blurred effect and velvety
textures endowed his portraits with
remarkable vitality and luminosity.

This portrait, which is in almost
perfect condition, is a very fine
example of his work, and demonstrates aptly Cotes's statement that
"crayon pictures, when finely painted, are superlatively beautiful, and
decorative in a very high degree in
apartments that are not too large;
for, having their surface dry, they
partake in appearance of the effect
of Fresco, and by candle light are
luminous and beautiful beyond all
other pictures."

Russell frequently incorporated
animals into his pastels, but the
inclusion of a ram in his portrait of
the Wiltshire wool merchant John
Collins (fl. 1771-99) is particularly
appropriate. (In his *Elements* Russell
noted: "Let the Embellishments of
the Picture, and introduction of
Birds, Animals, &c. be regulated by
the rules of propriety and consisten-
cy.") Described by the local historian
James Waylen as "an antiquary in
mind, manners and dress," Collins
bequeathed his library to the Baptist
Chapel at Broughton, Hampshire;
the Chapel subsequently acquired
this portrait. The circumstances of
its production are unknown, but the
pastel was still in Russell's studio
at his death and may have been a
rejected commission, by no means
an unusual occurrence for a professional portraitist of the period.
Russell was also an amateur astronomer, and one of his studies of the
moon is included in this catalogue
(cat. 57). GF

17

UNKNOWN ARTIST

Portrait of a Young Man

Watercolor and gouache on vellum; 3⅜ x 3 in. (8.6 x 7.6 cm), oval

PROVENANCE: Elizabeth Richard Simmons, New York, her sale, Christie's, 12 November 1968 (111), bt John Baskett, from whom bt. Paul Mellon, 1968

Paul Mellon Collection
B2001.2.1392

16

BERNARD LENS III (1682-1740)

The Reverend Dr. John Harris, 1707

Watercolor and gouache over graphite on ivory; 3¼ x 2½ in. (8.3 x 6.4 cm), oval

Signed in gold, lower left: BL in monogram, and inscribed in pen and brown ink on paper backing attached to ivory: *The Reverend | Dr Harris one of the | prebans of Rochester & | Chapplain of the Lord High | Chancellor of Great Britain | Earle Cowper | Bernard Lens fecit by the | Life 1707*; in a contemporary hand, in pen and brown ink, a similar inscription on a paper label attached to back of frame

PROVENANCE: ...; Reverend M. de la Hey; ...; Kennedy Galleries, New York, bt Paul Mellon, 1969

SELECTED EXHIBITIONS: YCBA, *English Portrait Drawings*, 1979-80, no. 21

SELECTED LITERATURE: Reynolds, 1952, p. 105; Long, 1929, pp. 268-9; Foskett, 1963, p. 90

Paul Mellon Collection
B1974.2.66

18

ANDREW PLIMER (1763-1837)

Mary and Nathaniel Jefferys

Watercolor and gouache on ivory; 3½ x 2¾ in. (9.0 x 7.0 cm), oval

Inscribed in ink on label on back: *25*

PROVENANCE: ...; sold Christie's, 2 June 1970, bt Fry, from whom bt Paul Mellon, 1970

Paul Mellon Collection
B1974.2.82

19

RICHARD COSWAY (1742-1821)

James Hope, 3rd Earl of Hopetoun, 1789

Watercolor and gouache on ivory; 3 x 2⁵/₁₆ in. (7.6 x 5.9 cm), oval

Signed, dated, and inscribed in pen and brown ink, on a paper label attached to back: *James | Earl of Hopetoun| R^dus Cosway R.A. | Primarius Pictor | Serenissimi Walliae | Principis | Pinxit | 1789*

PROVENANCE OF CATS 19 AND 20: ...; on loan to the Victoria and Albert Museum, London, 1945; A. P. Cunliffe, sold Sotheby's, 20 November 1945 (37), bt Sydney; ...; anon. sale, Christie's, 18 February 1969 (118), bt Fry, from whom acquired by Paul Mellon

SELECTED EXHIBITIONS: YCBA, *English Portrait Drawings,* 1979-80, no. 52; SNPG, *Cosway,* 1995, no. 67

Paul Mellon Collection
B1974.2.19

19

20

20

RICHARD COSWAY (1742-1821)

Elizabeth, Countess of Hopetoun, 1789

Watercolor and gouache on ivory; 3 x 2⁵/₁₆ in. (7.6 x 5.9 cm), oval

Signed, dated and inscribed in pen and brown ink, on a paper label attached to back: *Eliza | Countess of Hopetoun | R^dus Cosway R.A. | Primarius Pictor | Serenissimi Walliae | Principis | Pinxit | 1789*

PROVENANCE: As for cat. 19

SELECTED EXHIBITIONS: YCBA, *English Portrait Drawings,* 1979-80, no. 53; SNPG, *Cosway,* 1995, no. 68

Paul Mellon Collection
B1974.2.18

21

GEORGE ENGLEHEART (1753-1829)

Lady Grace Burnaby, 1790

Watercolor and gouache on ivory; 2¹/₈ x 1⁵/₈ in. (5.4 x 4.1 cm), oval

Inscribed in pen and brown ink, on paper label attached to back: *Lady Burnaby;* on back: hair interlaced with gold letters LB

PROVENANCE: ...; anon. sale, Christie's, 14 February 1945 (1612), bt Baker; ...; S.H.V. Hickson, sold Sotheby's, 10 November 1969 (57), bt Fry, from whom purchased by Paul Mellon

SELECTED EXHIBITIONS: YCBA, *English Portrait Drawings,* 1979-80, no. 55

Paul Mellon Collection
B1974.2.35

21

22

23

24

25

22

GEORGE ENGLEHEART (1753-1829)

A Lady of the Blunt Family

Watercolor and gouache on ivory;
3 ½ x 2 ⅞ in. (8.9 x 7.3 cm), oval

Inscribed in brown, lower right: *E*;
in pen and black ink, on a paper label
attached to back: *Miss Blunt | Property
of | Mrs. H. Grafton*; in pen and black
ink, on a paper label attached to back:
Edward Fletcher

PROVENANCE: Mrs. H. Grafton; ...;
Edward Fletcher (1763-1846), husband
of Dorothea Blunt; ...; Col. E. W.
Fletcher, sold Christie's, 28 October
1970 (88) bt Fry, from whom bt Paul
Mellon

SELECTED EXHIBITIONS: YCBA, *English
Portrait Drawings*, 1979-80, no. 56

Paul Mellon Collection
B1974.2.38

23

GEORGE ENGLEHEART (1753-1829)

Portrait of a Gentleman, 1787

Watercolor and gouache on ivory;
1 ⅝ x 1 5⁄16 in. (4.2 x 3.3 cm)

Engraved on reverse: *DD | Æt | Ap 27 | 1787*

PROVENANCE: ...; Michael Bertolini,
from whom bt Ann and Kenneth
Rapoport, 6 February 1973; given to the
Center, 2000

Gift of Ann and Kenneth Rapoport
B2000.10

24

JOHN SMART (1742/3-1811)

Major-General Sir Barry Close,
1794

Watercolor and gouache on ivory;
3 x 2⅜ in. (7.6 x 6.4 cm), oval

Signed and dated in gray, lower left:
J. S. | 1794 | I; on back, a lock of plaited
hair and in gold the initials: *BC*

PROVENANCE: ...; C. A. L. Bell, sold
Christie's, 15 April 1956 (104), bt
Murray; Dennis Ward, sold Christie's,
25 June 1968 (99), bt A. G. Tite; ...;
Kennedy Galleries, from whom bt Paul
Mellon, 1968

SELECTED EXHIBITIONS: YCBA, *English
Portrait Drawings*, 1979-80, no. 58

SELECTED LITERATURE: Foskett, 1964,
p. 64

Paul Mellon Collection
B1974.2.96

25

JOHN SMART (1742/3-1811)

General Stevenson, 1796

Gouache and watercolor on ivory;
3 x 2⅜in. (7.6 x 6.0 cm), oval

Inscribed on back of case: [?] *JDS* in
monogram

PROVENANCE: ...; sold Sotheby's,
1 June 1970, bt Fry, from whom bt
Paul Mellon, 1970

Paul Mellon Collection
B1974.2.99

THE PORTRAIT MINIATURE is
associated particularly with the sixteenth and seventeenth centuries,
but this distinctive form of drawing
retained its appeal throughout the
eighteenth century and indeed
increased in popularity as a middle-
class clientele for portraits evolved.
Although portrait miniatures were
exhibited publicly later in the century (at the Royal Academy they were
prominently displayed around the
fireplace in the Great Room), they
were generally, though not invariably, intended for private rather
than public uses. Usually commissioned to commemorate births,
marriages, friendships, love affairs,
or dynastic relationships – though
sometimes made as copies of large-
scale portraits – these delicate tiny
likenesses were often housed in
specially-made cases fashioned of
precious materials, and either worn
as jewelry or stored in cabinets with
other images of loved ones.

As Jean-Jacques Rousseau's concept of "natural" and close family
relationships became increasingly
influential towards the end of the
century, this most private form of
portraiture gained in popularity, as
did the family conversation piece
(see cats. 9-10). Because of the
inherently personal and private
nature of the genre, identities of sitters of miniatures have often been
mislaid over the centuries, particularly when they have left the families of their original owners and
entered museum collections; this
sense of loss adds a particular reso-
nance and poignancy to these commemorative images.

Miniatures in the sixteenth and
seventeenth centuries were painted,
or "limned," on vellum, but
Bernard Lens III popularized the
use of ivory supports for miniatures
in England early in the eighteenth
century. Lens's portrait of the
Reverend Dr. John Harris of 1707
(cat. 16) is the earliest dated English
miniature painted on ivory by an
English artist. Although ivory was
more durable than vellum, and
capable of a shimmering luminosity
when painted with thin, translu-
cent washes of watercolor, artists
initially found it a difficult support
to work on, and techniques for
painting on ivory were not perfected
until later in the century.

In the work of Richard Cosway
(cats. 19-20), George Engleheart
(cats. 21-3) and John Smart (cats.
24-5), the most accomplished proponents of the genre in the period,
the miniature achieved extraordinary
delicacy and luminosity, qualities
we can still appreciate today, since
many of these precious objects were
hidden from view and protected
from the damaging effects of light.
GF

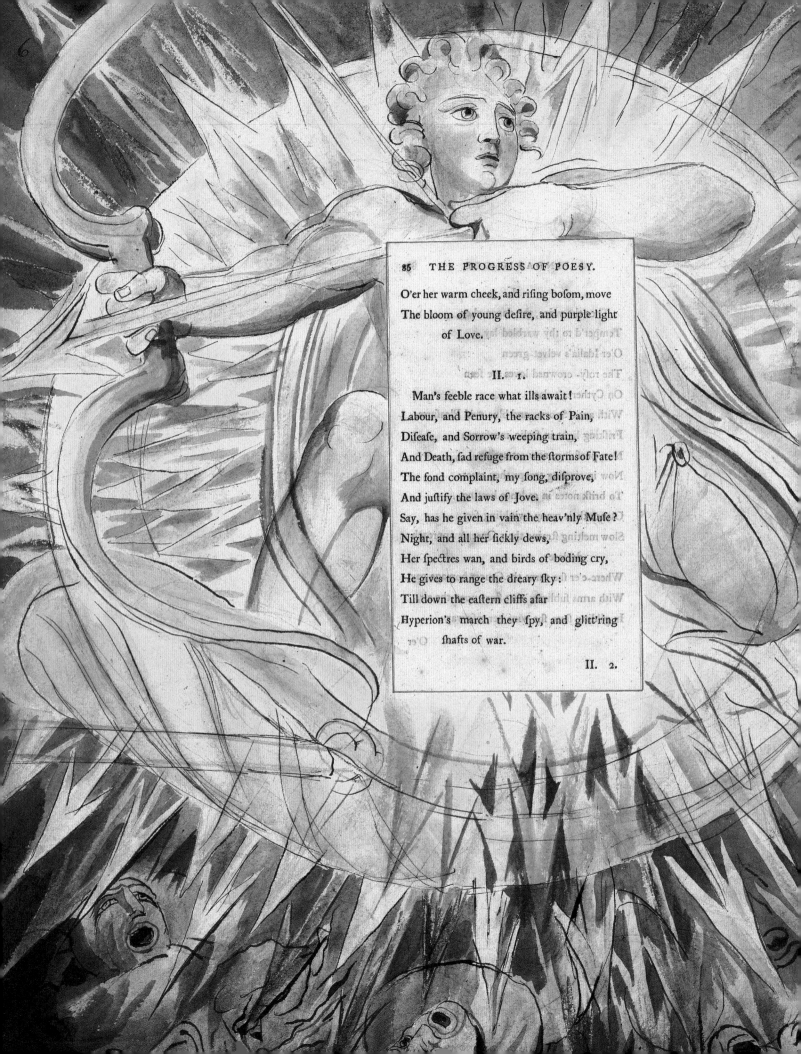

86 THE PROGRESS OF POESY.

O'er her warm cheek, and rising bosom, move
The bloom of young desire, and purple light
    of Love.

II.

Man's feeble race what ills await!
Labour, and Penury, the racks of Pain,
Disease, and Sorrow's weeping train,
And Death, sad refuge from the storms of Fate!
The fond complaint, my song, disprove,
And justify the laws of Jove.
Say, has he given in vain the heav'nly Muse?
Night, and all her sickly dews,
Her spectres wan, and birds of boding cry,
He gives to range the dreary sky:
Till down the eastern cliffs afar
Hyperion's march they spy, and glitt'ring
    shafts of war.

II. 2.

Literature, History and Mythology

IT WAS A CULTURAL COMMONPLACE in the eighteenth century that history painting, which gave pictorial embodiment to the great themes of literature, history, and religion, represented the pinnacle of artistic achievement. This exalted view of history painting underlies both Jonathan Richardson's writings and Sir Joshua Reynolds's later *Discourses on Art*. As Reynolds put it, it was the artist's appeal to the mind rather than the eye "which gives painting its true dignity, which entitles it to the name of a Liberal Art, and ranks it as a sister of poetry."

British artists found themselves trapped between such high-minded cultural pronouncements and the realities of the marketplace. In Protestant Britain, where there were no strong traditions of church or state patronage of the arts, opportunities for large-scale public cycles of history painting remained few and far between. Major schemes such as those indicated by James Thornhill's study for one of his paintings in the dome of St. Paul's (cat. 146), and his drawing for a staircase decoration (cat. 145), from the early years of the century, or Benjamin West's design for the Chapel of Revealed Religion at Windsor (cat. 151), from about 1780, are exceptional.

Although there was a thriving market in Old Master easel paintings of classical and religious subjects, there was no demand for comparable works by living British artists. For William Hogarth, intent on promoting his own art and that of his compatriots, this fixation on the Old Masters was anathema, and he railed against the imported "Ship Loads of dead *Christs, Holy Families, Madona's,* and other dismal Dark Subjects, neither entertaining nor Ornamental." But the taste for Old Masters did engender a particular line of work in the production of miniature versions of famous or historically significant works of the past. Bernard Lens's copies after Rubens (cat. 26) and Vogelaare (cat. 27) and Joseph Goupy's copy after Raphael (cat. 28) belong to this genre, which translated large public works into small images for private delectation.

Although British history painters did produce preparatory drawings, such as John Singleton Copley's figure studies for his paintings *The Death of Chatham* (cat. 157) and *The Victory of Lord Duncan* (cat. 158), the relative paucity of British history painting means inevitably that such drawings are scarce. In the case of George Romney, however, a vast body of drawings poignantly attests to his unfulfilled ambitions as a history painter (see cat. 38). In other instances, from Michael Rysbrack (cat. 30) to Richard Cosway (cat. 40) and Richard Westall (cat. 41), artists created drawings on literary or historical themes that point to no other works, either realized or not, but are ends in themselves. In the case of Rysbrack and Cosway there is a conscious emulation and extension of Old Master presentation drawings. Westall's watercolor stands outside the traditions of drawing altogether, being intended as an alternative to oil painting, though the history painting in watercolors that Westall pioneered never established itself as a viable ongoing tradition.

The ambitious draftsman had scope to deal with literature and history in the area of book illustration. Most frequently these illustrations were for publication, as was Hubert-François Gravelot's design for a title page (cat. 29), but at times they were special productions created for a specific patron. Such was the set of watercolor illustrations of the poems of Thomas Gray (cats. 36-7) that William Blake made for the wife of his friend John Flaxman. The sculptor Flaxman, the neoclassical linearity of whose drawings (see cats. 34-5) was eminently reproducible, was himself a noted illustrator of the classics.

SCOTT WILCOX

26

26

BERNARD LENS III (1682-1740),
after PETER PAUL RUBENS
(1577-1640)

*The Victorious Hero Takes
Occasion to Conclude Peace,*
1720

Watercolor and gouache heightened
with gold on vellum; 15½ x 18¾ in.
(39.4 x 47.6 cm)

Signed and dated in gold, lower right:
B. Lens Fecit. | July 21: 1720

PROVENANCE: ...; John Baskett, 1982,
from whom purchased

SELECTED EXHIBITIONS: YCBA, *First
Decade,* 1986, no. 100

SELECTED LITERATURE: Logan, 1986,
pp. 203-15

Paul Mellon Fund
B1982.6

27

BERNARD LENS III (1682-1740),
after LIVINUS DE VOGELAARE
(active 1567-8)

The Memorial of Lord Darnley,
1728

Gouache on vellum; 11¼ x 18¼ in.
(28.6 x 46.4 cm)

Signed in monogram, lower left;
inscribed on the verso: *Bernard Lens
Fecit after ye originall in ye cabbinet
of the Rt. Honble the Earl of Pomfret |
Sep: 21: 1728*

PROVENANCE: Commissioned from the
artist by Edward Harley, 2nd Earl of
Oxford, his sale, Mr. Cock "at his House
in the Great Piazza, Covent Garden,"
13 March 1742 (45); bt Edward Rudge,
the Abbey Manor, Evesham, Worcester-
shire; by descent; Sotheby's, 19
November 1987 (42), bt Ann and
Kenneth Rapoport, by whom given

SELECTED LITERATURE: Vertue, 1740,
p. 13

Gift of Ann and Kenneth Rapoport
B1998.9.2

28

JOSEPH GOUPY (1686-c. 1770),
after RAPHAEL (1483-1520)

The Death of Ananias, 1740

Gouache on vellum; 11⅞ x 18 in.
(30.2 x 45.7 cm)

Signed in pen and brown ink, lower left:
Jos. Goupy

PROVENANCE: Baron Kielmansegg;
James Brydges, 1st Duke of Chandos
(seal on verso of frame); ?Frederick,
Prince of Wales; Mr. Forman, 1800; Rev.
Alfred Chandler; W. E. Gladstone;
Christie's, 23 June 1875 (630); Lord
Downe, sale (six of set, 284-9),
Sotheby's, 19 June 1973 (289), bt David
Bindman, from whom purchased, 1986

SELECTED EXHIBITIONS: Museum of
London, *Quiet Conquest,* 1985, no. 291;
YCBA, *First Decade,* 1986, no. 89

Paul Mellon Fund
B1986.13

WHILE OPPORTUNITIES for Grand
Manner history painting were de-
cidedly limited in early eighteenth-
century England, a handful of
artists such as Bernard Lens and
Joseph Goupy enjoyed a healthy
business producing small-scale
copies in gouache or pastel of Old
Master paintings. Horace Walpole
described Lens as "an admirable
painter in miniatures," that is, a
portrait miniaturist (see cat. 16),
but, Walpole continued: "his excellence was copying works of great
masters, particularly Rubens and

Vandyck, whose colouring he imitated exactly."

Lens's *The Victorious Hero Takes Occasion to Conclude Peace* is a copy of a painting by Peter Paul Rubens, known today only in a workshop version in a museum in Siegen, Germany. Minerva places a lock of the hair of the nude Occasion in the hand of a victorious hero, watched by the figures of Ceres and Time. While Rubens seems not to have had a particular hero in mind, Lens's copy may have been intended to foster an association of the hero with John Churchill, 1st Duke of Marlborough, for whom the copy may well have been made. Lens made copies of other works by Rubens and Van Dyck owned by Marlborough.

The collector Edward Harley, 2nd Earl of Oxford, commissioned Lens's copy of the sixteenth-century *Memorial of Lord Darnley*. The original painting, then in the collection of the 1st Earl of Pomfret, is now in the Royal Collection and hangs in Holyrood-house in Edinburgh. A piece of anti-Mary Queen of Scots propaganda, it shows the young James vi kneeling before the tomb of his father Lord Darnley, in whose murder James's mother Mary was implicated. Behind James are members of his father's family, and an inset picture at the lower left shows Mary's defeat at the Battle of Carberry Hill.

In 1736 the French-born Joseph Goupy was appointed by Frederick, Prince of Wales, as his "cabinet painter." Goupy's duties included looking after Frederick's art collection and presumably painting copies after famous works such as *The Death of Ananias* from Raphael's

27

28

celebrated cartoons at Hampton Court (now in the Victoria and Albert Museum). Frederick certainly owned a set of Goupy copies after the Raphael cartoons, but it is not clear whether that was the same set earlier owned by the Duke of Chandos, from which this version of *The Death of Ananias* comes. sw

29

HUBERT-FRANÇOIS GRAVELOT
(1699-1773)

*Drawing for the Frontispiece
of "The Toast,"* 1735

Pen and black ink with gray wash on
laid paper; image: 7⅝ x 5 in. (19.4 x 12.7
cm); sheet: 8⅜ x 5⅝ in. (21.3 x 14.3 cm)

Signed and dated in black ink in margin, lower right: *Hubert f. Gravelot inv.
& delint. Londini. 1735.*

PROVENANCE: ...; Jocelyn Feilding,
December 1973, bt Paul Mellon

SELECTED LITERATURE: Stewart, 1989,
pp. 265-7

Paul Mellon Collection
B1975.4.881

AFTER STUDYING with the history
painter Jean Restout and working in
the studio of François Boucher in
Paris, Gravelot responded to an
invitation from the French engraver
Claude Du Bosc, who was working
in London and needed an assistant.
Gravelot traveled to England in 1732
or 1733, remaining there until 1745,
when anti-French sentiment precipi-
tated his return home. Writing
shortly after Gravelot's return to
Paris, George Vertue noted that the
Frenchman had gained the "reputation of a most ingenious draughtsman during the time he has been
in London." He had in fact played
a key role in the introduction of
elements of rococo style into
England and had significantly
advanced the art of British book
illustration.

During his years in London,
Gravelot illustrated over fifty books.
This drawing was engraved by
Bernard Baron as the frontispiece
for William King's *The Toast: An
Heroick Poem in Four Books*, privately
published in 1736. One of the tar-
gets of King's satirical poem was
Frances Brudenell, Countess of
Newburgh, the subject of the ador-
ing poem *Myra* by George Granville,
Baron Landsdowne. In Gravelot's
illustration Granville shows off a
portrait of a beautiful Myra to
Apollo, while a satyr delights in the
discrepancy between the painted
image and the actual appearance of
the sitter, to whom he points.
Gravelot's composition does not
illustrate a particular scene from
King's poem but echoes its attack on
Granville and Brudenell. Gravelot's
elegant draftsmanship in no way
vitiates the bite of the satire. sw

30

MICHAEL (JOHANNES MICHEL)
RYSBRACK (1694-1770)

Illustration to the Iliad, 1760s

Pen and brown ink with brown and gray
wash and gouache on laid paper, laid
down on original mount; 9¼ x 15⅛ in.
(23.5 x 38.4 cm)

Signed in brown ink on mount, lower
left: *Michl Rysbrack invt.*; inscribed in
brown ink on mount, lower right: *12/-*;
verso: *The Iliade of Homer. Book the V. |
Diomedes, fought Pandarus, and killed
him; Aeneas, going to | Revenge his
Death*[,] *Diomedes throws a large stone at
him and broke | both his Thighs, and the
nerve of his heel, when Venus seeing him |
in such danger took him away in a Cloud*;
verso, lower right: *No. 1*

PROVENANCE: ...; Christopher Powney,
from whom purchased, 1992

Paul Mellon Fund
B1992.19.2

FOR SEVERAL DECADES from his
arrival in London in 1720, the
Antwerp-born and -trained Rysbrack
was the foremost sculptor working
in England. He was also a prolific
and accomplished draftsman, producing highly finished drawings of
his sculptural projects for prospec-
tive patrons (see cat. 152). Rysbrack
created drawings independently of
his sculptural work as well; and, as
his health declined in the 1760s and
he could no longer work as a sculptor, drawing became increasingly
his chief artistic outlet. The collector
and connoisseur Charles Rogers,

who reproduced one of Rysbrack's
drawings in his *Prints in Imitation of
Drawings* of 1778, wrote of Rysbrack:
"From time to time he would amuse
himself with making high-finished
Drawings in an admirable taste;
these are generally of his own
invention, designed with a smart
pen, washed with bister, and heightened with white. This amusement
he continued to the last days of his
life."

Rysbrack's independent drawings
were generally of classical or biblical
subjects. This drawing of a scene
from Book v of Homer's *Iliad*,
described in the inscription on the
back of the mount, may well have
been the drawing titled "The Contest between Aeneas and Diomedes"
exhibited by Rysbrack at the Society
of Artists in 1765. SW

31

GAVIN HAMILTON (1723-98)

Illustrations to the *Iliad,*
c. 1760-3

31

*Achilles Lamenting the Death
of Patroclus*

Pen and brown ink with gray and brown
wash on laid paper; image: 5⅜ x 8¼ in.
(13.7 x 21 cm); sheet 6⅞ x 9 in.
(17.5 x 22.9 cm)

PROVENANCE: ...; Christie's, Rome,
11 June 1973 (3), bt John Baskett, from
whom purchased by Paul Mellon, 1973

SELECTED EXHIBITIONS: YCBA,
Visionary Company, 1997

Paul Mellon Collection
B1975.4.884

32

*Andromache Mourning the
Death of Hector*

Pen and brown ink with gray and brown
wash on laid paper; image: 5⅜ x 8⅛ in.
(13.7 x 20.6 cm); sheet: 6¾ x 9 in.
(17.1 x 22.9 cm)

PROVENANCE: As for cat. 31

Paul Mellon Collection
B1975.4.885

BASED IN ROME from the late
1750s, the Scottish artist Gavin
Hamilton enjoyed an international
reputation as a history painter.
Central to his reputation was the
series of six monumental paintings
of scenes from Homer's *Iliad,* painted over the course of about fifteen
years from 1760 and engraved by
Dominic Cunego. Although they
were commissioned from different
patrons, Hamilton thought of the
series as a single work and conceived of the engravings as a set.

The first in the series to be painted, though the final scene in Hamilton's narrative sequence, was *Andromache Mourning the Death of Hector,*

32

commissioned by Lord Compton and painted in the summer of 1760 (the painting has not survived). *Achilles Lamenting the Death of Patroclus*, commissioned by James Grant of Grant in 1760 and painted in 1763 (collection of the Earl of Seafield), came next. The pair of drawings mirrors the compositions of these first two paintings, although the role of the drawings in the genesis of the paintings and the subsequent Cunego prints is not clear. Within the series these two scenes – the furious grief of Achilles and the tragic sorrow of Andromache – are closely connect-ed, providing the kernel of the narrative that Hamilton expanded into six scenes.

In contrast to Rysbrack's *Iliad* illustration (cat. 30), Hamilton's compositions are more tightly focused on central figural groupings, enhancing both the clarity and the drama of the representations. Influenced by paintings of the seventeenth-century master Nicolas Poussin and by antique relief sculpture, Hamilton in these works announces the principles of neoclassicism in history painting. SW

33

JOHN HAMILTON MORTIMER
(1740-79)

Death on a Pale Horse, c. 1775

Pen and black ink on wove paper;
24⅝ x 18¼ in. (62.5 x 46.4 cm)

PROVENANCE: Hazlitt, Gooden & Fox,
1988, bt Paul Mellon

SELECTED EXHIBITIONS: Society of
Artists, 1775, no. 183; Eastbourne,
Mortimer, 1968, no. 44; PP, *Peinture
Romantique*, 1972, no. 198; YCBA,
Visionary Company, 1997

SELECTED LITERATURE: Ziff, 1970;
Sunderland, 1988, no. 100

Paul Mellon Collection
B1993.30.109

EDWARD EDWARDS in his *Anecdotes
of Painters* (1808) observed that "the
favourite subjects of Mr. Mortimer's
pencil, were the representations of
Banditti, or those transactions
recorded in history, wherein the
exertions of soldiers are principally
employed, as also, incantations, the
frolics of monsters, and all those
kind of scenes, that personify
'Horrible Imaginings.'" One of
those "Horrible Imaginings" is the
elaborate drawing of *Death on a Pale
Horse*, which Mortimer exhibited at
the Society of Arts in 1775 together
with a companion drawing illustrating the line from 1 Corinthians,
15:55: "O Death! Where is thy sting?
O Grave! Where is thy victory?"
After Mortimer's death, both drawings were etched by Joseph Haynes
and published by Mortimer's widow
Jane on January 1, 1784.

Mortimer's subject is the Fourth
Horseman of the Apocalypse from
the Book of Revelation, his imagery
drawn from the famous Dürer print
of the four horsemen and a seventeenth-century etching by Stefano
della Bella. A related working drawing owned by the connoisseur and
critic Richard Payne Knight is in the
British Museum.

If Mortimer's predilection for
"Horrible Imaginings" suggests an
excessive and morbid temperament,
Edwards confirms that the artist
was "imprudent in his conduct, and
intemperate in his pleasures, by
which he injured his health." Yet
his taste in subject matter went
beyond personal quirkiness or
pathology. His macabre and sensa-
tionalistic imagery was shared by
Henry Fuseli, and Mortimer's
Death on a Pale Horse is but an early
instance of an apocalyptic strain in
later eighteenth- and early nineteenth-century art. The subject of
the Fourth Horseman was subsequently taken up by James Gillray,
William Blake, and Benjamin West.
SW

34

JOHN FLAXMAN (1755-1826)

34

Get Thee Behind Me, Satan,
c. 1783-7

Graphite with pen and gray ink and gray
wash on laid paper; 15¹⁵⁄₁₆ x 21⁷⁄₈ in.
(40.5 x 55.6 cm)

PROVENANCE: ...; C. S. Bale; Charles
Thomas Milburn; J. S. Maas, 1963,
bt Paul Mellon

SELECTED EXHIBITIONS: YCBA, *Fuseli
Circle*, 1979, no. 133; YCBA, *Blake*, 1982-
83, no. 18; YCBA, *Visionary Company*,
1997

Paul Mellon Collection
B1977.14.6168

35

The Creation of the Heavens,
c. 1790

Pen and gray ink and gray wash on laid
paper; 9³⁄₁₆ x 9⁷⁄₈ in. (23.3 x 25.1 cm)

PROVENANCE: Christopher Powney,
from whom purchased by Paul Mellon,
1976

SELECTED EXHIBITIONS: YCBA, *Fuseli
Circle*, 1979, no. 135; YCBA, *Romantic
Vision*, 1995-6; YCBA, *Visionary Company*,
1997

Paul Mellon Collection
B1981.25.2586

LIKE MICHAEL RYSBRACK (see
cats. 30 and 152), John Flaxman was
a sculptor who was also a celebrated
draftsman. Indeed, Flaxman's spare,
unrelentingly linear drawings are the
quintessential statements of neoclassical draftsmanship. They take the
process of neoclassical simplification
of forms, seen in its early stages in
Gavin Hamilton's illustrations to the
Iliad (cats. 31-2), to a new level of
severity and abstraction.

Both these drawings demonstrate
the exchange of visual ideas between
Flaxman and his friend William
Blake (see cats. 36-7) as well as their
creative response to earlier art. In
Get Thee Behind Me, Satan the

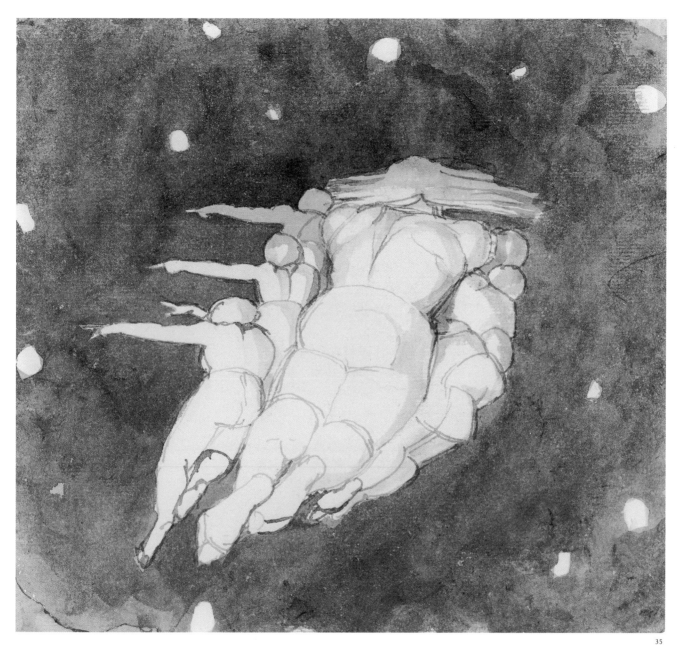

35

commanding figure of Christ is taken from Raphael's cartoon *Christ's Charge to St. Peter*. Blake made use of the same figure in his *Christ Appearing to the Apostles after the Resurrection*, one of his large color prints of the mid-1790s. Flaxman's fleeing Satan appears, rotated one hundred and eighty degrees, as the evil angel in *The Good and Evil Angels Struggling for Possession of a*

Child, another of Blake's large color prints. And the floating angels to the right of Christ in Flaxman's drawing, which also have their counterparts in Blake's art of the period, testify to a shared interest in the linear expressiveness of Gothic art. *The Creation of the Heavens* may have been inspired by Michelangelo's Sistine-ceiling image of God creating the heavens; but, in its expression of

cosmic energy through a radical simplification of the human form, it is even more Blakean. sw

36

WILLIAM BLAKE (1757-1827)

36

Illustrations to the *Poems of Thomas Gray,* 1797-8

Ode on a Distant Prospect of Eton College. "There shall the fury passions tear, The vultures of the mind"

Watercolor with pen and black ink over graphite on wove paper with letterpress inset; 16½ x 12¾ in. (41.9 x 32.4 cm)

Inscribed in black ink, upper left: *6*

PROVENANCE: Nancy Flaxman (née Denman, d. 1820), 1798; her husband, John Flaxman, his sale, Christie's, 1 July 1828 (85), bt Clarke for William Beckford; Beckford's daughter, Susan, Duchess of Hamilton, and by descent to Sir Douglas Douglas-Hamilton, 14th Duke of Hamilton, from whom purchased by Paul Mellon, 1966

SELECTED EXHIBITIONS: YCBA, *Blake,* 1982-3, no. 63c; YCBA, *Human Form Divine,* 1997

SELECTED LITERATURE: Keynes, 1971, pp. 46-7; Tayler, 1971, p. 37; Butlin, 1981, no. 335 18; Vaughan, 1996, pp. 51-2.

Paul Mellon Collection
B1992.8.11(9)

37

The Progress of Poesy. A Pindaric Ode. "Hyperion's march they spy, And glitt'ring shafts of war"

Watercolor with pen and black ink over graphite on wove paper with letterpress inset; 16½ x 12¾ in. (41.9 x 32.4 cm)

Inscribed in black ink, upper left: *6*

PROVENANCE: As for cat. 36

SELECTED EXHIBITIONS: Tate, *William Blake,* 1978, no. 129; YCBA, *Human Form Divine,* 1997

SELECTED LITERATURE: Keynes, 1971, p. 54; Tayler, 1971, pp. 86-7; Butlin, 1981, no. 335 46; Vaughan, 1996, pp. 69-70

Paul Mellon Collection
B1992.8.11(23)

THE TOWERING GENIUS of William Blake finds its most complete expression in the fusion of his poetry and visual imagery in his great illuminated books, yet Blake was also a forceful but sensitive artistic interpreter of other texts. His illustration of the work of other poets is at once both wonderfully imaginative and oddly literal-minded. Thus "the vultures of the mind" in Thomas Gray's "Ode on a Distant Prospect of Eton College" become phantasmagoric birdlike apparitions, and the "glitt'ring shafts of war" in "The Progress of Poesy" become a prickly aureole of arrows.

In about 1795 the London bookseller Richard Edwards commissioned William Blake to provide illustrations for a deluxe edition of Edward Young's *Night Thoughts*. A standard edition of the poem was taken apart and the pages mounted on large sheets of paper on which Blake drew and colored his designs. In all Blake created 537 illustrations on 269 sheets (now in the British Museum), only a fraction of which were actually published. With the model of Blake's watercolors for *Night Thoughts* in mind, Blake's friend John Flaxman commissioned a set of watercolor illustrations of the poems of Thomas Gray as a gift for his wife Nancy. Again the pages of a standard edition of the poems were mounted on large sheets, perhaps left over from the earlier project, on which Blake created his watercolor illustrations. Unlike his illustrations to *Night Thoughts*, these 116 watercolors on fifty-eight sheets (all now in the Yale Center for British Art) were never intended for publication. SW

37

38

38

GEORGE ROMNEY (1734-1802)

Howard Visiting a Prison,
c. 1790-4

Pen and black ink with gray wash over
graphite on laid paper; 12½ x 20⅛ in.
(31.8 x 51.1 cm)

Red oval Haas collection mark, lower
right, numbered 1132; blue-black circular Haas collection mark, upper left

PROVENANCE: ...; Xavier Haas, and his
heirs, from whom acquired in 1959 by
Mr. and Mrs. J. Richardson Dilworth;
given by them to the Yale University Art
Gallery, 1962; transferred to the Yale
Center for British Art, 1979

SELECTED EXHIBITIONS: Smith
College, *Romney*, 1962, no. 82; YCBA,
Visionary Company, 1997

Yale University Art Gallery Collection,
Gift of Mr. and Mrs. J. Richardson
Dilworth, B.A. 1938
B1979.12.667

39

ROBERT DIGHTON (1752-1814)

*Margaret Nicholson Attempting
to Assassinate His Majesty,
George III, at the Garden
Entrance of St. James's Palace,
2nd August 1786,* 1786

Watercolor and gouache over graphite
with pen and black ink on laid paper;
12⅞ x 10 in. (32.8 x 25.6 cm)

Inscribed in black ink, lower left: *576*

PROVENANCE: Collection of the family
of Carington Bowles, sold Sotheby's,
1953; bought by Jeffrey Rose, sold
Sotheby's, 23 February 1978 (36);
bought by John Baskett, from whom
purchased by Paul Mellon, 1978

SELECTED EXHIBITIONS: YCBA, *Crown
Pictorial*, 1990-1, no. 65

SELECTED LITERATURE: Rose, 1981,
p. 64

Paul Mellon Collection
B1986.29.373

THESE DRAWINGS by Romney and Dighton represent two approaches to contemporary history: one looking to the generalizing and universalizing traditions of Grand Manner history painting, the other arising from the world of the caricature.

From the 1770s the philanthropist John Howard campaigned for the reform of prison conditions first in England and Wales and later in Europe. He toured prisons throughout the Continent, finally dying in Russia in 1790 from a fever contracted during one of his prison visits. Howard had declined to be painted by Romney in 1785; but, after Howard's death, Romney set to work on what he hoped would be a series of paintings celebrating Howard's heroic efforts in alleviating human misery. In the early 1790s Romney produced a series of powerful drawings of nightmarish prison scenes in which Howard's experiences are transmuted into universal images of anguish and despair. Although Romney was one of the most fashionable society portrait painters of eighteenth-century England, success in the area of art he most valued – history painting – eluded him. As with so many of his other ambitious plans for history paintings, his projected paintings of Howard visiting prisons never progressed beyond the drawings.

On August 2, 1786, a mentally disturbed woman named Margaret Nicholson tried to stab George III; the monarch, escaping unharmed, pardoned his assailant, who was confined to Bethlehem Hospital. Dighton's drawing is a piece of visual reportage, attempting to convey the actual appearance of the

39

attempted assassination. For Dighton, the son of a printseller and himself a caricaturist and printseller, topicality and timeliness were of the essence. The print after the drawing was published just three days after the assault. Although there is nothing of caricature in his depiction of the attack on the king, neither is there any attempt to render the scene heroic or timeless. sw

51

40

RICHARD COSWAY (1742-1821)

Venus and Mars, c. 1790

Pen and brown ink on laid paper laid down on original mount; 8¾ x 7⅛ in. (22.2 x 18.1 cm)

Inscribed on mount in pen and brown ink, lower right: *Original Drawing by | Richard Cosway R.A.*

PROVENANCE: ...; Shamilt, September 1956; L. G. Duke from 1956 to 1961; P. & D. Colnaghi, April 1961

SELECTED EXHIBITIONS: SNPG, *Cosway*, 1995, no. 105

Paul Mellon Collection
B1977.14.5226

THE ELEGANCE apparent in Richard Cosway's portrait drawings and miniatures (cats. 19-20) pervaded every aspect of his art and life. While many eighteenth-century artists assembled useful working collections of prints, drawings, and paintings by their contemporaries and earlier masters, Cosway was a virtuoso collector. His acquisition of paintings, drawings, and prints, along with furniture and objets d'art, was part and parcel of his fashionable and extravagant lifestyle. But if Cosway's collecting could be flamboyant and at times eccentric, he was also a serious connoisseur and an artist sensitive to the lessons he could glean from the Old Masters. After seeing Cosway's collection of drawings in 1811, Thomas Lawrence had to revise his opinion of Cosway as an artist, impressed as he was by "the knowledge – the familiar acquaintance with, study; and often happy appropriation and even liberal imitation of the Old Masters, the fix'd Landmark of Art, of this little Being which we have been accustom'd never to think or speak of but with contempt." Lawrence, himself a serious collector of drawings, bought a number of sheets from the auction of Cosway's prints and drawings in 1822. As Lawrence's comment suggests, Cosway's collection of Old Master drawings informed his own drawings of subjects taken from the time-honored themes of classical literature and the Bible. In these drawings the grace and finesse of Cosway's draftsmanship is allied to a sensuousness that in subjects such as Venus and Mars becomes an elegant eroticism. sw

41

RICHARD WESTALL (1765-1836)

The Rosebud, 1791

Watercolor and gouache over graphite on wove paper; 12¾ x 15 in. (32.4 x 39.1 cm)

Signed and dated, lower right: *R. Westall 1791*

PROVENANCE: The Fine Art Society, 1969, bt Paul Mellon

SELECTED EXHIBITIONS: RA, 1791, no. 411; YCBA, *The Exhibition Watercolor*, 1981, no. 14; AFA, *British Watercolors*, 1985-6, no. 18

Paul Mellon Collection
B1977.14.4357

THE ASSOCIATION of the rising school of watercolor painting of the late eighteenth and early nineteenth century with landscape tended to marginalize the achievements of watercolorists who specialized in subject pictures. Thus Richard Westall's reputation has not proved as enduring as those of the preeminent landscape watercolorists of the time. Yet, to many of his contemporaries, Westall was a figure of comparable achievements. James Northcote (1746-1831) was of the opinion that "Westall is as much intitled to share in the honour of being one of the founders of the school of painting in water-colours, as his highly gifted contemporaries Girtin and Turner." In a series of articles titled "Observations of the Rise and Progress of Painting in Water Colours," which appeared in Ackermann's *Repository of Arts* in 1812 and 1813, the unnamed author (probably William Henry Pyne) concluded that "the entire development of that powerful union of richness and effect which at length elevated this art to vie with the force of painting in oil, was left for the genius of Richard Westall to complete."

In his exhibition watercolors, generally scenes from literature or classical mythology or rustic genre subjects, Westall combined elements of neoclassicism with rococo decorativeness. A frequent and prolific contributor to the Royal Academy exhibitions from 1784 to 1836, he exhibited *The Rosebud* there in 1792, the year in which he became an Associate. The watercolor is an illustration to Matthew Prior's poem "A Lover's Anger." A lover chides his mistress for being late (Westall shows him holding a watch in his left hand). She, seeking to deflect his anger, complains that a rosebud has fallen into her bodice and exposes her breast to exhibit the mark it has left. The lover, successfully distracted, forgets the rest of his rebuke. sw

42

WILLIAM YOUNG OTTLEY
(1771-1836)

Prospero Summoning Ariel,
c. 1800

Pen and black ink with brown and gray wash and white chalk and gouache over graphite on three joined pieces of wove paper; 12½ x 8⅛ in. (31.8 x 20.6 cm)

Inscribed in graphite, lower right: *WB*

PROVENANCE: (?)Artist's sale, Sotheby's, 14 June 1838 (14), bt Rodd; ...; Iolo A. Williams, bt Paul Mellon, 1973

SELECTED EXHIBITIONS: YCBA, *Fuseli Circle,* 1979, no. 146

Paul Mellon Collection
B1977.14.5645

A STUDENT OF JOHN BROWN (cat. 58) and a friend of John Flaxman (cats. 34-5), Ottley was a connoisseur, collector, writer on art, and an amateur draftsman of distinction. He studied with Brown at the Royal Academy shortly before Brown's death in 1787, at which time he acquired the contents of the artist's studio, including 219 drawings that formed the basis for Ottley's distinguished collection of Old Master drawings. During an extended period of study in Italy from 1791 to 1799, he added groups of drawings by Parmigianino, Raphael, and Michelangelo to his collection.

This drawing of a scene from the first act of Shakespeare's *The Tempest,* with its figure of Prospero clearly recalling Michelangelo's figure of Christ in the Sistine Chapel *Last Judgment,* probably dates from shortly after Ottley's return to London. It is almost certainly one of the group of drawings illustrating *The Tempest* included in the sale of Ottley's works in 1838. Other *Tempest* drawings by Ottley are in the British Museum and the Stanford University Museum of Art. That most of these drawings have traditionally been attributed to either John Brown (as is the case with *Prospero Summoning Ariel*) or John Flaxman is indicative of both Ottley's stylistic indebtedness to his mentor and his friend but also of the assured quality of his draftsmanship. sw

Landscape

IMAGINATIVE, PICTURESQUE AND NATURAL

IN THE EARLY YEARS of the eighteenth century, the painting and drawing of landscape fell into two distinct classes. One was imaginary or ideal landscape, based closely on models established in the seventeenth century by Continental masters such as Claude Lorrain and Gaspard Dughet. The other was the topographical record of actual scenes (see pp. 153-69). Each had its own set of conventions, but in the watercolors of William Taverner (cat. 44), an exponent of ideal landscape, or those of Jonathan Skelton (cats. 132-3), working in the topographical tradition, formula bends under the insistent pressure of natural observation.

Through the interplay of convention and a fresh naturalism, and through the formulation of new visual and mental constructs by which landscape could be perceived and created, the distinctions between ideal and topographical landscape were eroded. As Hogarth in his *Analysis of Beauty* set out principles for artistic creation, freeing the artist from servile imitation of the Old Masters, so Alexander Cozens (cat. 45) sought to provide similar principles and procedures for the creation of an expressive landscape art. That the elements of landscape composition could hold an emotional charge, either directly through their formal properties or through the associations they evoked, provided both fertile ground for aesthetic theorizing and new opportunities for landscape artists.

Edmund Burke's *Philosophical Enquiry into the Origin of our Ideas of the Sublime and Beautiful* (1757) set out not just a physiological explanation for human responses to the representation of extreme experiences but also a virtual blueprint for the landscape artist in the creation of imagery of nature at its most awesome. The Rev. William Gilpin's Picturesque (see cat. 46), articulated through a series of published tours of British scenery, identified picture-worthy characteristics in both art and the actual countryside, his standard for pictorial excellence being the landscape compositions of Claude Lorrain. Although Gilpin's approach, like that of Cozens, emphasized the generalized and the abstract over the particularity of topography, the Picturesque touring popularized by Gilpin had its effect both on the subject matter of topographical artists such as Thomas Hearne (cat. 51) and Francis Towne (cat. 53) and on the way they approached their subjects.

The concepts of the Sublime, the Beautiful, and the Picturesque were debated, refined, elaborated, popularized, and misconstrued by a succession of later commentators and pundits. In some versions the Picturesque came to represent a sort of middle ground between the Sublime and the Beautiful, which accounted for the appeal of the increasingly popular views of rural lanes with shaggy donkeys and tumbledown cottages populated by ragged peasants that were neither sublime nor conventionally beautiful.

This was the sort of rustic imagery that Thomas Gainsborough (cats. 47-9) made very much his own in a highly personal synthesis of the rhythms and formal structures of ideal landscape with humbler aspects of the English countryside. Only with later imitators did such imagery descend into Picturesque cliché. If the Sublime and the Picturesque were responsible for much artificial and formula-bound landscape art, these concepts provided necessary way stations on the road to the naturalistic landscape vision of the Romantics.

SCOTT WILCOX

43

43

BERNARD LENS III (1682-1740)

Classical Landscape, 1717

Gouache and gum over graphite on vellum; 7¹¹⁄₁₆ x 10¼ in. (19.5 x 26.0 cm)

Signed and dated in gold paint, lower left: *B. Lens Fecit 1717*

PROVENANCE: ...; John Morton Morris, London, May 1985, from whom purchased

SELECTED EXHIBITIONS: YCBA, *First Decade,* 1986, no. 101

Paul Mellon Fund
B1985.11.1

44

WILLIAM TAVERNER (1700-72)

Nymphs Bathing in a Glade, c. 1765-70

Watercolor with touches of gouache; 12 x 15¼ in. (30.5 x 38.7 cm)

Inscribed verso: *Nymphs bathing | Polinburg*

PROVENANCE: ...; John Manning, November 1965, bt Paul Mellon

SELECTED EXHIBITIONS: AFA, *British Watercolors,* 1985-6, no. 4

Paul Mellon Collection
B1975.4.1854

ALTHOUGH EARLY EIGHTEENTH-century miniature copies of Old Master paintings tended to reproduce figural subjects, as does Lens's copy after Rubens (cat. 26) and Goupy's after Raphael (cat. 28), Lens also made a number of small gouache versions of seventeenth-century classical landscapes. In exquisite diminutive paintings such as this one after an unidentified original, possibly by Gaspard Dughet, Lens responded to an existing taste for idealized landscape. At the same time, he was working as a topographical draftsman, producing documentary landscapes in pen and ink and wash.

The strands of ideal and topographical landscape, quite separate

44

and distinct at the beginning of the eighteenth century – and in the work of Lens – would become increasingly entwined over the course of the century. William Taverner, a lawyer and amateur draftsman and painter, felt less constraint in combining classical elements with observation of the English countryside. George Vertue credited Taverner with "a wonderful genius to drawing of Landskap in an excellent manner, adorned with figures in a stile above the common." The inscription on the verso of *Nymphs Bathing in a Glade*, just such a figure-adorned landscape, suggests that in this work Taverner echoed, if not copied, a composition by the seventeenth-century Dutch Italianate painter Cornelis Poelenbergh.

Despite his amateur status Taverner's landscapes were much admired and his drawings collected by professional artists such as Paul Sandby and connoisseurs such as Richard Payne Knight. At his death the *Gentleman's Magazine* deemed him "one of the best landscape painters England ever produced." He has continued to be regarded as one of the important early contributors to the rise of landscape painting in England. sw

45

45

ALEXANDER COZENS (1717-86)

Mountainous Landscape,
c. 1780

Gray and brown wash on laid paper
prepared with pale brown ground, laid
down on a contemporary mount;
9½ x 12½ in. (24.1 x 31.8 cm)

PROVENANCE: ...; John Baskett, bt Paul
Mellon, July 1971

SELECTED EXHIBITIONS: PML, *English
Drawings*, 1972, no. 27; YCBA, *English
Landscape*, 1977, no. 22; YCBA, *Cozens*,
1980, no. 23; YCBA, *Oil on Water*, 1986,
no. 16

Paul Mellon Collection
B1975.4.1480

46

WILLIAM GILPIN (1724-1804)

Forest Scene, 1771

Gray and brown wash with pen and
brown ink over graphite, heavily
gummed, on wove paper, on contemporary mount; 17¼ x 12⅞ in. (43.8 x
32.7 cm)

Inscribed in graphite on mount, lower
center: *W. Gilpin*; and on back of
mount: *Done in 1771.| Rev^d W Gilpin
of Boldre. 1771*

Collector's mark of H. J. Reveley
(Lugt 1356), lower left

PROVENANCE: H. J. Reveley; Colnaghi,
June 1948, bt L. G. Duke, to 1961;
Colnaghi, April 1961, bt Paul Mellon

SELECTED EXHIBITIONS: Kenwood,
Gilpin, 1959, no. 34

SELECTED LITERATURE: Barbier, 1963,
p. 34

Paul Mellon Collection
B1977.14.5442

DESCRIBED BY HIS FRIEND and
patron William Beckford as being
"almost as full of systems as the
universe," Alexander Cozens had a
strong pedagogical and theoretical
bent. In his teaching as a drawing-
master and in a series of treatises –
some published, others projected
but never realized – he sought to
establish a theoretical basis for a
landscape art that was neither topographical nor simply reliant on

copying the forms of seventeenth-century Continental models. *A New Method of Assisting the Invention in Drawing Original Compositions of Landscape,* published shortly before his death, illustrated the technique he had devised for using inkblots to stimulate the imagination in creating landscape compositions. Although not necessarily, and certainly not directly, blot-derived, *Mountainous Landscape* represents the kind of fantastic landscape that could result from the process. Much misunderstood, *A New Method* earned Cozens the soubriquet "Blot-master General to the town."

Cozens's landscape systems, though they found a receptive audience among certain artists, were too confusing and susceptible to ridicule and parody to gain wide public acceptance. The Rev. William Gilpin's writings on the Picturesque were, by contrast, hugely popular and influential with both artists and a wider public. Beginning with his *Observations on the River Wye,* published in 1782 but based on a trip down the river in 1770, Gilpin popularized the Picturesque as a distinct aesthetic category, a species of beauty appropriate to pictures but also applicable to natural scenery. In its simplest formulation the Picturesque was "that peculiar kind of beauty, which is agreeable in a picture."

Gilpin experimented with Cozens's blot method; and his own drawings, of which this brooding woodland scene is a particularly grand example, are indebted to Cozens in their bold, simplified forms and dark, monochromatic character. If the inscription on the verso, supplied by a descendant in the nineteenth

46

century, is accurate, Gilpin made the drawing between his Wye tour in 1770 and his tour of the Lakes in 1772 (published in 1786). It is unclear whether the drawing represents an actual location or is the kind of imaginary landscape Cozens's methods were meant to promote. sw

47

THOMAS GAINSBOROUGH
(1727-88)

47

A Hilly Landscape with Figures Approaching a Bridge, c. 1763

Watercolor and gouache on laid paper, on contemporary mount; 10⅞ x 14⅞ in. (27.6 x 37.8 cm)

Inscribed in pen and black ink, on back of mount, center: *Presented by Mr Gainsborough to Doctor Charlton at Bath | & purchased at the Doctors sale*

PROVENANCE: Dr. Rice Carlton; ...; Durlacher, New York, bt Mr. and Mrs. James Fosburgh, New York; given by them to the Yale University Art Gallery; transferred, 1998

SELECTED EXHIBITIONS: YUAG, *Alumni*, 1960, no. 172; Tate, *Gainsborough*, 1980-1, no. 15; Grand Palais, *Gainsborough*, 1981, no. 87; IEF, *Gainsborough Drawings*, 1983-4, no. 28

SELECTED LITERATURE: Hayes, 1971, no. 264

Yale University Art Gallery Collection, James W. and Mary C. Fosburgh Collection
B1998.14.1

48

A Woodland Pool with Rocks and Plants, c. 1765-70

Watercolor, black chalk and oil paint, with gum, on laid paper; 9 x 11⅛ in. (23 x 28.3 cm)

PROVENANCE: ...; David Rolt (a descendent of Dr. Thomas Monro); Colnaghi, bt Paul Mellon, March 1962

SELECTED EXHIBITIONS: VMFA, *Painting in England*, 1963, no. 58; Colnaghi-Yale, *English Drawings*, 1964-5, no. 12; PML, *English Drawings*, 1972, no. 37; YCBA, *English Landscape*, 1977, no. 25; Tate, *Gainsborough*, 1980-1, no. 22; Grand Palais, *Gainsborough*, 1981, no. 94; IEF, *Gainsborough Drawings*, 1983-4, no. 48; YCBA, *Oil on Water*, 1986, no. 25

48

SELECTED LITERATURE: Hayes, 1971, no. 311

Paul Mellon Collection
B1975.4.1198

49

Wooded Landscape with Figures, c. 1788

Black chalk with some white and red chalk, gray and brown wash, and touches of gouache on wove paper; 15½ x 12½ in. (39.4 x 31.7 cm)

Collector's mark of T. E. Lowinsky (Lugt 2420a), lower right

PROVENANCE: T. E. Lowinsky; by descent to Justin Lowinsky to 1963, Colnaghi, February 1963, bt Paul Mellon

SELECTED EXHIBITIONS: Arts Council, *Gainsborough Drawings*, 1960-1, no. 57; PML, *English Drawings*, 1972, no. 36; YCBA, *English Landscape*, 1977, no. 36; Tate, *Gainsborough*, 1980-1, no. 49; Grand Palais, *Gainsborough*, 1981, no. 113; IEF, *Gainsborough Drawings*, 1983-4, no. 88

SELECTED LITERATURE: Woodall, 1939, no. 208; Hayes, 1971, no. 803

Paul Mellon Collection
B1977.14.4697

THOMAS GAINSBOROUGH is perhaps the most naturally gifted and fluent of all British draftsmen. He seldom produced drawings as finished, saleable works; and, though he did make drawings in preparation for paintings, mostly he drew just for the pleasure it gave him. That pleasure informs the character and quality of his draftsmanship. It was in the act of drawing and in the creation of landscape compositions that he found an escape from the onerous business of painting portraits.

In Gainsborough's landscapes an early naturalism rooted in the

49

borough's friend Uvedale Price that he assembled in the studio "roots, stones and mosses, from which he formed, and then studied, foregrounds in miniature."

In the hands of theorists such as Price, the idea of the Picturesque was expanded from Gilpin's conception, based on the paintings of Claude, to include rustic and low-life genre scenes. Gainsborough's own taste for idyllic scenes of rustic peasant life played a key role in Price's thinking. *Wooded Landscape with Figures*, a drawing from the end of Gainsborough's life, together with the painting which he developed from it, *Peasant Smoking at a Cottage Door* (University of California at Los Angeles), represent the culmination and the most monumental statement of this line of imagery in Gainsborough's work. sw

example of seventeenth-century Dutch landscape painting is succeeded by, but never wholly gives way to, a more abstract language of landscape forms, which not only recalls aspects of Claude's and Dughet's landscapes but echoes the composite method of Alexander Cozens (cat. 45). Both *A Hilly Landscape with Figures Approaching a Bridge* and *A Woodland Pool with Rocks and Plants* date from Gainsborough's period of residence in Bath (1759-74). *A Hilly Landscape* with its flickering light effects and variety of touch embodies the devel-

oping Picturesque aesthetic. It also marks a movement away from the Dutch-inspired naturalism of his years in Suffolk to a more synthetic approach, in which his landscapes are constructed from a repertoire of recurring formal elements.

A Woodland Pool with Rocks and Plants demonstrates that Gainsborough had not wholly abandoned natural observation for the play of his fancy. Yet just how natural is this drawing? The Gainsborough scholar John Hayes has characterized the work as "a study from nature," yet we know from Gains-

50

50

PHILIPPE JACQUES DE
LOUTHERBOURG (1740-1812)

*Figures by a Stream with Cattle
Watering*

Gray wash over graphite on laid paper;
14 x 20 in. (36 x 51 cm)

PROVENANCE: ...; Michael Appleby; his
sale, Sotheby's, 29 November 2000
(60), bt Yale Center for British Art

Paul Mellon Fund
B2001.5

THE ALSATIAN ARTIST Philippe
Jacques de Loutherbourg arrived in
London in 1771, having already established himself in Paris as a successful painter of pastoral landscapes
and dramatic shipwreck scenes. With
an introduction to the actor-manager
David Garrick, Loutherbourg gained
employment designing scenery for
productions at the Drury Lane
Theatre. He also explored the beauties of the English and Welsh countryside, making pioneering use of
the actual scenery of Britain in his
theatrical work, in paintings exhibited at the Royal Academy, and in
publications.

This pastoral landscape, which
may well predate Loutherbourg's

move to England, is a decorative artificial construct rather than a tran-
script of nature. In that sense it is
not far removed from the synthetic
approach to landscape advocated by
Alexander Cozens, and its compo-
nents – the watering cattle in a shaded pool, the sleeping herd boy, the
tête-à-tête of hunter and milkmaid –
are very much the standard elements
of Thomas Gainsborough's landscape
creations, though rendered with a delicacy and fastidiousness of touch in
place of Gainsborough's bravura
draftsmanship. Loutherbourg and
Gainsborough were in fact friends,
and a portrait sketch of Gainsborough by Loutherbourg is in the Yale
Center for British Art. sw

51

51

THOMAS HEARNE (1744-1817)

View from Skiddaw over Derwentwater, c. 1777

Watercolor over graphite on wove paper, on contemporary mount; 7⅜ x 10⅝ in. (18.7 x 27.0 cm)

Signed in pen and black ink, lower left: *Hearne*

PROVENANCE: ...; Palser, bt Sabina Girtin, 1919; Tom Girtin, bt John Baskett, February 1970, from whom purchased by Paul Mellon

SELECTED EXHIBITIONS: PML, *English Drawings,* 1972, no. 52; YCBA, *English Landscape,* 1977, no. 55; NYPL, *Wordsworth,* 1987-8, no. 235; YCBA, *Fairest Isle,* 1989, no. 31

SELECTED LITERATURE: Morris and Milner, 1985, p. 8; Morris, 1989, p. 68

Paul Mellon Collection
B1977.14.4685

52

52

EDWARD DAYES (1763-1804)

Haweswater, Westmoreland,
c. 1795

Watercolor over graphite on wove paper;
11⅞ x 17⁹⁄₁₆ in. (30.2 x 44.6 cm)

Signed lower right, scratched into paper:
Dayes

PROVENANCE: ...; L.G. Duke; F. Nettlefold; Sotheby's, 23 November 1966
(224); Spink, Feb. 1967, bt Paul Mellon

SELECTED EXHIBITIONS: YCBA, *English
Landscape*, 1977, no. 92; YCBA, *Sandby*,
1985, no. 150

SELECTED LITERATURE: Grundy, 1933-
8, vol. 2, pp. 14-15

Paul Mellon Collection
B1981.25.2577

53

FRANCIS TOWNE (1739-1816)

Lake Windermere, 1786

Watercolor with pen and brown and
gray ink over graphite on two joined
sheets of laid paper, on artist's mount;
6⅛ x 18½ in. (15.6 x 47.0 cm)

Signed and dated in pen and black ink,
lower left.: *No 13 F Towne. del^t 1786*; inscribed on back of mount in pen and
brown ink: *No 13 | afternoon light from the
right hand | The Lake of Windermere taken
near Low Wood | August ye 9th 1786 by |
Francis Towne | Leicester Square | London | 1790*

PROVENANCE: John Merivale, by
descent to Dr. W.H.H. Merivale; Agnew,
1961, bt Paul Mellon

SELECTED EXHIBITIONS: ? Lower
Brook Street, London, 1805 (8); VMFA,
Painting in England, 1963, no. 72;
Colnaghi-Yale, *English Drawings*, 1964-5,
no. 54; YCBA, *English Landscape*, 1977,
no. 46; YCBA, *Fairest Isle*, 1989, no. 41;
Denver, *Glorious Nature*, 1993-4, no. 26;
Tate, *Towne*, 1997-8, no. 49

SELECTED LITERATURE: Andrews, 1989,
p. 157

Paul Mellon Collection
B1975.4.187

ALTHOUGH THE REV. WILLIAM GILPIN toured the Lake District in 1772, he did not publish his observations on the tour until 1786. By that date a number of artists including Loutherbourg and Gainsborough had already visited the area, and Thomas West had published his *Guide to the Lakes* (1778). Thus Gilpin's publication only confirmed and enhanced an existing appreciation of Lakeland scenery both as a subject for artists and an object of Picturesque touring.

Thomas Hearne visited the Lake District in 1777 and again in 1778 as part of longer tours of the north of England and Scotland on which he accompanied Sir George Beaumont. Hearne's extraordinary view of Derwentwater, the "most generally admired" of the Lakes according to Gilpin, emphasizes its austere beauty, capturing what an "ingenious person" quoted by Gilpin described as "Beauty lying in the lap of Horrour."

In the summer of 1786, the year of Gilpin's publication of his tour of the Lakes, Francis Towne undertook his own tour with two friends, one of whom was the first owner of this watercolor of Windermere. In a two-week period they visited most of the Lakes, and Towne filled two sketchbooks with drawings. Rather than consider these drawings as preliminary for other finished watercolors, Towne chose to work up the sketchbook pages themselves with watercolor and pen and ink outlines, extract the pages from the sketchbook, and mount them as finished drawings (the date of 1790 on the back of the mount indicates the year Towne mounted this drawing).

53

Although the watercolors have a carefully considered, even stylized appearance, the Towne scholar Timothy Wilcox maintains that, by retaining the format of the sketchbook page and by adding the insistent pen outlines, Towne was drawing attention to their origins as sketches done on the spot.

It is not known when Edward Dayes toured the Lakes. He exhibited "A View on Keswick Lake, Cumberland" at the RA in 1791 and another view of Keswick in 1802, suggesting a visit to the region in the years just prior to the earlier date, and perhaps a second visit in the later 1790s or early 1800s. While all these artists' tours must be seen in the context of Picturesque touring, changing popular conceptions of the Picturesque caused some artists, including Dayes, to object to the whole notion. In his *Essays on Painting*, published shortly after his death, Dayes maintained that the Picturesque should not apply to "objects 'rough and irregular,' or such as are deformed, aged, and ugly," and he railed against the taste for pictures "peopled with gypsies and vagabonds, dirty beggars, clothed with rags." In his view of Haweswater, the fisherman and the milkmaid in the foreground are fastidious in dress and elegant in manner. sw

54

54

JOHN WEBBER (1750-93)

Pont-y-Pair on the River Llugwy near Betws-y-Coed, Denbigh, 1791

Gray, brown and blue wash with watercolor over graphite on laid paper, on contemporary mount; 13½ x 18¾ in. (34.3 x 47.6 cm)

Signed and dated in pen and brown ink, lower right: *John Webber. 1791*; inscribed in graphite, lower left: *Ponte Pair Lanrwst | near*; on mount, lower center: *Ponte Pair in North Wales*

PROVENANCE: ... Mr. E. Martin, bt Colnaghi, March 1962, from whom purchased by Paul Mellon, June 1962

SELECTED EXHIBITIONS: RA, London, 1792, no. 512; YCBA, *Presences of Nature*, 1983, no IV.4; YCBA, *Fairest Isle*, 1989, no. 93; Bern, *Webber*, 1996, no. 61

Paul Mellon Collection
B1975.4.1966

55

WILLIAM DAY (1764-1807)

Matlock Baths, Derbyshire, c. 1789

Watercolor with pen and brown ink over graphite on laid paper; 13⅝ x 19⅛ in. (34.6 x 48.6 cm)

Signed in pen and brown ink, lower center: *W Day*; inscribed on mount, in pen and black ink: *16*; on fragment of old backing, now removed: *Matlock Baths, from the Guilderoy Mine at the Head of the Valley | Derbyshire*

PROVENANCE: ...; Sotheby's, 26 March 1975 (152), bt Paul Mellon through John Baskett

SELECTED LITERATURE: Hauptman, 1996, p. 203

Paul Mellon Collection
B1975.3.149

FROM 1776 TO 1780 JOHN WEBBER accompanied Captain James Cook as the official artist on Cook's third Pacific voyage. In the decade that followed Webber worked up his sketches from the voyage into engravings, oil paintings, finished

55

watercolors, even stage scenery (in collaboration with Philippe Jacques de Loutherbourg) for the pantomime *Omai* at Covent Garden. At the same time he made a number of sketching expeditions to those wilder reaches of Britain that were centers of Picturesque tourism: along the Wye, the mountains of Wales, the Lake District, and the Peak District of Derbyshire.

In 1789 Webber toured Derbyshire in the company of William Day, an amateur painter with a particular interest in geology and mineralogy. By the date of their visit, Matlock Baths had developed a reputation for its water cures, and Day's watercolor shows the buildings that had recently been constructed to accommodate visitors taking the waters nestling in the valley beneath Matlock Tor. Day's vantage point is the Guilderoy mine at the head of the valley, and in the foreground he represents characteristic activities of lead mining: breaking up large lumps of rock and lead ore, sieving and "buddling" the ore to separate it from other rock, and measuring out the amount of ore owed to the Crown as tithe.

Webber's drawings from his Derbyshire tour with Day, five of which are in the collection of the Yale Center for British Art, show, in addition to a Picturesque sensibility, a concern with the geology of the area that echoes the scientific orientation of his work for Captain Cook and must have formed the common ground of his friendship with Day. A similar concern with the specifics of geology informs his *Pont-y-Pair on the River Llugwy near Betws-y-Coed*, a drawing from the second of two tours to Wales in 1790 and 1791. His companion on the earlier of those tours was again Day. The village of Betws-y-Coed ("Chapel in the Wood") in northern Wales would become one of the most popular artists' haunts in this much visited region. Paul Sandby had made Pont-y-Pair ("Bridge of the Cauldron") the subject of one of his *XII Views in North Wales* in 1776. sw

"The Universal Law of Nature"
THE SCIENTIFIC DRAWING

THE EIGHTEENTH CENTURY in Britain was a period of intense intellectual and scientific curiosity, notable for the complex reciprocal relationships forged between science and the arts. Discrete disciplines had not yet been established within the general field of science, and it encompassed a broad range of subjects including astronomy, botany, chemistry, geology, medicine and anatomy, and physics. Such eclecticism encouraged the interchange of ideas between artists and scientists, who met through learned societies and formed networks which were often social as well as professional.

A number of the artists represented in this catalogue were actively involved with scientific endeavors. Joseph Wright of Derby (see cat. 12), who is well-known for his depiction of quasi-scientific scenarios, was a keen participant in the activities of the Lunar Society of Birmingham, a group of distinguished amateur scientists, and the pastellist John Russell (see cats. 15 and 57) was a highly-regarded lunar astronomer. Jonathan Richardson's life-long association with the Royal Society provided valuable opportunities to form friendships with its members, including the eminent natural historian and collector, Hans Sloane (see cat. 1), and to discuss his influential theoretical ideas. In his *Essay on the Theory of Painting* Richardson argued that visual culture not only gave pleasure but also functioned to "inform the Mind" about "Countries, Habits, Manners, Arms, Buildings Civil, and Military, Animals, Plants, Minerals, their Natures and Properties." Artists, conversely, benefited from scientific knowledge; they made use of optical devices, such as the camera obscura (see cat. 138), and advances in chemistry resulted in the development of new materials and processes. There were productive interactions between art, science, and manufacture, of which the collaboration between George Stubbs and Josiah Wedgwood on the production of enamels is just one example (see cat. 150).

Draftsmanship played an important role in the development of the sciences. Drawing was a quick and economical method of recording primary material accurately, and a draftsman such as Luigi Balugani (see cats. 60-3)

would have been considered an essential component of any scientific expedition. Drawings were used routinely as models for engravings, which were published to disseminate new information. Aesthetic considerations also seem to have been important to the scientific community: drawings produced ostensibly in the service of science often have a high degree of finish and sophistication beyond their practical requirements.

The relationship between draftsmen and anatomists was especially close. Anatomy was considered an essential subject for any aspiring artist, and at the foundation of the Royal Academy in 1768, Sir Joshua Reynolds established a Professorship of Anatomy and appointed the anatomist William Hunter as its first incumbent. One of the greatest contributions to an understanding of the subject in the eighteenth century was made by George Stubbs. Working in a tradition of "artist-anatomist" dating back to the Renaissance, Stubbs published his treatise on the anatomy of the horse in 1766 to acclaim from the scientific community, and the 125 drawings he made for his last great unfinished project, *A Comparative Anatomical Exposition of the Structure of the Human Body, with that of a Tiger, and Common Fowl* (see cats. 64-8), testify to his extraordinary mastery of this complex subject.

GILLIAN FORRESTER

56

PAUL SANDBY (1730-1809)

The Meteor of August 18, 1783, as Seen from the East Angle of the North Terrace, Windsor Castle, 1783

Watercolor on laid paper; 12½ x 19 in. (31.8 x 48.3 cm)

Signed in brown ink, lower left: *P! Sandby.* and inscribed on the verso in graphite, at top at center: *East end of Terrace | With the meteor*, and in graphite, above right, with two sketches of the meteor

PROVENANCE: ...;Paul Mellon, by whom given, 1993

SELECTED LITERATURE: Roberts, 1995, pp. 68-9, fig. 18.3; Olsen and Pasachoff, 1998, pp. 69-75, p. III, fig. 38

Paul Mellon Collection
B1993.30.115

METEORS AND COMETS were subjects of universal fascination in the eighteenth century. The traditional emblematic associations (comets were believed to portend the death of rulers or dramatic changes in the status quo) retained their currency in the popular imagination but were underpinned by greater knowledge of celestial phenomena, which was facilitated by increasingly sophisticated instruments, such as the telescope.

This watercolor is related to the extensive series of views of Windsor Castle and Great Park produced by Paul and Thomas Sandby (see cats. 134-5), and the circumstances of its production and circulation provide an illuminating example of how artists recorded and disseminated scientific knowledge in the period. The drawing commemorates one of the most celebrated astronomical events of the century, the transit of a meteor on the evening of August 18, 1783. The natural philosopher-physician Tiberius Cavallo published his recollections of the

episode in *Philosophical Transactions* in the following year:

> *Being upon the Castle Terrace at Windsor, in company with my friends Dr James Lind [the physician to the Royal household], Dr Lockman, Mr T. Sandby and a few other persons, we observed a very extraordinary meteor in the sky. ... Mr Sandby's watch was seventeen minutes past nine nearest; it did not mark seconds.*

The artist represented the progress of the meteor, somewhat surreally, by showing it three times within a single image, and his haunting depiction powerfully conveys the intense brightness it generated. (Cavallo observed that the meteor "lit up every object on the face of the country.")

The Sandbys made several drawings of the meteor (cat. 56 is attributed to Paul) and published an aquatint of the subject in October 1783 with a dedication to the celebrated natural historian Sir Joseph Banks, with whom Paul Sandby had toured Wales in 1773. The drawings and print were considered invaluable documentary records of this significant event. GF

57

JOHN RUSSELL (1745-1806)

A Drawing of a Part for the Map of the Moon, 1794

Graphite on wove paper; 7¹⁵⁄₁₆ x 6⅛ in. (20.2 x 15.7 cm)

Signed and dated in graphite, under the image: *J. Russell del^t June 10th 1794*; inscribed in ink at top: *Drawing of a part for the Map of the Moon,* and, in graphite, at right of center, and below, left of center, with shorthand notations

PROVENANCE: ...; Elizabeth Richardson Simmons, New York, sold Christie's, 12 November 1968 (164), bt Paul Mellon through John Baskett

SELECTED EXHIBITIONS: YCBA, *Pursuit of Happiness,* 1977, no. 99

SELECTED LITERATURE: Ryan, 1966, pp. 27-48

Paul Mellon Collection
B1975.4.920

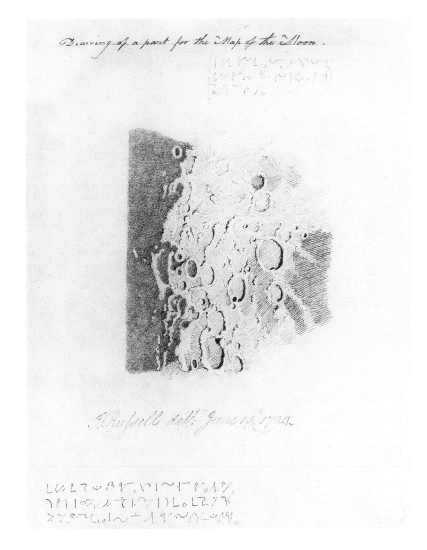

JOHN RUSSELL is best known for his portraits in pastel (see cat. 15), but he was also a distinguished amateur lunar astronomer. Russell was struck by the beauty of the "gibbous Moon" when he first viewed it through a telescope as a young artist "conversant with Light, and Shade." Dissatisfied with existing lunar cartography, he used his skills of observation and pictorial representation to produce moon-maps which were highly praised by his scientific contemporaries. Russell was encouraged in his endeavors by Sir Joseph Banks, President of the Royal Society, who advocated having lunar maps drawn by artists rather than astronomers.

Using a six-foot reflecting telescope with a six-inch mirror made by the astronomer Sir William Herschel and a refracting Dolland telescope, Russell made a large number of detailed working sketches, which he annotated with notes, using John Byrom's system of shorthand. Many of these remarkable drawings, together with other material relating to Russell's astronomical work, are now in the collection of the Museum of the History of Science in Oxford. Cat. 57 records an area of the moon near the crater Mersenious.

In 1795, thirty-one years after he embarked on his astronomical labors, Russell produced a pastel measuring four feet four inches by five feet, which was the largest and most accurate representation of the moon made up to that time. Russell also constructed a lunar relief globe, or "Selenographia," by pasting engraved pieces of paper onto a plain twelve-inch globe, with the intention of marketing it more widely, but the project was not a commercial success. Russell's studies culminated in *Luna Planispheres,* two prints illustrating the effects of direct and oblique illumination, engraved by the artist and published by his son after his death in 1806. GF

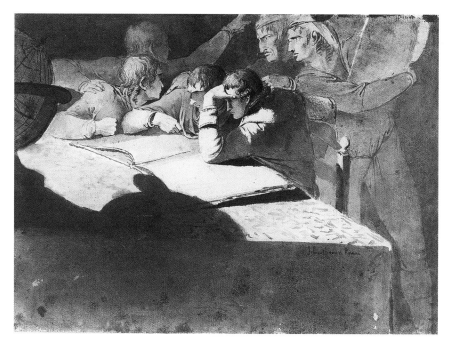

58

JOHN BROWN (1749-87)

The Geographers

Pen and ink and gray wash on laid paper; 7³⁄₁₆ x 10¹⁄₁₆ in. (18.3 x 25.6 cm)

Inscribed in graphite, lower right: *John Brown Romae*, and in top right corner: *61*; on verso in graphite: *J Brown del.*

Verso: graphite sketch of a seated man reading a book

PROVENANCE: William Young Ottley, his sale, T. Philipe, London, 20 June 1814 (1621); Sir Thomas Lawrence, his sale, Christie's, 17 June 1830 (105), bt Knowles; Lady North; Leon Suzor, Paris, by 1952; Faerber & Maison, London, from whom bt Paul Mellon, 1965

SELECTED EXHIBITIONS: MC, *Collections Parisiennes*, 1950, no. 94; PML, *English Drawings*, 1972, no. 59; YCBA, *Fuseli Circle*, 1979, no. 61; LACMA, *Visions of Antiquity*, 1993-4, no. 7

Paul Mellon Collection
B1977.14.4152

THE SUBJECT OF John Brown's enigmatic and atmospheric drawing has never been identified (it was untitled by the artist, and *The Geographers* is a later appellation), but the image seems to reflect contemporary interest in travel and cartography. The composition is dominated by the shadow of the globe looming menacingly over the foreground, and the volume over which the young men pore so intently may contain maps or be a travel book, though intriguingly it is depicted as a *tabula rasa*.

Brown spent most of the 1770s in Rome, where he met Henry Fuseli. *The Geographers*, originally a sheet in one of Brown's Roman sketchbooks, suggests something of the intense intellectual climate he experienced there and also reflects the preoccupation with supernatural and uncanny themes that informed the work of Fuseli and his circle.

The drawing also demonstrates Brown's fascination with physiognomy, a theoretical system dating back to the Renaissance and based on the premise that facial expressions were an index to human personality. Brown may have become interested in the subject through his association with Fuseli, who made several drawings for Johann Kasper Lavater's influential treatise, *Essays on Physiognomy, Calculated to Extend the Knowledge and the Love of Mankind*. The young man seated nearest the viewer in Brown's drawing has a classical profile, in physiognomonic terms indicative of nobility of character, whereas the hooked noses and scowling expressions of the standing men hint at their villainous nature. Brown, who made numerous drawings of heads, was described by one of his contemporaries as having "a peculiar talent in delineating the human physiognomy which he prosecuted with utmost diligence and perseverance, frequently following a remarkable character day after day until he completely succeeded in obtaining his resemblance and character."
GF

59

GIOVANNI BATTISTA BORRA
(1713-70)

Stromboli, 1750

Pen and ink and watercolor on laid
paper; 21¼ x 14⅞ in. (51.5 x 37.8 cm)

Inscribed in brown ink above at center:
STROMBOLI; and below at left: *Borra
Arch.ᵘˢ*; and below at center: *PIANTA DEL
VESVVIIO COME ERA NEL 1750.*; and with
border around image

PROVENANCE: ...; Edmund Neville-
Rolfe; bt Paul Mellon

Paul Mellon Collection
B1977.14.1015

ALTHOUGH GEOLOGY did not exist as
a self-contained discipline in the
mid-eighteenth century, there was
considerable interest in volcanoes
and other natural phenomena, and
the pioneering research conducted
by amateur natural historians such
as Sir William Hamilton proved
invaluable for the work of later professional geologists. Reflecting
Enlightenment views of the natural
world, one of Hamilton's geological
correspondents opined:

> *I know of no subject that fills the
> mind with greater ideas than the
> volcanic history of the world ... tis
> certainly a part of the great system
> of dissolution & renovation which
> seems the Universal Law of Nature,
> by which a sparrow, a city, a region
> or a world, probably, have their
> beginning & end.*

Volcanic activity also had considerable aesthetic appeal and provided
compelling subject matter for artists
interested in exploring the notion of
the Sublime.

The Italian architectural draftsman and civil engineer Giovanni
Battista Borra accompanied Sir
Robert Wood on his archaeological
expedition to Asia Minor and Syria
in 1750-1. Borra produced a large
group of drawings, ninety-eight of
which are in the Center's collection,
and a number of his architectural
subjects were engraved for Wood's
publications on the ruins of

Palmyra and Balbec (see cat. 118).
During the expedition Borra also
made studies of natural phenomena,
including this drawing of Stromboli,
the volcanic island north of Sicily.
Borra resisted the Sublime appeal of
Stromboli; maintaining a rigorous
architectural draftsman's approach,
he produced a precise and unembell-
ished delineation of the island, in plan
and elevation. GF

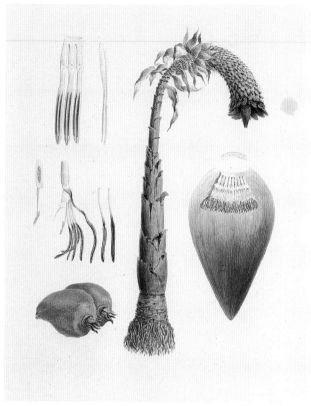

60

61

LUIGI BALUGANI (1737-70)

60

Ensete ventricosum
(African Wild Banana)

Watercolor over graphite on laid paper;
12½ x 9¾ in. (31.8 x 24.8 cm)

Inscribed, verso, in pen and brown ink:
Ensete No.10

PROVENANCE: By descent to Lord
Elgin of Broomhall, from whom bt Paul
Mellon, 1968

SELECTED LITERATURE: Hulton,
Hepper and Friis, 1991, p. 113

Paul Mellon Collection
B1977.14.8909

61

Carthamus tinctorius
(Safflower)

Watercolor and gouache over graphite
on laid paper; 15½ x 11¾ in. (39.4. x
30.0 cm)

Inscribed in pen and black ink, verso,
below at center: *Sussa Samf.*

PROVENANCE: As for cat. 60

SELECTED LITERATURE: Hulton,
Hepper and Friis, 1991, p. 77

Paul Mellon Collection
B1977.14.9100

62

Sphyrna Zygaena
(Hammer-headed Shark)

Watercolor and gouache on laid paper;
16 x 11⅝₆ in. (40.5 x 30.3 cm)

Inscribed in graphite, above right: *2*; and
in pen and brown ink, verso, above left:
[?*25*] *Hammer Fish*, and below at center:
Hammer headed Shark Loheia

PROVENANCE: As for cat. 60

Paul Mellon Collection
B1977.14.9129

63

Aspis Cornutus
(Horned Viper or Cerastes)

Watercolor and gouache on laid paper;
11⅞ x 9¾ in. (30.2 x 24.7 cm)

Inscribed in pen and brown ink, verso,
above left: *Cerastes No. 1 | to be engraved
as it stands*

PROVENANCE: As for cat. 60

Paul Mellon Collection
B1977.14.8926

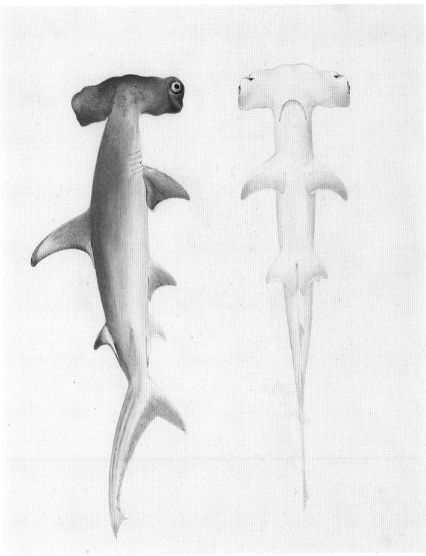

62

63

IN 1765 THE AMATEUR ARTIST and explorer James Bruce (1730-94) embarked on a private expedition to document Greek and Roman architectural remains in North Africa. After achieving his initial objective, he continued toward Ethiopia with the aim of locating the source of the Nile, then believed to rise there; his epic expedition continued until 1773. Bruce hired as his assistant Luigi Balugani, the accomplished young Bolognese architect and draftsman. Balugani is not known to have been a professional botanical artist, but he remained with Bruce after the expedition left North Africa, and his remarkable series of annotated field sketches and highly finished drawings of the flora and fauna they encountered in Ethiopia are notable both for their scientific and aesthetic qualities.

The simple terminology Balugani used for the extensive notes accompanying the drawings indicates that he was either self-taught or had a very limited botanical training, but he was a highly competent and assiduous observer, and his records of new species made an important contribution to the study of natural science. Bruce brought back the drawings intact to Britain against enormous odds, and they remained in the family together with journals, letters, and other archival records relating to the expedition until Paul Mellon acquired them in 1968; he gave the collection to the Center nine years later, and it provides an invaluable resource for the natural historian and a fascinating view onto eighteenth-century scientific endeavors.

The authorship of the drawings has been highly problematic and has only been elucidated in recent years. Bruce was an amateur artist and also made drawings during the expedition. Balugani died in Ethiopia, and after Bruce returned to Britain he claimed the draftsman's work as his own. Bruce seems to have been something of a fantasist (Sir Walter Scott recorded that the explorer Henry Salt, who followed in Bruce's footsteps and was one of his severest critics, "corroborated ... Bruce in all his material facts," but felt that he "considerably exaggerated his personal consequence and exploits"), and the temptation to appropriate his draftsman's achievements evidently was overwhelming.

In his published account of the expedition, *Travels to Discover the Source of the Nile*, Bruce stressed Balugani's shortcomings as an artist and lack of moral integrity, and it seems likely that he was jealous of the younger man's considerable and superior talents. Although some of Bruce's contemporaries harbored suspicions regarding the authenticity of "his" drawings, their authorship was not systematically investigated until the 1980s, when curators Patrick Noon and Paul Hulton, in collaboration with botanists Nigel Hepper and Ib Friis, undertook a thorough study of the plant drawings at the Center and revealed that all were almost certainly the work of Balugani.

The four finished watercolors included in this catalogue represent a tiny sample of the hundreds of drawings by Balugani in the Center's collection. Balugani made ten drawings of *Ensete ventricosum*, the African wild banana. Bruce noted that the wild banana "grows and comes to great perfection at Gondar, but it most abounds in that part of Maitsha and Goutto west of the Nile where there are large plantations of it"; he described the plant as "one of the most beautiful productions of nature, as well as most agreeable and wholesome food of man." *Carthamus tinctorius,* or safflower, has been used since ancient Egyptian times as an orange-yellow dye for textiles.

Balugani made several drawings of reptiles. Bruce conjectured, romantically, that *Cerastes* was most likely to have been the species of viper "which Cleopatra employed to procure her death." One day, when Bruce and his party were sailing in the Red Sea, their ship was surrounded by "a prodigious number of sharks ... of the hammer-headed kind." Bruce harpooned one of the sharks, possibly the one illustrated by cat. 62. He described the shark as "eleven feet seven inches from his snout to his tail, and nearly four feet round in the thickest part of him. He had in him a dolphin very lately swallowed, and about half-a-yard of blue cloth." GF

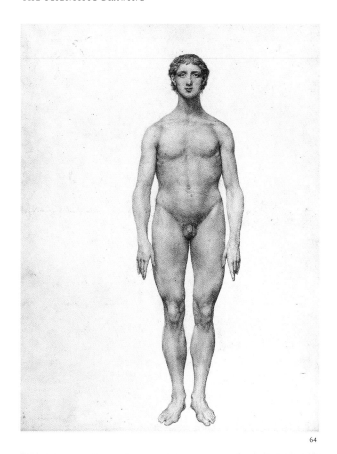

64

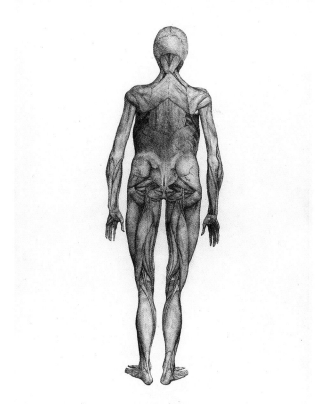

65

GEORGE STUBBS (1724-1806)

A Comparative Anatomical Exposition of the Structure of the Human Body, with that of a Tiger, and Common Fowl, 1795-1806

64

Human Figure, Anterior View, Undissected

Graphite on wove paper; 21½ x 16⅛ in. (54.6 x 41.0 cm)

PROVENANCE: Mary Spencer (Stubbs's common-law wife, d. 1817), sold by her executors, Phillips, 30 April 1817, presumably bt Richard Wroughton (1748-1822); his executors' sale, Sotheby's, 3 April 1822 (1636), bt "G", £24.3.0; ...; Thomas Bell F.R.S. (1792-1880) ...; Dr. John Green, Worcester, Massachusetts (1784-1865), by whom presented to the Worcester Public Library, 1 January 1863; bt Paul Mellon and presented to the Center, 1980

SELECTED LITERATURE: Doherty, 1974, pp. 111-247

SELECTED EXHIBITIONS: Arts Council, *Stubbs*, 1958, no. 11; Tate-YCBA, *Stubbs*, 1984-5, no. 142; YCBA, *Stubbs*, 1999, no. 75; Hall & Knight, *Stubbs*, 2000, no. 38

Paul Mellon Collection
B1980.1.6

65

*Human Figure, Posterior View,
Partially Dissected*

Graphite on wove paper; 21⅜ x 16 in.
(54.3 x 40.6 cm)

PROVENANCE: As for cat. 64

SELECTED LITERATURE: As for cat. 64

SELECTED EXHIBITIONS: Arts Council,
Stubbs, 1958, no. 23; Tate-YCBA, *Stubbs*,
1984-5, no. 144; Hall & Knight, *Stubbs*,
2000, no. 41

Paul Mellon Collection
B1980.1.33

66

Human Skeleton, Lateral View

Graphite on wove paper; 21½ x 16 in.
(54.6 x 40.6 cm)

PROVENANCE: As for cat. 64

SELECTED LITERATURE: As for cat. 64

SELECTED EXHIBITIONS: Tate-YCBA,
Stubbs, 1984-5, no. 139; YCBA, *Stubbs*,
1999, no. 81

Paul Mellon Collection
B1980.1.50

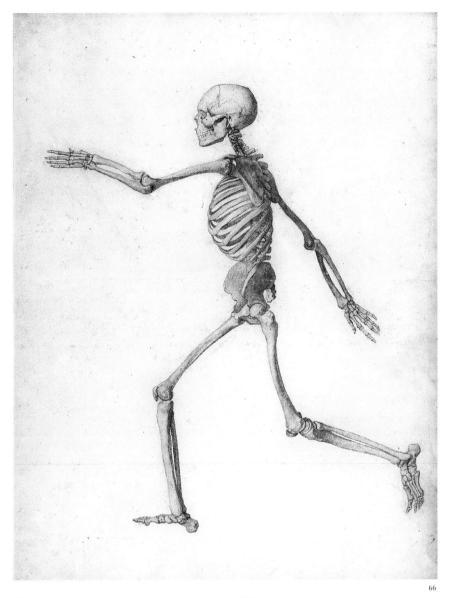

66

67

*Tiger, Lateral View, Partially
Dissected*

Graphite on wove paper; 16 x 21¼ in.
(40.8 x 54.0 cm)

PROVENANCE: As for cat. 64

SELECTED LITERATURE: As for cat. 64

SELECTED EXHIBITIONS: Arts Council,
Stubbs, 1958, no. 25; Tate-YCBA, *Stubbs*,
1984-5, no. 158; YCBA, *Stubbs*, 1999, no. 85

Paul Mellon Collection
B1980.1.79

68

*Fowl, Lateral View, Deeply
Dissected*

Graphite on wove paper; 21¼ x 16 in.
(54.0 x 40.6 cm)

PROVENANCE: As for cat. 64

SELECTED LITERATURE: As for cat. 64

SELECTED EXHIBITIONS: Arts Council,
Stubbs, 1958, no. 27; Tate-YCBA, *Stubbs*,
1984-5, no. 164; YCBA, *Stubbs*, 1999, no.
88; Hall & Knight, *Stubbs*, 2000, no. 43

Paul Mellon Collection
B1980.1.115

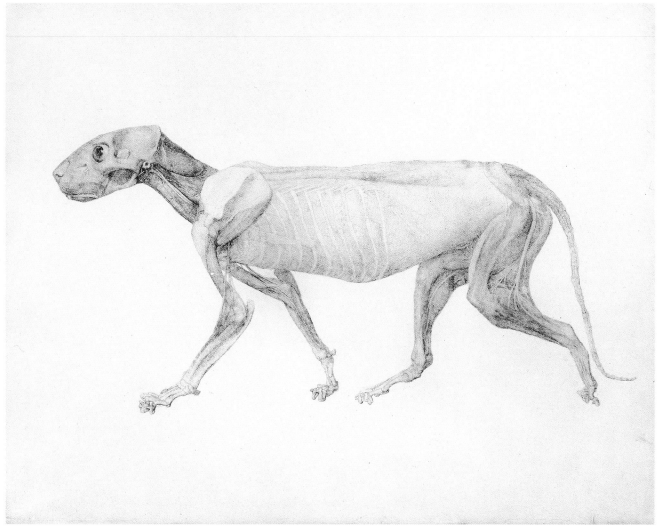

67

ALTHOUGH GEORGE STUBBS is celebrated primarily as a painter of animals, particularly horses, he was also an accomplished anatomist; indeed his exhaustive anatomical studies played a crucial role in the creation of his paintings. Stubbs's interest in anatomy was by no means innovative – the concept of the "artist-anatomist" was well established in the Renaissance period, with Michelangelo and Leonardo da Vinci as its prime exponents – but he showed extraordinary dedication to the subject, and his work was highly praised by his scientific contemporaries.

According to his earliest biographer Ozias Humphry, Stubbs demonstrated a precocious interest in anatomy, beginning his studies at the age of eight with the help of a Dr. Holt, who supplied him with bones to draw. After Stubbs moved to York to work as a portrait painter in 1745, he spent much of his time dissecting corpses at the hospital under the guidance of the surgeon Charles Atkinson, and he provided illustrations for John Burton's pioneering study of obstetrics, *Essay Towards a Complete New System of Midwifery* (1751). In 1756 Stubbs embarked on a study of equine

anatomy, spending sixteen months in a remote farmhouse in Lincolnshire dissecting and drawing the flayed carcasses of horses with the assistance of his common-law wife Mary Spencer. Stubbs intended to have his drawings engraved and published, but his attempts to find a professional engraver were unsuccessful, and he undertook the task himself. When *The Anatomy of the Horse* was eventually published in 1766, it was acclaimed by members of the scientific community, including Petrus Camper, the celebrated Dutch anatomist. Camper suggested that Stubbs might pursue his studies in equine anatomy further, but Stubbs replied, "What you have seen is all I meant to do, it being as much as I thought necessary for the study of Painting ... I looked very little into the internal Parts of a Horse, my search there being only matter of curiosity."

Stubbs's interest in anatomy was clearly more than merely utilitarian, however, as his highly sophisticated studies indicate, and in 1796, at the age of seventy-one, the artist embarked on his most ambitious anatomical investigation, a comparative anatomy of the human being, the tiger, and the common fowl. This choice of subject may sound eccentric today, but it reflected contemporary scientific theories regarding the shared structure of all living creatures, and Stubbs may been encouraged by the celebrated anatomists William and John Hunter, who had both commissioned him to produce paintings of exotic animals. Stubbs intended to publish his *Comparative Anatomical Exposition* as sixty engraved plates with explanatory letterpress in English and French editions, but only half of the plates had been published by the time of his death in 1806, although he had completed the preliminary drawings and had written four volumes of accompanying text. The project clearly had great personal significance for Stubbs: Mary Spencer recollected that on his death-bed, he lamented that "I had indeed hoped to have finished my *Comparative Anatomy* eer I went, for other things I have no anxiety."

The 125 studies and four manuscript volumes had a complex history prior to their acquisition by the Center. They were not included in

68

Stubbs's posthumous studio sale but remained with Mary Spencer until her death in 1817, when they were sold. The drawings were mounted on paperboard either by Edward Orme, who published an edition of the completed plates in 1817, or by a subsequent owner, Thomas Bell; they were eventually acquired by John Green of Worcester, Massachusetts, who gave them in 1863 to the Worcester Public Library, where they languished forgotten until they were discovered in the course of a cataloguing project in 1957. In 1980 Paul Mellon purchased the drawings with the manuscript volumes for the Center, where they were restored to their earlier condition through an extensive program of conservation work. GF

The Wider World
MARINE AND TRAVEL ART

As befits an island nation and the preeminent maritime power of the eighteenth century, marine painting and drawing were much valued in eighteenth-century Britain. Though ignored in the academic conception of the hierarchy of genres and unmentioned by Reynolds in his *Discourses*, marine art could be considered as analogous to both history, the most esteemed branch of painting, and portraiture, the most popular. Marine paintings in their celebration of the great naval victories were historical, and their recording of the appearance of ships was a form of portraiture. Yet it cannot be denied that the associations of marine art, and particularly marine draftsmanship, were mostly utilitarian.

Students destined for naval careers were taught drawing so that they could record coastal profiles, harbors, and types of ships (see pp. 188-9). If professional seamen were expected to have some knowledge of drawing, professional artists who supplied the demand for documentary images of ships and coastlines were expected to have a detailed nautical knowledge. Consequently, they tended to specialize, and the specialty was often passed along from father to son and brother to brother, as with the families of Robert Cleveley (cat. 69) and John Thomas Serres (cats. 72-3).

Britain's imperial expansion in the eighteenth century was less a matter of government policy than of commercial enterprise. By the end of the century, despite the loss of the American colonies, Britain was the dominant colonial power. With commercial and strategic interests around the world, the British outlook was increasingly global. Artists were recruited to document the far-flung reaches of empire, commercial missions to distant capitals, and voyages of exploration. The draftsman in the employ of a colonial administrator, such as Thomas Hearne in the service of Sir Ralph Payne in Antigua (cat. 77), not only documented the topography of empire but did so in a manner calculated to convey certain messages about the values of British control. For John Webber, with Captain Cook in the Pacific, and William Alexander (cat. 82), with Macartney's embassy to the Emperor of China, the responsibility to produce an official documentary record led to opportunities to publish and further exploit for an interested public the visual material they had gleaned on their travels. Other artists, such as Thomas and William Daniell, with their monumental *Oriental Scenery* (cats. 79-81), recognized the potential profit in bringing back accurate images of exotic locales, laying the groundwork for a thriving industry in travel art in the nineteenth century.

SCOTT WILCOX

69

69

ROBERT CLEVELEY (1747-1809)

An English Man-of-War Taking Possession of a Ship, 1783

Watercolor with pen and black ink, over graphite on heavy laid paper; 13½ x 19⅞ in. (34.3 x 50.5 cm)

Signed and dated in pen and black ink, lower left on wreckage: *R! Cleveley del 1783*

PROVENANCE: ...; John Baskett, July 1970, bt Paul Mellon

SELECTED EXHIBITIONS: AFA, *British Watercolors,* 1985-6, no. 12

Paul Mellon Collection
B1975.4.1476

70

WILLIAM ANDERSON (1757-1837)

A Frigate Awaiting a Pilot, 1797

Watercolor with pen and gray and brown ink on wove paper; 7⅞ x 11¾ in. (20 x 29.8 cm)

Signed and dated in pen and brown ink, lower right: *W Anderson 1797*

PROVENANCE: ...; Palser, 1908, bt T. Girtin; Tom Girtin; John Baskett, February 1970, bt Paul Mellon

SELECTED EXHIBITIONS: YCBA, *Masters of the Sea,* 1987, no. 58

Paul Mellon Collection
B1975.3.1090

71

JOHN HARRIS THE ELDER (1767-1832)

Men-of-War Lying off Sheerness

Watercolor with pen and black ink and gouache over graphite on laid paper; 16¼ x 21¼ in. (41.3 x 54.0 cm)

Signed in pen and black ink, lower right: *John Harris pinxt*

PROVENANCE: ...; Frank T. Sabin, November 1964, bt Paul Mellon

SELECTED EXHIBITIONS: YCBA, *Masters of the Sea,* 1987, no. 62

Paul Mellon Collection
B1975.4.1999

MARINE DRAWING in eighteenth-century Britain was largely a specialist production aimed at an expert audience. The marine draftsman was required to provide a documentary record of ships, naval engagements, harbors, and coastlines for a knowledgeable public of active and retired seamen. As John Thomas Serres (cats. 72-3) observed in his *Liber Nauticus and Instructor in the Art of Marine Drawing* (1805), proficiency in the art demanded a working knowledge both of the construction of ships, what Serres termed "naval architecture," and of seamanship. Consequently, it was common for the marine draftsman or painter to have turned to art after an actual involvement in the building or sailing of ships.

Like his father and his twin brother, Robert Cleveley became a marine painter after working in the Royal Dockyard at Deptford. The Scottish-born William Anderson was likewise a shipwright before becoming an artist. John Harris, like the Cleveleys, grew up in the neighborhood of the Deptford dockyard. His boyhood surroundings inspired an early interest in shipbuilding, manifested in the building of a model sloop, though apparently not in any actual employment in the shipbuilding trade. As an artist, Harris pursued marine drawing as but one of several specializations. He worked as a book designer and illustrator and natural-history draftsman.

With its documentary nature the marine watercolor of the period was the nautical equivalent, in both function and technique, of the topographical watercolor. The combination of precise pen outlines and del-

70

71

icate washes of color that characterize the "stained" or "tinted" drawings of the topographical tradition was equally well-suited to the depiction of ships and rigging. Robert Cleveley's brother John studied with the topographical landscape artist Paul Sandby, who was one of a number of watercolorists employed by naval and military schools to teach their young cadets the art of drawing. sw

JOHN THOMAS SERRES (1759-1825)

72

View of Castle Cornet, Guernsey, Channel Islands, with Shipping, c. 1800

Watercolor with pen and black ink over graphite on wove paper; 9⅜ x 26¼ in. (23.8 x 66.7 cm)

Signed in pen and black ink, lower right: *J.T. Serres*

PROVENANCE: ...; Frank T. Sabin, December 1968, bt Paul Mellon

SELECTED EXHIBITIONS: YCBA, *Masters of the Sea*, 1987, no. 60

Paul Mellon Collection
B1975.3.194

73

A Hoy and a Lugger with other Shipping on a Calm Sea

Watercolor with pen and black ink on wove paper; 13⅛ x 18⅝ in. (33.3 x 47.3 cm)

PROVENANCE: ...; Colnaghi, December 1965, bt Paul Mellon

SELECTED EXHIBITIONS: YCBA, *Masters of the Sea*, 1987, no. 61

Paul Mellon Collection
B1986.29.549

ROBERT CLEVELEY (cat. 69) belonged to a family of marine painters. So too did John Thomas Serres. His father Dominic Serres, from a well-off Gascon family, ran away to sea and arrived in England as a prisoner of war in the 1750s. After studying with the marine painter Charles Brooking, the elder Serres achieved considerable success in that line, becoming Marine Painter to George III in 1780.

Unlike Robert Cleveley, John Thomas Serres had no practical experience of ships and the sea. But he was a pupil of his father and, on his father's death in 1793, succeeded him as Marine Painter to George III. In 1800 John Thomas Serres was also appointed Marine Draughtsman to the Admiralty. One of his duties was to provide detailed elevations of the coastlines of Britain, France, and Spain. His *View of Castle Cornet, Guernsey, Channel Islands, with Shipping* may be related to the production of these official coastal views. The more modest but also more charming *A Hoy and a Lugger with other Shipping on a Calm Sea* depicts two of the types of small vessels that plied the coastal trade around England and Holland in the eighteenth century. SW

74

74

JOHN "WARWICK" SMITH
(1749-1831)

Bay Scene in Moonlight, 1787

Watercolor over graphite on wove paper;
13⅜ x 20 in. (34.0 x 50.8 cm)

Signed and dated lower right: *J. Smith
1787*

PROVENANCE: Earl of Warwick; ...;
Colnaghi, May 1967, bt Paul Mellon

SELECTED EXHIBITIONS: YCBA,
Presences of Nature, 1982-3, no. 11.1;
YCBA, *Masters of the Sea*, 1987, no. 48

Paul Mellon Collection
B1977.14.4383

75

THOMAS ROWLANDSON
(1756-1827)

*A Dutch Packet in a Rising
Breeze*, 1791

Watercolor with pen and gray ink over
graphite on laid paper; 7¾ x 10¾ in.
(19.7 x 27.3 cm)

Signed and dated in pen and brown ink,
lower left: *Rowlandson 1791*; and
inscribed, lower center: *Dutch Packet*

PROVENANCE: ...; Sir Bruce Ingram;
C.A. Hunter; Christie's, 11 March 1969
(97); John Baskett, 1969, bt Paul Mellon

SELECTED EXHIBITIONS: YCBA,
Rowlandson Drawings, 1977-8, no. 32;
YCBA, *Masters of the Sea*, 1987, no. 52

SELECTED LITERATURE: Hayes, 1972,
p. 41; Baskett and Snelgrove, 1977,
no. 272

Paul Mellon Collection
B2001.2.1150

75

In 1799 a new periodical, the *Naval Chronicle*, lamented that "Marine Painting is at present in its infancy in this country." The problem was "that this noble branch of the art is cramped, and greatly confined to portraits of particular ships, or correct representations of particular actions, which forbid the artist from indulging in the fine rolling phrenzy of imagination." In the nineteenth century this call for a more imaginative sea painting would be answered by Romantic artists such as J.M.W. Turner. But already in the eighteenth century non-specialist artists had found in the sea and ships and coast, subject matter that was dramatic, evocative, or at times humorous.

John "Warwick" Smith was celebrated in his own time as one of the great innovators in the development of a national school of watercolor painting. In his *Bay Scene in Moonlight* Smith attempts in watercolor the type of atmospheric moonlit coastal view that the French painter Claude Joseph Vernet had made popular in oils.

For such a keen observer of all aspects of contemporary life as Thomas Rowlandson, ships and sailors and the bustling life – and lowlife – of ports and harbors provided an inexhaustible source of subject matter. Rowlandson visited Holland and Germany in 1791. From that tour comes this shipboard view of a Dutch packet-boat crossing the

Channel, conveying vividly both the pleasure and the discomfort inherent in such a voyage. sw

76

DIRK LANGENDIJK (1748-1805)

British Troops Disembarking,
1799

Watercolor with pen and gray ink over
graphite on wove paper; 9⅛ x 13⅞ in.
(23.2 x 35.2 cm)

Signed in pen and brown ink, lower left:
Dirk Langendijk ad vivum 1799

PROVENANCE: ...; Banfather of
Blunsdon; John Baskett, November
1970, bt Paul Mellon

Paul Mellon Collection
B1986.29.429

ALTHOUGH MANY BRITISH and
Dutch artists of the eighteenth century made their careers as marine
painters, documenting and celebrating the great naval battles of the
period, the Dutch painter, etcher,
and draftsman Dirk Langendijk's
specialization in military scenes was
more unusual. In carefully wrought
drawings, which in their combination of pen and ink and watercolor
mirror the topographical and
marine drawings of his British contemporaries, he recorded the military campaigns waged for control of
his native Holland in the later years
of the century.

This watercolor is one of two by
Langendijk in the Yale Center for
British Art showing British troops
in the Netherlands during the

Anglo-Russian expedition in 1799.
It depicts British troops disembarking in North Holland in the late
summer at the start of a short,
unsuccessful campaign to instigate
a counter-revolution against the
French-supported Batavian Republic
and secure the restoration of the
House of Orange. The faint inscription "ad vivum" indicates that
Langendijk was an eyewitness to the
scene, although the fine detail and
careful finish of the drawing hardly
suggest a work executed on the
spot. SW

77

Thomas Hearne (1744-1817)

A View on the Island of Antigua: the English Barracks and St. John's Church Seen from the Hospital, c. 1775-6

Watercolor with pen and gray ink over graphite on wove paper; 20¼ x 29 in. (51.4 x 73.7 cm)

PROVENANCE: Ralph Payne, 1st Baron Lavington, his sale, Jaubert, 5 July 1810 (15); ...; Squire Gallery; ...; Walker's Galleries, February 1951, bt Ray Livingston Murphy; Christie's, 19 November 1985 (38); bt Paul Mellon

SELECTED LITERATURE: Morris and Milner, 1985-6, pp. 24, 37; Morris, 1989, pp. 9-13

Paul Mellon Collection
B1993.30.78

IN 1771 THOMAS HEARNE, fresh from an apprenticeship with the engraver William Woollett, became the official draftsman for Sir Ralph Payne. Payne was taking up an appointment as Captain-General and Governor-in-Chief of the Leeward Islands – an important post, given the role of the sugar-producing slave economy of the Leewards in Britain's commercial empire. Hearne spent three and a half years in the Islands, documenting the life and landscape. After his return to England with Payne in 1775, he produced for Payne a set of twenty large watercolors based on the drawings he had made in the Leewards. This view of Antigua is one of only a handful of these watercolors that are now known.

It records the appearance of the new military barracks constructed during Payne's governorship. Against a backdrop of contemporary fears of a slave insurrection as well as mounting anti-slavery sentiment, the barracks in Hearne's grand watercolor functions as an emblem of British military authority and of the security and stability of Payne's tenure. To the same end, the inclusion of a group of black slaves gambling in the left foreground suggests that they are a contented, if feckless, lot. SW

78

78

SAMUEL DAVIS (1757-1819)

Tassisudon, 1783

Watercolor over graphite on wove paper, on contemporary mount; 20⁵⁄16 x 30¼ in. (51.6 x 76.8 cm)

Inscribed in graphite on the back of the mount: *Tassisudon | House in which the embassy was lodged*

PROVENANCE: By descent in the artist's family, bt Paul Mellon, 1967

SELECTED LITERATURE: Aris, 1982, p. 84

Paul Mellon Collection
B1977.14.283

IN HIS ATTEMPTS to consolidate British East India Company control in northern India, the Governor-General Warren Hastings sent two missions through Bhutan to Tibet. The first was in 1774; the second, in 1783, was headed by Samuel Turner. Its "draughtsman and surveyor" was Samuel Davis, who had arrived in India in 1780. One hundred and forty-four of Davis's drawings of Bhutan from this expedition, both working studies and finished watercolors, are in the collection of the Yale Center for British Art. Of Davis's work Turner wrote: "His subjects indeed, in themselves, are not more remarkable for their grandeur and beauty, than for the judgement, fidelity, and taste with which he has seized on and recorded their features." Turner had nine of the drawings engraved as illustrations to his *An Account of an Embassy to the Court of the Teshoo Lama in Tibet; Containing a Narrative of a Journey through Bootan, and Part of Tibet* in 1800.

Tassisudon (Tashichö Dzong) was the site of the Bhutanese summer capital. According to a narrative of the 1774 mission, the palace had three thousand residents, all men and a third of them Buddhist monks. In his account Turner commented on his party's accommodation, the subject of this watercolor by Davis: "Our habitation, which was within a stone's throw of the palace, was extremely commodious, and well adapted to our use." sw

79

THOMAS DANIELL (1749-1840)

Tremal Naig's Choultry, Madura, 1792

Graphite on three joined sheets of laid paper; 15¹⁵/₁₆ x 24 in. (40.5 x 61.0 cm)

Inscribed in graphite on paper attached to mount: *Tremal Naig's Choultry, Madura | Drawn by Thoˢ. Daniell – published Nov. 1798 – engraved by Thoˢ. & Wᵐ. Daniell | No. XVIII*

PROVENANCE: ...; Paul F. Walter, by whom given

Gift of Paul F. Walter
B2000.6.9

80

THOMAS DANIELL (1749-1840) and WILLIAM DANIELL (1769-1837)

Main Entrance of the Jami Mosque, Jaunpur, c. 1802

Watercolor over graphite on wove paper; 22 x 32⅛ in. (55.9 x 81.6 cm)

PROVENANCE: ...; Bromley-Davenport family, to 1951; Sir Donald Anderson for the P. & O. Steam Navigation Co., 1952 to 1974; Spink, November 1974, bt Paul Mellon

Paul Mellon Collection
B1977.14.6140

79

81

WILLIAM DANIELL (1769-1837)

Sankrydroog, Madras, c. 1792

Watercolor over graphite on laid paper; 17⅝ x 21⅛ in. (44.8 x 53.7 cm)

Inscribed on modern mount, in graphite, lower left: *150*; also: *151/33*; and lower center: *Part of Sankrydroog.*

PROVENANCE: ...; Walker Galleries; Agnew, 1961, bt Paul Mellon

Paul Mellon Collection
B1977.14.6144

IN 1784 THOMAS DANIELL set out for India with his nephew William. India offered a rich lode of material for the topographical artist, with large potential markets for Indian views among both the British in India and back home. William Hodges's *Select Views in India,* based on his travels between 1780 and 1783, pointed the way. The Daniells sought to surpass Hodges both in

the extent of their travel and view-taking and in their topographical accuracy. They remained in India until 1794, when they returned to England and began working up their Indian drawings for publication. Their monumental *Oriental Scenery,* with 144 aquatints, was issued in six volumes from 1795 to 1808.

During their travels around India, the Daniells employed a camera obscura (see cat. 138) to produce detailed pencil drawings such as the one of Tremal Naig's Choultry in Madura. The drawing, made in July 1792 during a tour of south India, shows the Choultry or Thousand-pillared Hall of the Rajah Tremal Naig. The aquatint based on the drawing was published as Plate 18 in the second volume of *Oriental Scenery* in 1798. In the commentary to the plate, the Choultry is described as "one of the first works of its kind in the south of Hindoostan."

The Daniells drew the Jami Mosque at Jaunpur in November 1789. Their imposing watercolor of

80

81

the mosque's main entrance is an example of the finished watercolors that they worked up from their Indian field drawings after their return to England. It was reproduced in aquatint in 1802 as Plate 9 in the fourth volume of *Oriental Scenery*.

Thomas and William seem to have worked together on both their field drawings and their finished watercolors, making it difficult to distinguish their individual contributions. The unfinished drawing of Sankrydroog (Sankjaridrug) has been attributed solely to William, but the evidence is inconclusive. In the journal that William kept of their Indian travels, he records being at Sankrydroog on May 24, 1792. Although the Daniells did include several views of Sankrydroog in *Oriental Scenery*, this particular composition was not published. SW

82

82

WILLIAM ALEXANDER
(1767-1816)

*City of Lin Tsin, Shantung,
with a View of the Grand
Canal,* 1795

Watercolor over graphite on laid paper;
11¼ x 17⅜ in. (28.6 x 44.1 cm)

Signed and dated in brown ink, lower
right: *W Alexander 95*; inscribed in
graphite, verso: *Lin Tsin, from canal*

PROVENANCE: Direct descent through
artist's family; Spink, 1964, bt Paul
Mellon

SELECTED EXHIBITIONS: PML, *English
Drawings,* 1972, no. 83; YCBA, *English
Landscape,* 1977, no. 94

SELECTED LITERATURE: Legouix, 1980,
p. 66; Legouix and Conner, 1981, p. 36

Paul Mellon Collection
B1975.4.1450

FROM 1792 TO 1794 William
Alexander accompanied Lord
Macartney's embassy to the
Emperor of China as its official
draftsman. Alexander owed his
appointment to Julius Caesar
Ibbetson (cat. 93), who had been
his teacher when he moved to
London from his native Maidstone
in 1782. Ibbetson had been the
draftsman on an earlier, aborted
embassy to China; when offered
the post of draftsman with Lord
Macartney's embassy, he declined,
suggesting that Alexander replace
him.

Although the embassy failed in its
ostensible mission to open up a
Chinese market for British goods, it
engendered in the British public a
fascination for all things Chinese.
With his virtual monopoly on accurate visual information about China,
Alexander was strategically situated
to take advantage of this interest.

Throughout the rest of his life, he
produced finished watercolors from
his Chinese sketches and provided
illustrations to a number of books
on China. His first published
Chinese views appeared in 1797
illustrating Sir George Staunton's
*An Authentic Account of an Embassy
from the King of Great Britain to the
Emperor of China.* This view of Lin
Tsin was one of the illustrations.
Indeed, it seems to have been particularly popular. Four other watercolor versions of it are known, and
Alexander exhibited one of these
versions (very possibly this one) at
the Royal Academy in 1796 under
the title *Pagoda near Lin-tchin-four.*
SW

"The Age of Pastime, the Golden Reign of Pleasure"
URBAN AND RURAL LIFE AND LEISURE

EVERYDAY LIFE in eighteenth-century Britain was transformed by the development of a new culture of leisure, stimulated in part by the evolution of a middle class and greater prosperity. Cultivation of the "polite arts" was widespread and was considered to play a crucial role in maintaining a civilized society as life increasingly came to be lived in the public sphere. London saw unprecedented growth and development, and early in the century Joseph Addison in the *Spectator* characterized the city as "a kind of Emporium for the whole Earth." As a highly sophisticated consumer culture evolved, an extensive array of recreations became available in the metropolis, including attending plays, operas, concerts, and scientific lectures, visiting circulating libraries, sports, and, inevitably, shopping.

In 1763 the indefatigable and infatuated James Boswell noted in his journal:

> I have often amused myself with thinking how different a place London is to different people. *They, whose narrow minds are contracted to the consideration of some one particular pursuit, view it only through that medium. A politician thinks of it merely as the seat of government in its different departments; a grazier, as a vast market for cattle; a mercantile man, as a place where a prodigious deal of business is done upon 'Change; a dramatick enthusiast, as the grand scene of theatrical entertainments; a man of pleasure, as an assemblage of taverns, and the great emporium for ladies of easy virtue. But the intellectual man is struck with it, as* comprehending the whole of human life in all its variety, the contemplation of which is inexhaustible.

London's wealth and diversity impressed many visitors, who ignored or were unaware of the harsh and brutal lives of its more impoverished inhabitants that Hogarth recorded so unflinchingly (see cat. 148). The development of leisure was not confined to the metropolis, however, and it was also a feature of provincial and rural life.

The visual arts played a significant and complex role in this new leisure culture. Artists were commissioned to decorate places of recreation, most notably Jonathan Tyers's rococo Vauxhall Gardens, which became the first public showcase for contemporary painting and decorative arts (see cat. 87). Later in the century viewing and buying art, previously the domain of the aristocratic, became a popular pastime with the creation of public exhibition spaces such as the Society of Artists and the Royal Academy. Draftsmanship fulfilled an important function in this increasingly sociable and self-reflexive society, since drawing was an ideal medium for providing more or less instant records of contemporary events and newsworthy personalities that could be readily engraved and circulated. A number of artists made successful careers as dedicated draftsmen, notably Thomas Rowlandson, whose observant eye and elegant drawing style made him the consummate chronicler of his times. Drawing also became a popular amateur pastime; artists were often employed as drawing-masters, and technical and theoretical manuals proliferated (see cats. 155-6, and pp. 187-95). As travel became easier, Britons began to discover their own country, and this new phenomenon created a market for travel guides, as well as topographical and antiquarian drawings and prints.

GILLIAN FORRESTER

83

SAMUEL HIERONYMUS GRIMM
(1733-94)

83

The English Lady at Paris, 1771

Gray wash with pen and black ink over
graphite on laid paper; 12½ x 9¾ in.
(31.8 x 24.8 cm)

Signed and dated in artist's hand in pen
and gray ink, lower left: *S H Grimm fecit
1771*, and inscribed within image: *To
Alderman | Paris*; inscribed above right,
with stamp of Thomas Lowinsky (Lugt
2420a), and in pen and brown ink,
verso: *The English Lady at Paris – N°. 8*

PROVENANCE: ...; Thomas Lowinsky
(1892-1947); Justin Lowinsky, 1963,
from whom bt Paul Mellon

SELECTED EXHIBITIONS: University of
Missouri-Columbia, *British Comic Art*,
1988

Paul Mellon Collection
B1977.14.6037

84

The French Lady in London,
c. 1771

Gray wash with pen and gray ink,
heightened with white gouache over
graphite on laid paper; verso prepared
for transfer; 11½ x 9¹⁄₁₆ in. (29.2 x
23.0 cm)

Signed in pen and gray ink, lower right:
S.H. Grimm fecit; and inscribed within
image: *the Geese watching the Capitole,
and Representation of the Pic of Teneriffe,
and Lecture | upon | Heads*; inscribed
above right with stamp of Thomas
Lowinsky (Lugt 2420a), and in pen and
brown ink, verso: *The French Lady in
London N°. 9*

PROVENANCE: As for cat. 83

SELECTED EXHIBITIONS: YCBA, *English
Caricature*, 1984-5, no. 58; University of
Missouri-Columbia, *British Comic Art*,
1988

Paul Mellon Collection
B1977.14.6038

ANXIETIES THAT AFFLUENCE and
luxury were corrupting the nation
were commonplace throughout the
eighteenth century in Britain and
deepened during times of national
crisis. The issue was often characterized as a debate between doughty
old-fashioned (masculine) British
values and subversive (effeminate)
Continental notions of refinement.
French hairdressers, valets, and
dancing-masters were often singled
out for particular opprobrium; a
character in one of Samuel Foote's
popular anti-French plays of the
1750s claimed

*the importation of these puppies
makes a part of the politics of your
old friends, the French; unable to*

resist you, whilst you retain your ancient roughness, they have recourse to these minions, who would first, by unmanly means, sap and soften all your native spirit, and then deliver you an easy prey to their employers.

The pervasive influence of French culture was an especially pressing concern for British artists striving to establish the concept of an authentic and indigenous art in the face of connoisseurship that favored the work of their Continental counterparts and the Old Masters. The contrast between over-refined and mannered French mores and robustly British ones was frequently articulated in the work of artists such as Thomas Rowlandson (see cat. 86) and William Hogarth and was a popular subject for caricature.

Samuel Hieronymus Grimm's pair of drawings, which were published as engravings in 1771, satirize the vogue for French fashions in Britain. A Frenchwoman with a terrifyingly over-elaborate hairstyle is compared with her dowdy English counterpart, whose risible attempts to imitate French finesse are parodied by the image of the bear walking a tightrope in the painting on the wall behind her. Contemporary accounts indicate that the extraordinary height of the Frenchwoman's hair in Grimm's parody may be only slightly exaggerated. Such hairstyles were created by a costly and labor-intensive process. Hair was padded using a variety of materials, including horsehair and cotton wool, and then powdered and ornamented, sometimes using lard and plaster (in 1768, a Dublin hairdresser advertised his skills in "stuccowing"). One commentator patriotical-

ly noted that "Parisian ladies wear high towers with an extraordinary number of flowers, pads and ribbons. The English find such boundless display extremely ill-bred, and if any such lady comes to London, people hiss and throw mud at her." Despite their apparently hostile reception, these extraordinary hairstyles became extremely fashionable in England.

Another opponent of sartorial excess ingeniously invoked Hogarth's concept of the "Line of Beauty" to support his argument. In his *Treatise on the Principles of Hair-*

Dressing, in which the Deformities of Modern Hair-dressing are pointed out, and an elegant and natural Plan recommended, upon Hogarth's immortal System of Beauty (c. 1785), William Barker advocated that straight lines should be avoided in dress, as well as in hairstyles, where the "oval is lengthened to a risible stretch," and recommended that his readers should study Hogarth's "admirable 'Analysis of Beauty'" if they mean to attain to elegance of dress and deportment." GF

85

SAMUEL HIERONYMUS GRIMM
(1733-94)

Kennington Common, 1776

Watercolor with pen and gray ink and
gouache over graphite on laid paper;
13⁵⁄₁₆ x 20⁷⁄₁₆ in. (33.8 x 51.9 cm)

Signed and dated in pen and black ink,
within image, on fence: *S.H. Grimm fecit
1776*

SELECTED EXHIBITIONS: NGA, *English
Drawings*, 1962, no. 38; AFA, *British
Watercolors*, 1985-6, no. 8

Paul Mellon Collection
B1975.4.1531

THE SWISS WATERCOLORIST and poet
Samuel Hieronymous Grimm settled
in London in 1768 and became well
known for his topographical views
and caricatures (see cats. 83-4). Situated on the edge of the expanding
metropolis less than two miles from
Westminster, Kennington was still a
rural neighborhood at the time of
Grimm's watercolor but was developed as a residential area soon thereafter. The opening of Westminster
Bridge in 1750 and Kennington Road
in the following year facilitated access
to the West End, and the construction
of Blackfriars Bridge and its approach
roads between 1760 and 1769 made
the relatively pastoral Kennington a
desirable home for merchants working in the City. In the mid-nineteenth
century the remnants of the common
land were enclosed, and it was des-
ignated as a Royal Park.

Grimm's charming portrayal of
bucolic activity and genteel recreation alludes neither to the area's
traditional associations with radical-
ism and free speech, nor to its grim
function as a place of execution
until the end of the century. Kennington Common was regularly
used in the eighteenth and nineteenth centuries as a platform for
political activists and dissenting religious preachers, including John
Wesley, who addressed a crowd of
20,000 in the fall of 1739. The park
is still used as an assembly-point for
political gatherings today. The south-
west corner of the Common was the
site of a public gallows, where, most
notoriously, nine Catholic members
of the Manchester Regiment were
hung, drawn, and quartered after
the Jacobite rebellion on July 30,
1746. GF

86

THOMAS ROWLANDSON
(1756-1827)

Place des Victoires, Paris, c. 1783

Pen and black ink and watercolor over
graphite on laid paper; 13¾ x 21 in.
(34.9 x 53.3 cm)

PROVENANCE: ...; Somerville and
Simpson, London, from whom bt, 1981

SELECTED EXHIBITIONS: ?Society of
Artists, 1783, no. 223; YCBA, *English
Caricature*, 1984-5, no. 83; YCBA, *First
Decade*, 1986, no. 118

Paul Mellon Fund
B1981.17

THE INIQUITIES AND EXCESSES of
ancien régime France were a popular
target for British satirical art (see
cats. 83-4). Thomas Rowlandson's
watercolor draws on a number of
stereotypes commonly associated
with the French at this period – the
superstitious adherence to the
Catholic faith, indicated by the procession of monks and the looming
presence of Notre-Dame (flaunting
topographical accuracy, Rowlandson
has placed the cathedral immediately behind Place des Victoires); an
unquestioning devotion to the
monarchy, signaled by the man in
the sedan chair gazing raptly at the
monument erected to Louis XIV in
1686; and a frivolous attachment to
sartorial considerations, represented
by the fashionably-dressed figures
and the poodle dog wearing a wig.
Two other versions of the composition are known, but it is likely that

cat. 86 was the original watercolor
exhibited by Rowlandson at the
Society of Artists in 1783. The image
was engraved and published in
Britain shortly after the outbreak of
the French Revolution in 1789, presumably in response to the considerable public interest generated by
the tumultuous events in France.

Rowlandson clearly derived pleasure from ridiculing the French and
produced many watercolors on this
theme, but his relationship with
France seems to have been more
complex than his John Bullish
stance might suggest. Raised by his
French-speaking aunt Jane (née
Chevalier), Rowlandson visited the
country on a number of occasions,
and his sophisticated and refined
drawing style, which often seems at
odds with his robust subject matter,
owes much to French rococo art.
GF

87

THOMAS ROWLANDSON
(1756–1827)

87

Vauxhall Gardens, c. 1784

Pen and ink and watercolor over
graphite on wove paper; 13½ x 18¾ in.
(34.3 x 47.6 cm)

Collector's stamp of L. S. Delatigny
(Lugt 1768a), lower left

PROVENANCE: ...; Sir William
Augustus Grazer, Bt, his sale, Christie's,
3 December 1900 (47); L. S. Delatigny;
...; Leggatt Bros., February 1963, from
whom bt Paul Mellon

SELECTED EXHIBITIONS: VMFA, *Paint-
ing in England*, 1963, no. 492; PML,
English Drawings, 1972, no. 71; YCBA,
Pursuit of Happiness, 1977, no. 110;
YCBA, *Vauxhall Gardens*, 1983, no. 92;
YCBA, *Rowlandson Drawings*, 1977-8, no. 4;
YCBA, *Pleasures and Pastimes*, 1990, no. 213

SELECTED LITERATURE: Falk, 1949,
p. 78; Hardie, 1967-8, vol. I, p. 212;
Baskett and Snelgrove, 1977, no. 12;
Hayes, 1990, pp. 66-9, no. 20

Paul Mellon Collection
B1975.4.1844

88

*An Audience Watching a Play
at Drury Lane*, c. 1785

Pen and black ink and watercolor over
graphite on laid paper; 9⁷⁄₁₆ x 14⅜ in.
(24.0 x 36.5 cm)

PROVENANCE: ...; Baskett and Day,
from whom bt Paul Mellon, 1976

SELECTED EXHIBITIONS: YCBA,
Rowlandson Drawings, 1977-8, no. 5;
YCBA, *Pleasures and Pastimes*, 1990,
no. 118

SELECTED LITERATURE: Baskett and
Snelgrove, 1977, no. 242

Paul Mellon Collection
B1977.14.149

88

VAUXHALL PLEASURE GARDENS had been a fashionable resort since the time of Charles II. In 1732 the gardens reopened to the public after extensive renovations under the proprietorship of Jonathan Tyers. The entrepreneurial Tyers had the gardens embellished with walks, ruins, statues, Chinese pavilions, triumphal arches, and a "Gothick" orchestra, and his continuing program of improvements included several important art commissions, most notably Louis-François Roubiliac's celebrated statue of Handel, four patriotic modern history subjects by Francis Hayman, and an extensive sequence of decorative paintings designed for the supper-boxes by Hayman and William Hogarth.

Vauxhall was almost universally popular, despite (or because of) its reputation for frivolity and moral laxity, and typified the egalitarian nature of British social life of the period. James Boswell, an inveterate commentator on metropolitan life, observed

> Vauxhall Gardens is peculiarly adapted to the taste of the English nation; there being a mixture of curious show – gay exhibition, musick, vocal and instrumental, not too refined for the general ear; – for all which only a shilling is paid. And, though last, not least, good eating and drinking for those who wish to purchase that regale.

Rowlandson frequently visited Vauxhall, finding there, as his friend Henry Angelo noted, "plenty of employment for his pencil." The subject of his watercolor is the orchestra outside the Rotunda during an evening concert. The orchestra was one of the few professional ensembles of the period and renowned for the high quality of its playing. Many of the figures can be tentatively identified, including the Prince Regent whispering to the actress "Perdita" Robinson, his former lover, shown arm-in-arm with her husband, and, in the foreground, the playwright and dandy Edward Topham peering through his monocle or "quizzing glass" at Georgiana, Duchess of Devonshire, and her sister Harriet (see cat. 7).

Rowlandson frequently depicted the interiors of Drury Lane and Covent Garden, which were the only two London theaters granted full patents as "royal theatres" by the

89

Licensing Act of 1737. Theater-going was a relatively inexpensive and popular pastime in eighteenth-century Britain, and was enjoyed by a wide cross-section of the public. Theophilus Cibber, the son of the famous actor-playwright and former Drury Lane proprietor Colley Cibber, noted: "Noble, Gentle, or Simple, who fill the Boxes, Pit, and Galleries ... as K-ng, L–rds and COMMONS ... make the great body of the Nation." The theatrical portrait became a popular genre, and images of actors, usually in character, were widely circulated through engravings (see cat. 8).

Theaters, concert-halls, and opera houses were important social centers, and the fashionable attended to meet their friends and acquaintances, observe their enemies, and to be seen by the public. This practice evidently annoyed more serious theater-goers, including an anonymous writer in the *Theatrical Monitor* of 1768, who complained testily:

During the time of the representation of a play, the quality in the boxes are totally employed in finding out, and beckoning to their acquaintances, male and female; they criticize on fashions, whisper cross the benches, make significant nods, and give hints of this and that, and t'other body.

In this watercolor Rowlandson slyly played on this performative aspect of theater-going, by depicting the audience as if they were actors in a play, and placing the viewer in the role of the spectator. GF

89

THOMAS ROWLANDSON (1756-1827)

The Prize Fight, 1787

Pen and ink and watercolor over graphite on laid paper; 18¼ x 27⅜ in. (46.4 x 69.5 cm)

Inscribed in ink, lower left:
T. Rowlandson

PROVENANCE: ...; Christie's, 12 February 1912 (112), bt Huggins; M. Knoedler & Co., February 1915 (no. 83 in catalogue); Frank T. Sabin, 1956; Arthur Reader, bt Paul Mellon, 1960

SELECTED EXHIBITIONS: YCBA, *Pursuit of Happiness*, 1977, no. 156; YCBA, *Rowlandson Drawings*, 1977-8, no. 14

SELECTED LITERATURE: Baskett and Snelgrove, 1977, no. 114; Hayes, 1972, p. 45, pl. 37; Plumb, 1975, p. 145

Paul Mellon Collection
B1993.30.113

90

MICHAEL "ANGELO" ROOKER
(1746-1801)

*A Game of Bowls on the
Bowling-Green outside the
Bunch of Grapes Inn, Hurst,
Berkshire*

Watercolor on wove paper; 8½ x 10¾ in.
(21.6 x 27.3 cm)

Signed, lower left: *MA Rooker*

PROVENANCE: ...; Mr. Tompkins of
Palser and Sons until 1932; L.G. Duke;
Colnaghi, from whom bt Paul Mellon,
1961

SELECTED LITERATURE: Egerton, 1974,
p. 24

Paul Mellon Collection
B2001.2.1128

90

SPORTS OF VARYING DEGREES of
brutality and gentility flourished
during the eighteenth century.
Boxing, hitherto an unregulated
amateur sport, became professional-
ized and commercialized. John
Broughton, the most celebrated
pugilist of the day, drew up rules
which were introduced on August
16, 1743, and enforced until 1838,
when they were superseded by the
London Prize Ring Rules. In 1747
Broughton opened an academy in
London where gloves were worn for
the first time. The subject of
Rowlandson's ambitious watercolor
has never been identified conclusively, but it may commemorate the
celebrated fight between Richard
Humphries (the "Gentleman Boxer")
and Samuel Martin which took place
at Newmarket on May 3, 1786. The

contest was attended by several hundred people, including members of
the English and French nobility. The
London Chronicle reported that "the
long contended battle between
Martin, the Bath Butcher, and the
famous Humphries ... lasted about
an hour and a half, when the latter
beat the former in a terrible manner; upwards of 4000 l. were won
and lost on the occasion."

Michael "Angelo" Rooker's drawing depicts a rather more sedate if
less thrilling sporting activity, the
game of bowls. Dating back to the
Middle Ages, and still popular in
Britain today, bowls is played on
grass by rolling heavy balls, known
as "woods" so that they rest as closely as possible to the target ball,
known as the "jack." The woods
have a built-in bias that causes them
to move in a curving rather than a
straight trajectory. Bowling greens
were frequently attached to country
inns. In his *Account of a Visit to
Hurst* of 1747, James Belchin

described a convivial evening at the
Bunch of Grapes: "This house is
very pleasantly situated, and has
belonging to it a large and handsome bowling-green for the diver-
sion of those gentlemen who please
to play. Being all assembled together
we sat down and smoked our pipes,
and drank some wine in a very
sociable manner." GF

91

FRANCIS WHEATLEY (1747-1801)

Donnybrook Fair, 1782

Pen and ink and watercolor on wove
paper; 12¹¹⁄₁₆ x 21½ in. (32.2 x 54.6 cm)

Signed and dated on cart wheel, lower
left: *Wheatley | del! 1782*

PROVENANCE: ...; Frank T. Sabin, from
whom bt Paul Mellon, 1961

SELECTED EXHIBITIONS: Victoria,
British Watercolour Drawings, 1971,
no. 50; PML, *English Drawings*, 1972,
no. 53

Paul Mellon Collection
B1986.29.579

FRANCIS WHEATLEY is chiefly known
today for his *Cries of London*, a series
of paintings of itinerant merchants
that were widely circulated as
engravings. After studying at the
newly-established Royal Academy
Schools, the versatile artist quickly
consolidated his reputation in
London as a painter and draftsman.
Although his portraits, landscapes,
and history and genre subjects were
favorably received, Wheatley was
constantly in debt, and in 1779 he
fled to Ireland to escape his creditors.

Wheatley established a thriving
portrait practice in Dublin, and he
also produced landscapes and genre
subjects, including a large group of
watercolors depicting two traditional
peasant fairs, Donnybrook and
Palmerston. These attractive drawings were extremely popular with his
fashionable Irish clientele, but neither Wheatley's choice of subject
matter nor his mode of representation are as straightforward as they
may seem at first sight. Founded in
1204, and held on the periphery of
Dublin, Donnybrook Fair was notorious for drunkenness, licentiousness,
and violence (indeed, the term "donnybrook" is still used today as a syn-
onym for a disorderly brawl), and in
the late eighteenth century it provided the Irish ruling classes with a
potent reminder of the ever-present
possibility of social unrest.

In 1778 a writer in the *Freeman's
Journal* noted "how irksome it was
to friends of the industry and well-
being of the Society to hear that
upwards of 50,000 persons visited
the fair on the previous Sunday, and
returned to the city like intoxicated
savages." Such complaints were
commonplace, and Donnybrook
Fair was eventually abolished in
1867. This refined and neutrally-
colored watercolor, with its subdued
and cheerless groups of peasants,
betrays no hint of the Saturnalian
character of the fair that Wheatley's
contemporaries found so disturb-
ing, and, like many other examples
of Picturesque genre art of the period, seems to have been produced
with the intention of reassuring his
respectable clientele. GF

92

ROBERT HEALY (1743-71)

Tom Conolly of Castletown Hunting with his Friends, 1769

Pastel, chalks, and gouache on two sheets of joined laid paper; 20¼ x 53½ in. (51.4 x 135.9 cm)

Signed and dated, lower left: *R Healy delin.̣ 1769.*

PROVENANCE: The Conolly family; by descent to Lord Carew, from whom bt the Hon. Desmond Guinness; Christie's, 15 July 1983 (10), bt Paul Mellon

SELECTED EXHIBITIONS: Dublin, *Irish Portraits,* 1969, no. 76

SELECTED LITERATURE: Guinness, 1982, pp. 84-5; Crookshank, 1994, pp. 63-4

Paul Mellon Collection B2001.2.880

THE SON OF A SUCCESSFUL architect and decorator, Robert Healy studied at the Dublin Society's Drawing Schools under the pastellist Robert West. The Schools' curriculum in the late eighteenth century did not include oil painting, and, like his fellow-student Hugh Douglas Hamilton (see cat. 11), Healy specialized in pastel and chalk drawings. Healy's promising career was cut short when he died at the age of twenty-eight, and the few works by him known to have survived are distinctive drawings in grisaille, that is, a subtle blend of monochrome and color pigments. Healy may have been influenced by the Irish artist Thomas Frye's monochrome chalk portrait heads, but his accomplished drawings go far beyond Frye's in terms of finish and sophistication. The pseudonymous Dublin critic Anthony Pasquin observed that they were "proverbial for their exquisite softness: – they look like fine proof prints of the most capital mezzotinto engravings."

In his memoirs the actor John O'Keeffe recalled that his friend Healy "excelled at drawing in chalks, portraits, etc., but his chief forte was horses which he delineated so admirably that he got plenty of employment from those who had hunters, mares, or Ladies palfreys." The only known evidence of Healy's work in this genre, however, is a remarkable series of drawings made for the Conollys of Castletown in the late 1760s. Castletown in County Kildare was built in the 1720s by the wealthy Whig politician William Conolly. At his death in 1729 the Palladian mansion was still unfinished, but, when his greatnephew Tom and his wife Louisa settled on the estate in 1759, they undertook an extensive program of renovations. Castletown was renowned for its informal hospitality, and in 1768-9 Healy chronicled the traditional recreations of hunting, shooting, and skating enjoyed by the Conollys. The centerpiece of the group is cat. 92, an ambitious frieze-like drawing with close affinities with the work of George Stubbs (see cats. 64-8). GF

93

JULIUS CAESAR IBBETSON
(1759-1817)

St. James's Park, Summer, 1796

Watercolor on wove paper;
17⅜ x 23½ in. (44.1 x 59.7 cm)

Signed and dated on table, below right:
Julius Ibbetson 1796

PROVENANCE: ...; A. Gilbey; J.T.T.
Fletcher; Sotheby's, 23 March 1966 (28),
bt Paul Mellon through Colnaghi

SELECTED EXHIBITIONS: RA, 1796,
no. 383

SELECTED LITERATURE: Clay, 1948,
pp. 45-6

Paul Mellon Collection
B1977.14.6207

94

JOHN NIXON (c. 1760-1818)

Skating in St. James's Park,
c. 1789

Watercolor with pen and brown ink over
graphite on wove paper; 12¾ x 27¾ in.
(32.4 x 70.5 cm)

PROVENANCE: Sir William Fraser, Bt.;
J.S. Maas, from whom bt, 1963

SELECTED EXHIBITIONS: University of
Missouri-Columbia, *British Comic Art*,
1988

Paul Mellon Collection
B1977.14.6234

ST. JAMES'S PARK is the oldest of London's royal parks, which first opened to the public in the early seventeenth century. After the Restoration Charles II extended the park by thirty-six acres, stocked it with deer, planted fruit trees, and built The Mall, the tree-lined avenue which still exists today. The rapid expansion of London in the eighteenth century was accompanied by a concern to retain, or even introduce, if necessary, rural elements into the city, and the therapeutic and social value of the parks was widely acknowledged. In 1774 Oliver Goldsmith commented, "if a man be splenetic [i.e., afflicted with melancholia or hypochrondria], he may every day meet companions in the seats of St James's Park, with whose groans he may mix his own and pathetically talk of the weather." Londoners' enthusiasm for their parks was reflected in the popularity of picturesque sub-urban pastorals like Julius Caesar Ibbetson's water-color of St. James's Park. Ibbetson, who lived in London from 1777 to 1798, produced a large group of drawings and paintings depicting metropolitan park scenes, often pairing summer and winter subjects. There was a dairy in St. James's Park, and milk fairs were regularly held there in the eighteenth century.

Ice skates were introduced in England in the late seventeenth century, and skating became a popular winter recreation. John Nixon's humorous depiction of skating and sliding on the frozen canal in St. James's Park probably commemorates the severe winter of 1788-9, when the river Thames froze over for the first time since 1683. The frost fair held on the river was a popular attraction and proved lucrative for the many enterprising vendors of food, drink, and souvenirs. The *Public Advertizer* noted on January 5, 1789: "This Booth is to let. The present possessor of the premises is Mr Frost. His affairs, however, not being on a permanent footing, a dissolution or bankruptcy may soon be expected, and a final settlement of the whole entrusted to Mr Thaw." The Thames was soon to be the permanent domain of "Mr Thaw," since the demolition of Old London Bridge in 1831 improved the flow of the river to such an extent that it no longer froze over. GF

93

94

"Magick Land"
ARTISTS AND THE GRAND TOUR

FOR THE BRITISH GENTLEMAN in the eighteenth century, the Grand Tour – travel on the Continent culminating in an extended stay in Italy – was a necessary component of a complete education. In a culture permeated with knowledge of the classical world, the firsthand experience of the remains of that world was a prerequisite for full participation in the culture.

The art and architecture of antiquity were there in Italy to be admired and studied, as were the great achievements of the Renaissance and Baroque, the worthy inheritors of the classical legacy. The Italian landscape itself, steeped in classical associations, was to be savored and then commemorated through paintings and drawings.

Artists were rarely Grand Tourists as such: they were rarely gentlemen, though they could, through a combination of talent, erudition, and charm, occasionally move in those circles. But Italy was for them as well the object of pilgrimage, often made possible by Grand Tourists in whose entourage they could make the trip or from whose purses they obtained the funding for their travels. British artists went to study, though not in formal academies like that of the French in Rome. They pursued their artistic training in a more ad hoc manner, visiting ruins, churches, and great collections. Drawing everywhere they went, they amassed stocks of images that they would be able to incorporate into their own artworks for years to come. The artists also went to Italy in the hope of making contacts among the Grand Tourists who could help to subsidize their stay and continue as patrons when they returned to Britain. If there were practical and mercenary reasons for following the Grand Tourists to Italy, there was also the allure of what the artist Thomas Jones called "Magick Land."

The British were but part of a larger international community of artists in Italy that included history painters, portraitists, sculptors, architects, and printmakers. There is scarcely a section of this catalogue in which the influence of Italy and of the international exchange of ideas that took place there is not very much in evidence. In the genre of landscape, and in the landscape watercolor particularly, British artists in Italy made important strides. Alexander Cozens, in Rome in 1746, was one of the earliest of a long succession of British landscape artists who traveled to Italy either to imbibe the principles of classical landscape painting or to provide topographical records of the fabled sites. Richard Wilson and Jonathan Skelton were there in the 1750s, William Marlow in the mid-1760s. But it was the group of watercolorists who were there in the later 1770s – William Pars, John "Warwick" Smith, Francis Towne, Thomas Jones, and John Robert Cozens – often living and working together, trading ideas and techniques, who expanded and enriched the technical range of watercolor and fused classical landscape and topography into a new art of landscape watercolor.

With the French invasion of Italy in 1796, the age of the Grand Tour came to an end. After the Napoleonic Wars the British tourists and artists returned, but tourism was increasingly less exclusive. And the experience of Italy was less imperative for the cultured British gentleman or the aspiring British artist.

SCOTT WILCOX

95

WILLIAM MARLOW (1740-1813)

Nîmes from the Tour Magne,
c. 1765-68

Watercolor with pen and brown ink over
graphite on laid paper, on original
mount; 14⅜ x 21 in. (36.5 x 53.3 cm)

Signed in pen and brown ink, lower left:
W. Marlow; inscribed in pen and brown
ink, lower center of mount: *Nîmes*

PROVENANCE: ...; Palser; ...; T. Girtin,
1908; Tom Girtin, bt Paul Mellon
through John Baskett, 1970

SELECTED EXHIBITIONS: Guildhall,
Marlow, 1956, no. 59; NGA, *Jefferson*,
1977, no. 350; YCBA, *English Landscape*,
1977, no. 47

Paul Mellon Collection
B1977.14.366

WITH ITS CLUSTER of famous Roman
ruins, Nîmes in the south of France
was a popular stop for classically
minded Grand Tourists. William
Marlow visited the city during his
travels in France and Italy between
1765 and 1768. Like Richard Wilson
in the previous decade, or the generation of British landscape watercolorists who worked in Italy in the
1770s, Marlow was profoundly
affected by his Continental sojourn,
which provided him with a major
source of subject matter after his
return to England.

For this general view of Nîmes,
Marlow takes a vantage point on
Mont Cavalier near the Tour Magne,
a Roman monument probably dating from the second century B.C.
Within the city the well-preserved
amphitheater and the temple known
as the Maison Carrée, both from the
first century A.D., are clearly visible.
Another watercolor by Marlow
showing a closer view of the amphitheater is also in the collection
of the Yale Center for British Art.
SW

96

JOHN ROBERT COZENS (1752-99)

Near Chiavenna in the Grisons,
c. 1779

Watercolor with rubbing out over graphite on laid paper; 16¾ x 24½ in. (42.5 x
62.2 cm)

PROVENANCE: ...; F.J.C. Holdsworth;
C. Morland Agnew; Hugh L. Agnew;
Lady Mayer; Agnew, 1971, bt Paul Mellon

SELECTED EXHIBITIONS: PML, *English
Drawings,* 1972, no. 62; YCBA, *English
Landscape,* 1977, no. 71; Munich, *Englische
Malerei,* 1979-80, no. 76; YCBA, *Cozens,*
1980, no. 95; AGO, *Cozens,* 1987, no. 138

SELECTED LITERATURE: Bell and
Girtin, 1935, no. 47

Paul Mellon Collection
B1977.14.4634

FOR MANY GRAND TOURISTS the trip
across the Alps provided a sublime
prelude to the civilized pleasures of
Italy. In 1776 John Robert Cozens
crossed the Alps and traveled in Italy
with the connoisseur, collector, and
classical scholar Richard Payne Knight.
Payne Knight was an aficionado of
sublimity in landscape, who would
later make his own significant contributions to the growing body of literature on aesthetics and landscape.
On their trip or immediately after,
Cozens produced for Payne Knight
a series of fifty-seven monochrome
drawings of Swiss views, five of which
are in the Yale Center for British Art.

Near Chiavenna in the Grisons,
Cozens's most dramatic and sublime expression of alpine scenery,
was not created for Payne Knight,
nor was the 1776 drawing (now in
the Leeds City Art Gallery) on which
Cozens based this impressive watercolor part of the Payne Knight set.
Nonetheless, Payne Knight's preoccupation with sublime landscape
may well be reflected in Cozens's
composition, which exaggerates the
scale of the mountains to enhance
the awesome grandeur of the scene.
In the angular, almost abstract treatment of the rocky forms, Cozens
also shows a debt to the fantastic
mountainous landscapes of his
father, Alexander Cozens (cat. 45).
SW

Borra Arch.ᵘˢ Del.   TERME ROVINATE NELLA VILLA D'ADRIANO A TIVOLI

97

GIOVANNI BATTISTA BORRA
(1713-70)

View of the Ruined Baths at Hadrian's Villa at Tivoli, c. 1750

Gray wash with pen and gray ink over graphite on laid paper; image: 9 x 14¼ in. (22.9 x 36.2 cm); sheet: 15 x 21¼ in. (38.1 x 54 cm)

Signed in pen and brown ink beneath image, lower left: *Borra Arch.ᵘˢ del*; inscribed in pen and brown ink beneath image, lower center: *TERME ROVINATE NELLA VILLA D'ADRIANO A TIVOLI*

PROVENANCE: ...; Edmund Neville-Rolfe; bt Paul Mellon

Paul Mellon Collection
B1977.14.1011

OF THE GROUP of ninety-eight drawings in the Yale Center for British Art by the Piedmontese architect, engineer, and draftsman Giovanni Battista Borra, most are of sites in Asia Minor that he visited as draftsman to Robert Wood's archaeological expedition (see also cats. 59 and 118). However, the drawings do include some views of Rome and Tivoli, presumably also derived from sketches made in the company of Wood.

The summer palace of the emperor Hadrian, built between 118 and 134 A.D., was from the time of the Renaissance a source of fascination and inspiration for classical scholars, architects, and artists. Robert Wood in a diary entry described Hadrian's Villa as "this immense heap of ruins, which show nothing but such magnificent confusion and disorder as will admit of no regular description: the remains of the palace, naumachia, amphitheatre, theatre, temples, etc., covering a circumference of nearly six miles." sw

RICHARD WILSON (c. 1713/14-82)

98

Temple of Minerva Medica, Rome, 1754

Black and white chalk on blue laid paper on original mount; 14 x 19¼ in. (35.6 x 48.9 cm)

Signed and dated in black chalk on mount, lower left: *R. Wilson f. 1754;* inscribed on mount in pen and brown ink, lower center: *T. of Minerva | Medica;* and in black chalk, lower right: *No. 19*

PROVENANCE: Drawn for 2nd Earl of Dartmouth, by descent to the 8th Earl; Agnew, bt Paul Mellon, February 1961

SELECTED EXHIBITIONS: Birmingham, *Wilson,* 1948-9, no. 87; PML *English Drawings,* 1972, no. 25; YCBA, *English Landscape,* 1977, no. 16; YCBA, *Classic Ground,* 1981, no. 73

SELECTED LITERATURE: Ford, 1948, p. 345; Ford, 1951, pl. 55; Constable, 1953, no. 88b

Paul Mellon Collection
B1977.14.4654

99

The Arbra Sacra on the Banks of Lake Nemi, c. 1754-6

Black chalk, heightened with white chalk, on gray wove paper, 15⅛ x 21⅞ in. (38.4 x 55.6 cm)

Collector's stamp of the Earl of Warwick, lower right (Lugt 2600)

PROVENANCE: ...; George Guy, 4th Earl of Warwick (1818-93); ...; Mrs. Arthur Clifton; ...; Agnew, bt Paul Mellon, May 1964

SELECTED EXHIBITIONS: PML, *English Drawings,* 1972, no. 26; YCBA, *English Landscape,* 1977, no. 18; Munich, *Englische Malerei,* 1979-80, no. 104; Tate, *Wilson,* 1982-3, no. 52; YCBA, *Sandby,* 1985, no. 15

Paul Mellon Collection
B1977.14.4655

ACCORDING TO JOSEPH FARINGTON, who was Richard Wilson's pupil in the early 1760s, it was to improve his art as a portrait painter that Wilson traveled to Italy in 1750. During the years he spent there, until 1756 or 1757, he gave up portraiture and devoted himself to landscape. In a series of lectures in 1836 devoted to the history of landscape painting, John Constable credited Wilson with "opening the way to the genuine principles of Landscape in England," and stated that "it was in Italy that [Wilson] first became acquainted with his own powers."

Although he was primarily a painter, over the course of his stay in Italy Wilson also developed into a draftsman of great subtlety and delicacy. One of the crowning achievements of his years in Italy is the series of finished landscape drawings for William Legge, 2nd Earl of Dartmouth. Lord Dartmouth, who made the Grand Tour in 1752-3, acquired two views of Rome in oils from Wilson (one of which, *Rome from the Villa Madama,* 1753, is in the Yale Center for British Art) and sixty-eight drawings. Of the drawings, twenty-some are known today. *The Temple of Minerva Medica* is one of two from the set now in the Yale Center for British Art. While Wilson's drawings for Dartmouth are topographical in that they depict actual views in Rome and its environs, his choice of media – black and white chalk on blue paper – reflects not the standard practice of the topographical draftsman, which would have been pen and ink with watercolor, but the techniques employed at the French Academy in Rome, redolent of the traditions of Old Master drawing.

Similar to the Dartmouth series in date and in the sensitivity of its draftsmanship is Wilson's drawing of a plane tree on the banks of Lake Nemi. The tree is presumably the one mentioned by Wilson's pupil Thomas Jones, when he visited Nemi in April 1778: "All went to make sketches about the Lake of Nemi – particularly a large *Plane* tree call'd the Arbor Santa, which has a hollow within that I believe w'd contain about a dozen persons & I was told that my Old Master *Willson* when in this Country made use of it as a Study to paint in."
sw

98

99

100

100

WILLIAM PARS (1742-82)

A View of Rome Taken from the Pincio, 1776

Watercolor over graphite on laid paper; 15⅛ x 21⅛ in. (38.4 x 53.7 cm)

Signed and dated in pen and black ink, lower left: *W Pars Rome 1776*

PROVENANCE:...; Rimell; ...; T. Girtin, c. 1907; Tom Girtin, bt Paul Mellon through John Baskett, 1970

SELECTED EXHIBITIONS: PML, *English Drawings*, 1972, no. 50; YCBA, *English Landscape*, 1977, no. 50

Paul Mellon Collection
B1977.14.4704

IN 1764 THE SOCIETY OF DILETTANTI, an association of gentlemen formed to promote the appreciation of ancient art, commissioned the young classical scholar Richard Chandler to record the classical ruins of Asia Minor. William Pars, a twenty-two-year-old portrait painter, was chosen to accompany Chandler as draftsman. Pars's watercolors from the expedition were published by the Society in 1769 as illustrations to Chandler's account under the title *Ionian Antiquities*. The following year one of the Society's members, Lord Palmerston, asked Pars to accompany him on a tour of Switzerland. As part of Palmerston's entourage, Pars visited Rome for the first time.

In 1775 the Society of Dilettanti's first award to an artist for study in Rome allowed Pars to return to the city. He lived there for the last seven years of his life, at the heart of a community of visiting British water-colorists that included John "Warwick" Smith (cat. 74), Francis Towne (cat. 53), and Pars's good friend and housemate Thomas Jones (cat. 101). Pars's watercolor of the view from the Pincian Hill, in which the heat and haze hanging over the city are almost palpable, shows the area around the Spanish Steps where British artists in Rome congregated. SW

101

THOMAS JONES (1742-1803)

*The Claudean Aqueduct and
Colosseum*, 1778

Watercolor over graphite on laid paper;
10¾ x 16¼ in. (27.3 x 41.3 cm)

Inscribed in graphite, upper right: *2*;
upper center: *part of the Antique Aqua-
duct that convey'd water to M. Palatine-* |
May 1778 | *2 the Collosseo-*; and lower
right: *vinyard*

PROVENANCE: By descent to Canon J.H.
Adams, step-great-great grandson of the
artist, sold Sotheby's, 27 November 1975
(90), bt Paul Mellon through John Baskett

SELECTED EXHIBITIONS: Marble Hill,
Jones, no. 38; YCBA, *Classic Ground*, 1981,
no. 68; YCBA, *Presences of Nature*, 1982-
83, no. III.14

SELECTED LITERATURE: Gowing, 1986,
pl. 31

Paul Mellon Collection
B1981.25.2637

TODAY THOMAS JONES is best
remembered for his memoirs and
oil sketches. The memoirs, based
in part on diaries kept during his
stay in Italy between 1776 and 1783
but published only in 1951, provide
an invaluable insider's view of the
life of British artists in Italy in the
period. His remarkably modern-
looking oil sketches, virtually unknown until a group of them came
on the market in 1954, are now
seen as a significant early achievement in the history of plein-air
sketching in oils.

While Jones's Italian watercolors
have neither the appeal to modern-
ist sensibilities nor the claim on the
art-historical imagination of the oil
sketches, they have their own clear-
eyed forthrightness and delicate
beauty. In his memoirs Jones recorded "making some Drawings in
the garden belonging to the English
colledge upon Mount Palatine" on
May 21, 1778. Presumably this watercolor was done at that time, though
it seems quite highly finished for a
sketch made on the spot. Despite
their finish Jones's watercolors of
this type seem not to have been
intended either for sale or exhibition, and the annotations prominently placed on the drawings suggest that they were made for personal reference. sw

102

ABRAHAM-LOUIS-RODOLPHE
DUCROS (1748-1810)

*Ruins of the Basilica of
Maxentius in the Roman
Forum*, 1779

Watercolor with pen and black ink over
graphite on laid paper; 20⅞ x 29⅛ in.
(53 x 74 cm)

Signed and dated in watercolor, lower
right: *DuCros 1779*

PROVENANCE: ...; Somerville and
Simpson, 1977, bt Paul Mellon

SELECTED EXHIBITIONS: YCBA, *Classic
Ground*, 1981, no. 62

SELECTED LITERATURE: Chessex, 1985,
pp. 48-9

Paul Mellon Collection
B1977.14.141

THE SWISS PAINTER Louis Ducros
traveled to Rome in 1776 and remained in Italy until 1807. There he
became known for his large, elabo-
rately worked watercolors of Italian
scenes, frequently featuring ancient
ruins, which were much sought
after by British visitors to Italy. One
of the most important of his British
patrons was the antiquary Richard
Colt Hoare, who wrote in 1787 that
four drawings that Ducros had done

for him "will be the admiration of
the whole town & put all our English
artists, even the great Mr. Smith
[John 'Warwick' Smith] to the blush."
 In 1822 Colt Hoare, who eventually owned thirteen watercolors by
Ducros, credited the artist with a
key role in the development of
watercolor painting in Britain:
*The advancement from drawing to
painting in water-colours did not
take place till after the introduction
into England of the drawings of
Louis du Cros, a Swiss artist who
settled at Rome. His works proved
the force as well as the consequence
that could be given to the unsub-
stantial body of water-colours, and
to him I attribute the first knowledge*

123

103

*and power of watercolours. Hence
have sprung a numerous succession
of Artists in this line.*

Colt Hoare's partiality toward
Ducros led him to overestimate the
Swiss artist's influence on British
watercolorists; there is no evidence
that the achievements in watercolor
by "Warwick" Smith (cat. 74), John
Robert Cozens (cats. 103-4 and 142),
and other British artists working in
Italy were based on a knowledge of
Ducros' work. Colt Hoare was, however, an important early patron of
J.M.W. Turner (cat. 144), and it is
very probable that Turner's large
dramatic landscape watercolors of
the early years of the nineteenth
century reflect his awareness of the
Ducros watercolors he would have
seen in Colt Hoare's collection. sw

JOHN ROBERT COZENS (1752-99)

103

*The Lake of Albano and Castel
Gandolfo,* c. 1779

Watercolor over graphite on wove paper;
17½ x 25¼ in. (44.5 x 64.1 cm)

PROVENANCE: ...; C. Morland Agnew;
C. Gerald Agnew; D. Martin Agnew;
Agnew, bt Paul Mellon, 1967

SELECTED EXHIBITIONS: PML, *English
Drawings,* 1972, no. 60; YCBA, *English
Landscape,* 1977, no. 73; YCBA, *Cozens,*
1980, no. 93

SELECTED LITERATURE: Bell and Girtin,
1935, no. 147 v; Hawcroft, 1971, p. 19

Paul Mellon Collection
B1977.14.4635

104

*The Lake of Albano and Castel
Gandolfo,* c. 1783-5

Watercolor over graphite on wove paper;
17 x 24⅜ in. (43.2 x 61.9 cm)

Inscribed in pen and black ink, lower
left: *Cozens* [partially trimmed off]

PROVENANCE: Dr. T. C. Girtin; by
descent to Tom Girtin, bt Paul Mellon
through John Baskett, 1970

SELECTED EXHIBITIONS: YCBA, *English
Landscape,* 1977, no. 72; YCBA, *Cozens,*
1981, no. 134; YCBA, *Classic Ground,*
1981, no. 16

SELECTED LITERATURE: Bell and
Girtin, 1935, no. 147 VI; Hawcroft, 1971,
p. 19

Paul Mellon Collection
B1977.14.360

104

JOHN ROBERT COZENS returned from his first visit to Italy in the spring of 1779. Three years later he made a second Italian tour, this time in the company of his father's pupil, patron, and friend William Beckford. Back in London in 1783, Cozens created finished watercolors for Beckford and other collectors based on sketches from his recent tour but also returning to the more striking and popular of his drawings from the earlier Italian visit.

As did many other landscape painters and draftsmen of the period (one thinks of Richard Wilson with his many repetitions of his paintings of Italy), Cozens produced numerous versions of his more popular compositions. *The Lake of Albano and Castel Gandolfo* was certainly one of the most popular, known in at least ten variants. The differences in tone and handling of the two versions in the Yale Center for British Art suggest that these watercolors date from different periods in the artist's life and stylistic evolution. Andrew Wilton has suggested that the darker, richer, more densely worked version (cat. 103) can be associated with Cozens's first visit to Italy, while the lighter, freer handling of cat. 104 reflects the artist's manner of working in the years following his second Italian trip.

In both versions the Alban hills are given full weight and solidity by Cozens's technique of building form through the massing of delicate touches of subdued color. While Cozens's technical achievement was considerable and influential, it was also at the service of a sensibility that the great Romantic landscape painter John Constable described as "all poetry." The sense of light and atmosphere, as well as mystery and melancholy, that Cozens created in watercolors such as these, set him apart from other contemporaries working in Italy, such as William Pars (cat. 100) or John "Warwick" Smith (cat. 74), and provided an important model for a younger generation of watercolorists, which included Thomas Girtin (cat. 143) and J.M.W. Turner (cat. 144). SW

105

105

ALEXANDER COZENS (1717-86)

Roman Sketchbook, 1746

Eighty-seven pages of laid paper
(27 removed), bound in vellum; each
sheet: 7¼ x 5 in. (18.5 x 12.7 cm)

Shown: *A View of the Roman Forum*,
graphite

PROVENANCE: By descent in the artist's
family to Ralph George Norwood Young;
his sale, Sotheby's, 16 March 1978 (46),
from whom purchased

SELECTED EXHIBITIONS: YCBA, *Cozens*,
1980, no. 2; YCBA, *Classic Ground*, 1981,
no. 89; YCBA, *First Decade*, 1986, no. 79

SELECTED LITERATURE: Oppé, 1928,
pp. 81-93; Oppé, 1952, pp. 13-20; Sloan,
1986, pp. 9-20

Paul Mellon Collection
B1978.43.166

106

RICHARD WILSON (1713-82)

Italian Sketchbook, 1754

Thirty-one pages of blue laid paper
bound in vellum; each sheet 11¼ x
8¼ in. (28.1 x 21 cm)

Inscribed in pen and brown ink on fly-
leaf: *Studies by R.Wilson | at Rome 1754*;
in black chalk: *Brockwell Bushes near Mr.
Broc|kmans in Kent*; and in brown ink:
*The gift of O. Bowles | to his Dear friend |
Sir George Beaumont | Dec.! 2ᵈ 1784*

Shown: *View of the Falls and Temple of
the Sibyl at Tivoli*, black chalk

PROVENANCE: Oldfield Bowles; by
whom given to Sir George Howland
Beaumont; by descent in the Beaumont
family; Colnaghi, 1963, bt Paul Mellon

SELECTED EXHIBITIONS: YCBA, *English
Landscape*, 1977, no. 15; Tate, *Wilson*,
1982-3, no. 39; YCBA, *Classic Ground*,
1981, no. 90; Beinecke, *Grand Tour*,
1998

SELECTED LITERATURE: Sutton, 1968

Paul Mellon Collection
B1977.14.359

107

THOMAS PATCH (1725-82)

Sketchbook of Portrait Studies,
1760s

Seventy-seven pages (five removed)
of laid paper bound in patterned carta
fiorentina; each sheet: 8¾ x 6⅜ in.
(22.2 x 16.1 cm)

Inscribed in pen and brown ink inside
front cover: *These Sketches executed by
Patch at Florence 1770*

Shown: *Portrait of a Man, called Edward
Gibbon*, red crayon

Inscribed in graphite, lower right: *May
be Gibbon*

PROVENANCE: ...; Sotheby's, 21 March
1974 (44), bt Paul Mellon through John
Baskett

SELECTED EXHIBITIONS: YCBA, *English
Portrait Drawings*, 1979-80, no. 44;
Beinecke, *Grand Tour*, 1998

Paul Mellon Collection
B1977.14.309

108

GEORGE ROMNEY (1734-1802)

Italian Sketchbook, 1773

One hundred and seventy pages of laid
paper bound in vellum; each sheet:
6⅜ x 4½ in. (16.2 x 11.4 cm)

Signed and dated in pen and brown ink
on verso of flyleaf: *Geo. Romney June 5
1773*

Shown: *Sketch of Michelangelo's Statue of
Lorenzo de Medici from the Medici
Chapel, San Lorenzo, Florence*, graphite

PROVENANCE: ... ; Harry L. Stern,
Chicago, from whom purchased

109

JOHN FLAXMAN (1755-1826)

Italian Sketchbook, 1787

Seventy-nine pages of laid paper bound
in vellum; each sheet: 8⅝ x 6 in. (21.9 x
15.2 cm)

Inscribed in graphite inside front cover
and again in pen and black ink on the
flyleaf: *John Flaxman | sculptor | began at
Florence November the 4th | 1787*

Shown: *Christ Driving out the Money
Changers, from Lorenzo Ghiberti's
Baptistery Doors, Florence,* pen and gray
ink and gray wash

Inscribed in pen and gray ink, verso:
*Our Saviour driving the buyers, sellers, |
& money changers out of the Temple |
Ghiberti*

106

107

For the British artist studying in Italy, the sketchbook was a crucial tool. There on "classic ground" the act of drawing focused the attention and aided the understanding. Back in Britain the sketchbook provided not only a record of the art and landscape encountered but also a repertoire of poses, figural groupings, and compositional ideas from the ancients and the masters of the Renaissance and Baroque or of richly evocative landscape elements that could be incorporated into their own art.

Alexander Cozens, one of the first British landscape painters to travel to Italy, arrived in Rome in 1746. His sketchbook from his Roman visit includes records in pencil outline of the Roman landscape and antiquities, compositional studies, and lists of procedures for drawing and study. His pedagogical and theoretical orientation is already very much in evidence.

Richard Wilson's sketchbook of 1754 is the second of two extant sketchbooks from his years in Italy. The earlier sketchbook (Victoria and Albert Museum), dated 1752, includes both quick studies from nature and imaginary landscape compositions of his own invention. Such landscape capriccios are absent from the later sketchbook, which is largely devoted to sensitive and more highly finished studies in chalk of antique sculpture, copses and gnarled trees, and recognizable views of Rome and the Campagna, such as the drawing of Tivoli shown here. The falls at Tivoli, with the circular temple known as the Temple of the Sybil perched above, was one of the most popular motifs for foreign landscape artists in Italy.

While their sketchbooks show them to have been eager and receptive students, both George Romney and John Flaxman made their visits to Italy as mature well-established artists. Romney interrupted a successful practice as a portrait painter to travel in Italy between 1773 and 1775. Flaxman by 1787 had earned enough as a sculptor to afford a more extended stay in Italy, remaining there until 1794. The sketchbooks by Romney and Flaxman are each filled with drawings after antique sculpture and works of the early and high Renaissance in both Florence and Rome. Romney's sketches are freer and are interspersed with original compositional studies; Flaxman's drawings are more disciplined, frequently worked up with pen and ink and wash.

The sketchbook attributed to Thomas Patch is of a different nature. It records not the beauties of Italian art and the Italian countryside but a gallery of British Grand Tourists. Although the attribution of the sketchbook as well as the accuracy of the inscribed identifications have been questioned, the lively studies are plausibly the work of Patch, and the displayed portrait could well be that of the twenty-seven-year-old Edward Gibbon, future author of the *History of the Decline and Fall of the Roman Empire*. After being banished from the Papal States for an unnamed indiscretion, Patch took up residence in Florence. There he became a close friend of Sir Horace Mann, the British Minister to Florence, through whom he was introduced to all the visiting British worthies, including, in 1764, the young Gibbon. sw

108

109

"Great Manner and Exquisite Taste"
ARCHITECTURAL DRAWINGS

AT THE BEGINNING of the eighteenth century the architect was regarded as merely "a tradesman and an artificer." Yet in 1768 the founders of the Royal Academy considered architecture a branch of art. Drawing played a central role in the radical transformation of the education and social position of the architect, as it connected the practice of the architect to that of other artists. As significant Renaissance theorists such as Leon Battista Alberti and Sebastiano Serlio indicated, *disegno*, or design conveyed through line, was a central tenet of both painting and architecture.

These theorists, along with the influential Andrea Palladio, suggested that the architect convey his designs through drawing, namely through two-dimensional projection: plan, section, and elevation. At the time Palladio was writing, in the 1570s, most of the building in England was done by master masons under the auspices of the Office of the Royal Works. Inigo Jones, an admirer of Palladio who was later acclaimed as the first English "architect," provided a model for architectural education adopted in the eighteenth century: extensive visits abroad to study Italian masters and a period of apprenticeship or pupilage to an established architect. Looking to these Italian masters, Jones presented his designs in the standard method of plan, section, and elevation. Jones headed the Royal Works, and throughout the eighteenth century appointments to its offices represented an official stamp of approval: Sir Christopher Wren, Sir John Vanbrugh, and Sir Nicholas Hawksmoor all held positions there. In an age notable for the diverse backgrounds of its most prominent architects, from the playwright-soldier-architect Vanbrugh to the Oxford-educated Wren, the Royal Works functioned as an unofficial academy for practical and theoretical training. In this context, James Gibbs's training in Rome with the architect Carlo Fontana was highly unusual. As the century progressed, however, such experience would come to represent the ideal.

Admirers of Palladio gathered at the informal neo-Palladian academy formed by the aristocratic amateur architect Richard Boyle, 3rd Earl of Burlington, William Kent, and Colen Campbell. Architecture became a genteel pursuit, and the study of the architect in Italy became associated with the Grand Tour. William Chambers and Robert Adam, for example, combined the social and cultural functions of the Grand Tour with architectural training. Like other aspiring architects such as Sir John Soane, they also met potential patrons in the process.

Chambers and Adam, while in Italy on separate occasions, both met the influential Italian architect and designer Giovanni Battista Piranesi and French neoclassical architects working in Italy, such as Charles-Louis Clérisseau. Through these contacts they brought a new type of architectural drawing to England: the perspective drawing of a planned structure in a landscape setting, often with color or other decorative effects. Like architects before them, both men advocated study in Italy and trained pupils in their offices. In addition, they also trained draftsmen and perspectivists to depict their designs as well as execute studies of existing structures. The establishment of the Royal Academy encouraged the drawing skills of architects and promoted the development of architectural draftsmen such as John Yenn and Thomas Malton. Henry Holland exhibited the first perspective architectural drawing at the Royal Academy in 1776, and such works became a regular feature at the annual Academy exhibitions.

MORNA O'NEILL

110

SIR JOHN VANBRUGH (1664-1726)

King's Weston House, Gloucestershire, Entrance Elevation, 1712

Watercolor over pen and graphite on laid paper; 14½ x 18½ in. (36.8 x 47 cm)

PROVENANCE: ...; Colen Campbell, bt Sir Thomas Robinson, 3rd Baron Grantham, c. 1729; by descent to Harry Vyner of Studley Royal, Yorkshire; bt Marlborough Rare Books; bt Paul Mellon, 1966

SELECTED EXHIBITIONS: YCBA *Architectural Drawings,* 1982, no. 37; AIA, *Architect and the Country House,* 1985, no. 16

Paul Mellon Collection
B1977.14.1237

ALONG WITH SUCH LUMINARIES as Sir Christopher Wren and Sir Nicholas Hawksmoor, Sir John Vanbrugh popularized a mix of exuberant Italian baroque forms with classical elements inspired by the writings of the first century B.C. Roman architect and theorist Vitruvius. In 1711 Vanbrugh began plans to rebuild King's Weston near Bristol for Edward Southwell. This drawing of the front elevation of the mansion house was possibly used by Vanbrugh to present his ideas to his patron, since elevations were the principal means to portray the size, proportion, and appearance of a building without conveying technical information. In a typical blending of elements, the irregular placement of the giant-order Corinthian pilasters flanking the entrance lightens the bold simplicity of the symmetrical façade, while the decorative urns mark the corners of the structure. The use of gray watercolor wash to fill in the windows and add shadows gives a sense of depth to this essentially two-dimensional image. In a naturalistic gesture Vanbrugh has added the smoke coming from the arcade of linked chimneys, perhaps to indicate that they are not decorative. This design, with minor alterations, was reproduced by Colen Campbell (cat. 112) in the first volume of his study of English architecture *Vitruvius Britannicus* (1715-25). MO

111

James Gibbs (1682-1754)

Elevation and Plan for a Town or Country House, c. 1720

Watercolor over pen and graphite on laid paper; 18 ¾ x 14 ⁹⁄₁₆ in. (47.5 x 37 cm)

PROVENANCE: ...; John Harris; bt Paul Mellon, 1975

SELECTED EXHIBITIONS: YCBA, *Architectural Drawings*, 1982, no. 15

Paul Mellon Collection
B1975.2.342

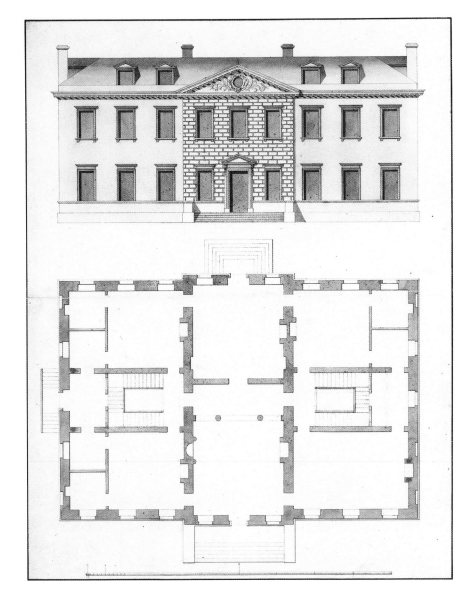

As the designer of such London churches as St. Mary-le-Strand and St. Martin-in-the-Fields, James Gibbs is today best remembered as an ecclesiastical architect. However, one of the hallmarks of his practice was his versatility; he completed designs for government buildings, libraries, garden buildings, mansions, and country homes. This drawing is characteristic of Gibbs's symmetrical and rectangular domestic structures.

While not featured in his publication, this illustration resembles some of the plates in Gibbs's influential *A Book of Architecture* (1728). Intended for "such Gentleman as might be concerned with Building, especially in the more remote parts of the Country, where little or no assistance for Designs can be procured," the publication spread Gibbs's influence throughout Great Britain and abroad. In this drawing he presents the house in plan and elevation, two traditional methods of non-perspective projection used to convey a structure in the eighteenth century. This practice isolates the structure from its surroundings, making it unclear whether this house was intended for the town or the country. As in Vanbrugh's drawing (cat. 110) subtle shading indicates the three-dimensionality of the elevation, while the plan conveys practical information, such as room layout. MO

112

COLEN CAMPBELL (1676-1729)

Elevation of Garden Front of Lowther Castle, c. 1718-20

Watercolor, pen, and graphite on wove paper; 13¾ x 20¾ in. (34.9 x 52.7 cm)

PROVENANCE: ...; B. Weinreb, 1966, bt Paul Mellon, 1966

SELECTED EXHIBITIONS: YCBA, *Architectural Drawings*, 1982, no. 6

SELECTED LITERATURE: Colvin *et al.*, 1980, nos. 27-30

Paul Mellon Collection
B1977.14.1072

COLEN CAMPBELL, along with the architect William Kent and the architect-patron Richard Boyle, Lord Burlington, was one of the chief proponents of the Palladian revival of the first part of the eighteenth century. Campbell was hired by a group of booksellers to act as the author, draftsman, and organizational force of *Vitruvius Britannicus* (1715-25), a three-volume edition of 100 plates each of plans, elevations, and sections. Planned as a review of contemporary English secular architecture, Campbell's text instead focused attention on the "antique simplicity" of buildings in the Palladian style, derived from the buildings and writings of Italian architect Andrea Palladio (1508-80). Campbell used these volumes to inveigh against the excesses of the "foreign" baroque style as "affected and licentious," and he advocated the restrained classicism of a Palladian style, seen as "native" to England in the work of Inigo Jones. The volume was hugely influential, and its large distribution sparked a vogue for architectural publications.

His reputation and architectural theories established with *Vitruvius Britannicus*, Campbell was able to concentrate on his own architectural practice. Although he courted government commissions, he found his greatest success as an architect of country houses. He submitted this design to Henry, 3rd Viscount Lonsdale, for the rebuilding of his fire-damaged Lowther Castle. Although never executed, the design shows Campbell's begrudging appreciation for baroque architects such as Sir John Vanbrugh in the use of decorative urns (cat. 110) and giant-order pilasters. However, Campbell here preserves the strict structural symmetry that would become one of the hallmarks of this early neo-Palladian style. This façade would have faced the elaborate garden landscape that surely accompanied the renovations. MO

113

WILLIAM KENT (bap. 1685-1748)

Design for an Octagonal Temple at Shotover Park, Oxfordshire, c. 1738-45

Pen and brown wash over graphite on laid paper; 11⅛ x 12³⁄₁₆ in. (28.3 x 31 cm)

Inscribed in graphite, lower right: *D*; in pen, lower left, in artist's hand: scale indicating measurements. Verso in artist's hand in pen and ink: *Coll Tyerell | in Oxfordshire; W.K.*

PROVENANCE: ...; John Harris; bt Paul Mellon, 1975

SELECTED EXHIBITIONS: YCBA, *Architectural Drawings*, 1982, no. 19; YCBA, *Country Houses*, 1979, no. 54

SELECTED LITERATURE: Harris, 1986, p. 147

Paul Mellon Collection
B1975.2.152

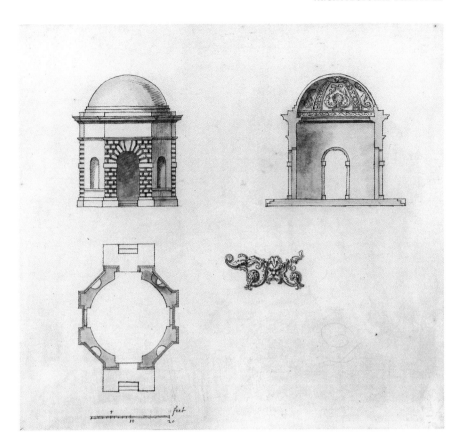

TRAINED IN ROME AND FLORENCE as a painter, "Il Kentino," as his critics mockingly called him, was lured home from Italy in 1720 by Richard Boyle, 3rd Earl of Burlington, to work as interior decorator for Burlington House, Piccadilly. As the leading proponent of the revival of the Palladian style in England and an architect himself, Boyle was influential in establishing this classical style as the predominant architectural language of the mid-eighteenth century. The Italian architect's *I quattri libri dell'architettura* was first translated into English in 1715, the same year as the appearance of the first volume of Colen Campbell's homage to Palladio, *Vitruvius Britannicus.* Kent's interior decoration, architecture, and garden design repeatedly return to the classicism and rationalism of Palladio for inspiration.

General James Tyrell continued his father's plans to renovate the house and gardens of Shotover Park when he inherited the property in 1718, and Kent's design indicates Tyrell's desire for the latest style, to transform his grounds into a landscape inspired by the paintings of Claude. Kent's temple, erected near the west front of the house, displays the even proportions, solid masses, and plain exterior characteristic of his interpretation of the Palladian style. The drawing depicts the traditional plan, elevation, and cross-section of the structure. However, Kent has also included an ornate grotesque design that does not correspond to his depiction of the decorated ceiling of the temple interior. This drawing could represent an alternative decorative scheme or indicate Kent's well-known habit of doodling on his drawings. MO

114

JEAN-BAPTISTE-CLAUDE
CHATELAIN (C. 1710-C. 1758)

*A View of the Rotunda in the
Garden at Stowe,
Buckinghamshire,* 1753

Watercolor over ink and graphite on laid
paper; 9⅛ x 12⅞ in. (23.3 x 32.7 cm)

PROVENANCE: ...; Christie's, 17
November 1970 (64) bt John Baskett,
1970; bt Paul Mellon, 1970

SELECTED EXHIBITIONS: YCBA, *Country
Houses,* 1979, no. 58; YCBA, *Georgian
Landscape Garden,* 1983, no. 28; YCBA,
Pope, 1988, no. 49

Paul Mellon Collection
B1975.4.1058

A WELL-KNOWN TEACHER, draftsman, and engraver of landscapes,
Chatelain often assisted topographical landscape artists with their
work. This drawing was part of a
series of views of Stowe engraved in
1753 by George Bickham Jr. for his
*Sixteen Perspective Views, Together
with a General Plan of the
Magnificent Buildings at Stowe.*
While not an architect himself,
Chatelain's role in depicting and
disseminating architecture to a larger public was an important part of
architectural practice, as it raised
public awareness of architectural
styles and important structures.

The gardens at Stowe, the home
of Richard Temple, Viscount Cob-
ham, were a subject of popular
interest because of their reconstruc-
tion throughout the early eighteenth
century by Temple and Charles
Bridgeman. They attracted architects such as Sir John Vanbrugh
(cat. 110), who designed this rotunda (1721), and William Kent (cat.
113). Lancelot "Capability" Brown
was head gardener at Stowe in 1741.
Chatelain presents the landscape at
Stowe as a pastoral idyll; framed by
the Ionic columns of the rotunda on
the left and majestic trees on the
right, diminutive picturesque work-
ers rest or assume classical poses.
This view would change drastically
soon afterward, as the monument
and canal in the distance, as well as
surrounding trees, were removed to
provide a central vista from the garden façade of the house. MO

115

HUMPHRY REPTON (1752-1818)

Bird's-eye View of Sarsden House and Gardens, Oxfordshire, c. 1795

Watercolor over graphite; 9½ x 12⅞ in. (24.1 x 32.7 cm)

Inscribed below image in graphite: *perspective view of Saresdan, seat of Sir John [...]*

PROVENANCE: ...; John Harris; bt Paul Mellon, 1975

SELECTED EXHIBITIONS: YCBA, *Architectural Drawings*, 1982, no. 28

Paul Mellon Collection
B1975.2.386

AS THE IDEOLOGICAL HEIR to Lancelot "Capability" Brown and an advocate of the Claudian ideal of the "natural" landscape, Repton coined the term "landscape gardening" to describe his method for the artful arrangement of nature. In his 1795 treatise *Sketches and Hints on Landscape Gardening* he aimed to "establish fixed principles on the art of laying out ground" in his attempt to elevate landscape gardening to a "polite art" on a par with drawing. This type of drawing was one of Repton's preferred methods for introducing clients, in this case James H. Langston, to his ideas. Here he provides an ichnographic or "bird's-eye" view, a form of architectural drawing mentioned by Vitruvius and advocated by Leonardo da Vinci. Traditionally, it was a popular method in England for representing country houses.

Repton would compile his many drawings for each project into a red leather-bound "Red Book" for presentation to the client, complete with written descriptions and "before-and-after" overlays to demonstrate his plans for the landscape. Although he was not the architect of Sarsden House, Repton was the architect of Sarsden's landscape, and this drawing provides insight into his art. The formal gardens of parterres and terraces near the garden façade of the house give way to a picturesque treatment in the distance, complete with serpentine lake and a classically-inspired pavilion. MO

116

WILLIAM CHAMBERS (1723-96)

Elevations with Details of Mouldings and Entablatures for Gateways at the Hoo, Kimpton, Hertfordshire, c. 1760-4

Watercolor over pen and graphite on laid paper; 12 x 19½ in. (30.5 x 48.9 cm)

Inscribed below left in pen: *The Wall is 14° thick | the Rusticks projects 2 ½° | before the Wall and the pillasters project <¼ of | their width with >5 inches.*

PROVENANCE: The Hoo; bt Mrs. Brand of Glynde Place, Sussex; bt Rupert Gunnis Esq.; bt B. Weinreb, 1966; bt Paul Mellon, 1966

SELECTED EXHIBITIONS: YCBA, *Architectural Drawings*, 1982, no. 8

SELECTED LITERATURE: Harris, 1970, pp. 210-11

Paul Mellon Collection
B1977.14.1073

SIR WILLIAM CHAMBERS was the foremost architect of his generation and architectural advisor to King George III. A founding member of the Royal Academy, he was placed in charge of all government building in his capacity as Surveyor General of the Board of Works (1782). In contrast to the baroque training and interests of Vanbrugh (cat. 110) and Gibbs (cat. 111), Chambers and the neoclassical architects of his generation looked to ancient Roman architecture and archaeological findings for inspiration.

In 1759 Chambers published his *Treatise on Civil Architecture*, a volume devoted to "sound precepts and good designs" that considered, for the most part, the decorative aspects of architecture such as doors and gateways. One of these "good designs" was a doorway by the Italian architect Palladio. In a practice common at the time, Chambers showed his skill and knowledge of classical forms by adapting Palladio's design in his own work, these gateways for Thomas Brand at his country home The Hoo. This drawing gives the viewer some indication of Chambers's working process, as he has noted the thickness of the wall and the projection of the architectural elements, while more technical drawings to the left of each gateway explain the proportions and construction methods. Placed side by side, these two gateways illustrate the diversity of his practice. While the rusticated stone and the large central keystone that breaks through the entablature in the gateway on the left indicate vestigial traces of the baroque, the sleek lines of the gateway on the right announce neoclassical elegance.

MO

117

WILLIAM CHAMBERS (1723-96)

Façade for a Temple of Peace, Kew Gardens, Surrey, 1763

Watercolor over pen and graphite on laid paper; 12¾ x 18¹³⁄₁₆ in. (32.4 x 47.8 cm)

Inscribed below left in pen: numbers indicating the scale of measurement in feet

PROVENANCE: ...; B. Weinreb, 1966; bt Paul Mellon, 1966

SELECTED EXHIBITIONS: YCBA, *Architectural Drawings*, 1982, no. 9; YCBA, *Georgian Landscape Garden*, 1983; no. 76

SELECTED LITERATURE: Harris, 1970, p. 38; Harris and Snodin, 1996, pp. 55-67

Paul Mellon Collection
B1977.14.1074

CHAMBERS SPENT THE EARLY 1750S in Rome, and his friendships with visiting noblemen became advantageous business contacts, as Lord Bute recommended him as tutor in architecture to George, Prince of Wales (the future King George III), in 1756. Through these royal connections, the Dowager Princess Augusta, the widow of Prince Frederick, commissioned Chambers to design Prince Frederick's mausoleum, and she enlisted him in her project to redesign Kew Gardens. Lord Bute, director of the project, planned to create a scientific botanic garden amid this royal retreat in the Surrey countryside; new greenhouses were built, existing buildings were moved, and Chambers set about designing new garden structures in a variety of architectural styles.

Although it was never built due to financial concerns on the part of the patroness, the Temple of Peace was planned as part of an excursion through classical themes and motifs in a garden that presented a tour of world architecture, including Chambers's celebrated Chinese-style Pagoda. Chambers presents the viewer with the elevation of the Temple, appropriately shaded to give some indication of depth. The Ionic columns would have echoed those of the diminutive Temple of Arethusa located nearby, while the sculpted pediment and entablature surpassed it in grandeur.

In 1763 Chambers recorded his involvement in the redesign of Kew Gardens with the publication of *Plans, Elevations, Sections, and Perspective Views of the Gardens and Buildings at Kew in Surry*, and he remained architect there until the death of Princess Augusta in 1772.
MO

118

GIOVANNI BATTISTA BORRA
(1713-70)

The Members of a Corinthian Temple in Ruins at Ephesus, c. 1750

Pen with watercolor on laid paper; 12⅜ x 8 in. (31.4 x 20.3 cm)

Inscribed in pen in top left: *XLVIII* and in pencil: *XXXXII*

PROVENANCE: . . .; Edmund Neville-Rolfe; bt Paul Mellon

Paul Mellon Collection
B1977.14.935

THIS STUDY OF THE ARCHITECTURAL elements of a Corinthian temple at Ephesus, in modern day Turkey, dates from Giambattista Borra's travels with Robert Wood, (cats. 59, 97). The studies of ancient architecture and architectural ruins executed by Borra throughout the course of this journey provided illustrations for Robert Wood's 1753 *The Ruins of Palmyra* and his 1757 *The Ruins of Balbec.* This drawing is one of a group of ninety-eight finished drawings in the Center's collection that were intended to illustrate a further publication that was never produced. Attention to ancient architecture was an important part of a gentleman's education. Borra's drawings, engraved and published in Wood's volumes, aided the gentleman in his quest for knowledge and refinement; as Wood himself wrote in *The Ruins of Balbec,* "we shall ... refer our reader almost entirely to the plates, where his information will be more full and circumstantial, as well as less tedious and confused, than could be conveyed by the happiest precision of language."

The careful study of all aspects of classical building provided the cornerstone of the architect's education. Architects like Borra trained as draftsmen in part to produce carefully measured renderings of ancient ruins. He delineates the details of the Corinthian order and its decoration, following certain accepted standards such as the rendering of both the bottom and the top of the column to indicate its tapering, and he provides a rubric to indicate scale. The depiction of different examples of the classical orders of columns was an important aspect of architectural drawing, as each order had its own particular forms and subsequent uses. The Corinthian, shown here, was one of the more elaborate and fanciful orders. Most architects traveled to view the buildings for themselves, while others had to rely on publications and the drawings of others for their education. MO

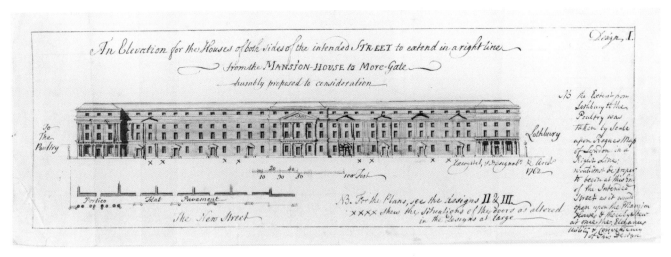

119

STEPHEN RIOU (1720-80)

Design for "the Houses of Both Sides of the Intended Street to Extend in a Right Line from the Mansion-House to More-Gate Humbly Proposed for Consideration," 1762

Watercolor over pen and graphite on laid paper; 7¹⁵⁄₁₆ x 20⅞ in. (18.6 x 53 cm)

Signed and dated in pen, right below design: *Excogitat & Designat SR* [in monogram] *1762.* Inscribed top center in pen: *An Elevation for the Houses of both sides of the Intended Street to extend in a right line | from the* MANSION-HOUSE *to More-Gate | humbly proposed for consideration*; top right in pen: *Design I*; far right in pen: NB *The extent from | Lothbury to the Poultry was taken | by Scale upon Roque's Map | of London in a | Right line; would it not be proper | to begin at this End | of the Intended | Street as it would | open upon the Mansion | House & thereby shew at once the Elegance | Utility, & Convenience of this Design*; at immediate right of design: *Lothbury*; at immediate left of design: *to | the | Poultry*; below center in pen: measurement of scale, and below: *Portico Flat Pavement and | The New Street*; below right in pen: NB *for the Plans, see the designs* II & III | *xxxx shew the situations of the doors as altered | in the Designs at large*

PROVENANCE: ...; D. & R. Blissett, 1997; bt Yale Center for British Art, 1998

Paul Mellon Fund
B1998.19.1

ALTHOUGH STEPHEN RIOU published widely on architecture and exhibited his designs publicly, he never executed a single building. His writings and sketches, however, document a lifelong interest in the application of classical form to contemporary building.

Trained as an architect in Geneva, Riou traveled throughout Greece and Italy in the 1750s, acting as a guide to Grand Tourists and eventually meeting up with James "Athenian" Stuart and Charles Revett. He accompanied the pair to Athens, and he shared their goal of increasing public knowledge and acceptance of classical Greek architecture. To this end, he published *The Grecian Orders of Architecture delineated and explained from the Antiquities of Athens* in 1768 and dedicated it to James Stuart.

This design appears in simplified form as Plate VI in the second volume of *Grecian Orders* as "The Design for a New Street in the City." With these designs he hoped to illustrate the adaptability of forms such as the pedimented façade and Doric colonnade to the building projects of London, in this instance the planned construction of a new street leading from Mansion House to Moorgate. Riou's design maintains class distinctions even within the new city dwelling through architectural language: "the center house, and those at the extremities, are larger than all of the intervening ones" to indicate "a difference in the fortunes and rents of the citizens." With his incorporation of Grecian features into Palladian designs, Riou was at the forefront of the Greek Revival movement. MO

ROBERT ADAM (1728-92)

120

Headfort House, Eating Parlor, Chimney Side, 1771

Watercolor over pen and graphite on laid paper, 14½ x 25¹¹⁄₁₆ in. (36.8 x 65.2 cm)

Signed and dated lower left in pen: *Robert Adam archt. 1771*; inscribed in pen in artist's hand: *Design for finishing the Chimney Side of the Eating Parlor. For The Right Honble The Earl of Bective. | Adelphi Decr. 2 d 1775*; verso in graphite in different hand; *Chimney side of my Parlor*; bottom in pen in artist's hand: *scale*

PROVENANCE: ...; bt Paul Mellon, 1967

SELECTED EXHIBITIONS: YCBA, *Architectural Drawings,* 1982, no. 2; Wash U, *Spirit of Antiquity,* 1984, no. 10; Cooper-Hewitt, 1982, no. 86

SELECTED LITERATURE: Harris, 1973, pp. 1-2; Harris, 1985, p. 165, fig. 45; Cooper-Hewitt, *Adam & His Style,* 1982, pp. 4-5, fig. 1

Paul Mellon Collection
B1975.2.793

121

Headfort House, Staircase, Side Section, 1775

Watercolor wash over pen and graphite on laid paper; 21¼ x 14⅝ in. (53.8 x 37 cm)

PROVENANCE: ...; bt Paul Mellon, 1967

SELECTED EXHIBITIONS: RIBA, *Headfort House,* 1973, no. 15; Cooper-Hewitt, *Adam & His Style,* 1982, no. 81

SELECTED LITERATURE: Cooper-Hewitt, 1982, p. 5; Harris, 1973, pp. 1-2

Paul Mellon Collection
B1975.2.798

SIR THOMAS TAYLOR became Earl of Bective in 1766, and at that time he apparently decided that his family home of Headfort House, in Co. Meath, Ireland, also needed to increase its stature. Taylor at one point contemplated razing the structure, described by later commentators as "a long range of tasteless buildings," and rebuilding it along more fashionable lines to plans devised by Sir William Chambers in 1765 (also in the Center's collection). While Chambers's redesigned exterior was never executed, his rival Robert Adam was commissioned to decorate the interior in 1771, completing designs for the Hall, Staircase, Eating Parlor, Saloon, and Lady's Room, including furniture and structural fittings.

The Scottish-born Adam reputedly boasted that he "brought about in this country a kind of revolution in the whole system of this useful and elegant art." After a Grand Tour of Italy and extended study of both actual Rome ruins and their interpretation by Giovanni Battista Piranesi, Adam brought the new neoclassical style to London. Informed by an intense study of ancient Roman and Renaissance architecture, he demonstrated his skill at combining the two, as in his decorative scheme for the Eating Parlor at Headfort House. The wood and stucco decorations appropriate classical motifs such as the Three Graces, while the central painting of picturesque figures lounging beside the Pyramid of Gaius Cestius in Rome recalls fashionable eighteenth-century *capricci*. The design for the staircase, never executed as shown, displays Adam's talent for adapting his decorative style to different spaces.

Adam's revolution was one of both form and practice. He received instruction in Rome from the master French Academic architect and draftsman Charles-Louis Clérisseau, and the practice he established in London around 1760 in partnership with his brother James is an early example of modern architecture and design firms. Serendipitously, Adam's rise to prominence accompanied an increase in country-house building in Great Britain perhaps fueled by new-found commercial wealth. His beautiful and elaborate

121

drawings, often with watercolor washes, were a persuasive way to communicate his designs to potential patrons. MO

143

George Richardson Invt 1773.

122

GEORGE RICHARDSON
(c. 1736-1813)

Design for a Chimney Piece, 1773

Watercolor over pen on laid paper;
10⁷⁄₁₆ x 14³⁄₈ in. (26.5 x 36.5 cm)

Signed in graphite lower left: *George Richardson Invt 1773*

PROVENANCE: ...; John Harris; bt Paul Mellon, 1975

SELECTED EXHIBITIONS: YCBA, *Architectural Drawings*, 1982, no. 29

Paul Mellon Collection
B1975.2.675

TRAINED AS A DRAFTSMAN in the studio of Robert Adam and his brother James, George Richardson even accompanied Adam on his Grand Tour of Italy from 1760 to 1763. In addition, he shared the interest of the Adam brothers in interior decoration as an integral part of the architectural whole. When he left the Adams in 1765, he was already established as a ceiling painter, and he would later publish *A Book of Ceilings Composed in the Stile of the Antique Grotesques.*

Throughout his career Richardson displayed an interest in the "antique grotesque," a form of design adapted from both Renaissance sources such as Raphael and from the recent discovery of wall decorations in Pompeii, unearthed in 1748. These influences are evident in this design for a chimney piece with its delicate scroll work and dancing maidens adapted from classical wall paintings. Perhaps motivated by Giovanni Battista Piranesi's 1769 folio *Diverse maniere d'adornare I cammoni*, featuring designs for fireplaces influenced by classical and ancient Egyptian architecture, Richardson published his *New Collection of Chimney Pieces Ornamented in the Style of Etruscan, Greek, and Roman Architecture* in 1781. Unlike Piranesi, however, he showed his chimney pieces in the traditional manner, without roaring fires. MO

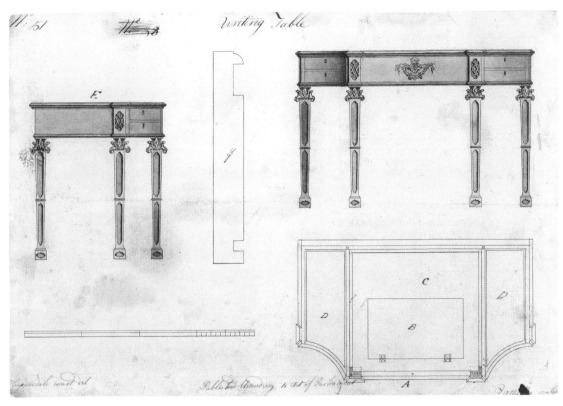

123

THOMAS CHIPPENDALE
(bap. 1718-79)

Design for a Writing Table, 1754

Watercolor over pen and graphite on wove paper; 8⅝ x 12¹⁵⁄₁₆ in. (21.9 x 32.9 cm)

Inscribed in pen over graphite, upper left: *No. 51; No. 53* erased; center left: *Writing Table*; inscribed in pen over graphite, throughout drawing labeling parts of table: *A-F* in upper case and also *f*; inscribed in pen over graphite, lower left: *Chippendale invert del*; left center: *Published According to Act of Parliament*; lower right: *M[...] sculp*

PROVENANCE: ...; William Fowkes; John L. Marks, Esq. to 1972; sold Sotheby's, 20 April 1972 (38, repr. pl. IV); bt John Baskett, 1972, from whom bt Paul Mellon, 1972

SELECTED LITERATURE: Chippendale, 1754, pl. 51; Chippendale, 1762, pl. 74

Paul Mellon Collection
B1975.4.1630

THOMAS CHIPPENDALE worked with architects to execute their designs for interior fittings, and he also produced designs for interiors, sometimes conferring with the architect of the exterior. As an interior decorator, he conceived decorative schemes as well as designing wallpaper, chimney pieces, carpets, and even silverware for an array of aristocratic and fashionable clients such as David Garrick. Trained as a cabinetmaker and as a draftsman, he put both talents to use, although it is thought that he stopped personally executing his furniture designs after the 1750s.

This design for a writing table appeared as Plate LI in Chippendale's important 1754 publication *The Gentleman and Cabinet-Maker's Director*, consisting of "most elegant and useful designs of household furniture in the most fashionable taste." This influential publication was the first pattern-book to consider a wide array of household furnishings, and it was unique in that it united the patron (the Gentleman of the title) with craftsman (the Cabinet-Maker) in a sense of shared endeavor: "to assist the one [the patron] in the Choice, and the other [the craftsman] in the Execution of the Designs." Echoing the accepted mode of architectural drawing, Chippendale provides the viewer with elevation, plan, and section of the writing table.

The popularity of this volume made the name Chippendale into an adjective describing English rococo furniture. Characterized by the influence of the curvilinear French ornament with continuous curves and foliage, the rococo style is evident in the elaborate drawer-pull and acanthus-topped legs of the table. MO

124

SIR JOHN SOANE (1753-1837)

Sketch of a Half-Façade for a Royal Palace, Hyde Park, London, c. 1779

Watercolor wash and graphite on laid paper; 3½ x 8¼ in. (8.9 x 21 cm)

Signed in graphite, lower right: *J. Soane;* lower right in graphite in different hand: *Sir J. Soane Palace*; lower right in graphite in a third hand: *sketch by J. Soane*

PROVENANCE: ...; Iolo A. Williams; bt Paul Mellon from the estate of Iolo A. Williams, 1970

SELECTED EXHIBITIONS: YCBA, *Architectural Drawings*, 1982, no. 34

SELECTED LITERATURE: Du Prey, 1972, pp. 145-9.

Paul Mellon Collection
B1977.14.5594

SIMILARLY TO PAINTERS of the period who depicted imaginary landscapes, Sir John Soane and his colleagues invented ideal structures. The interest in conceptualizing ancient architectural ruins as complete structures was combined with the influence of architectural fantasies by Piranesi to allow architect-draftsmen to give free expression to the visual vocabulary of ancient architecture. They imagined grand structures for London as the new Rome. Soane conceived of this design while working in Rome, and in his memoirs he describes it as a mix of ancient Roman and Italian Renaissance sources, part Pantheon, part Villa Farnese. Here he uses the popular neoclassical forms of the domed roofs and Corinthian pilasters in his fanciful sketch of a Royal Palace for Hyde Park. The pedimented temple façade and tall dome mark the center of the structure, and he includes the right wing in his depiction.

Soane commissioned his chief architectural draftsman Joseph Michael Gandy to depict this structure in a perspective watercolor (Soane Museum, London). Gandy, an architectural draftsman like Thomas Malton (cat. 129), specialized in the perspectival depiction of imagined, ideal structures of his own or other's invention, as well as acting as chief draftsman for Soane's architectural practice. He was a frequent and popular exhibitor at the Royal Academy, an indication of the increasing acceptance of architectural drawings as works of art as well as utilitarian documents. MO

Carlton House. Section through the Portico Hall & Tribune

125

HENRY HOLLAND (1745-1806)

Section through the Portico, Hall, and Tribune of Carlton House, Pall Mall, c. 1787

Watercolor over pen and graphite on laid paper; 14 x 28⅛ in. (35.6 x 71.6 cm)

PROVENANCE: ...; John Harris; bt Paul Mellon, 1975

SELECTED EXHIBITIONS: YCBA, *Architectural Drawings*, 1982, no. 18; AIA, *Architect and the Country House*, 1985, no. 50

SELECTED LITERATURE: Harris, 1985, pp. 174-5; Harris, 1991, pp. 251-3.

Paul Mellon Collection
B1975.2.640

CARLTON HOUSE became a Royal residence in 1732, and the Prince of Wales, the future King George III, took possession of it in 1783. His first act was to hire Henry Holland to renovate the exterior and refurbish the interior to suit the Prince's luxurious lifestyle. In the 1780s Holland traveled to France and was influenced there by the neoclassical architects associated with the French Academy of Architecture such as J.G. Soufflot, designer of the Roman-inspired Panthéon in Paris. Following the widespread influence of neo-Palladianism, late eighteenth-century neoclassicism favored newly discovered monuments of classical antiquity over Palladian interpretations of classical architecture.

From the right to left this cross-section presents the portico as a *porte-cochère* (with the outline of a carriage sketched in), a vestibule with a cast of the Apollo Belvedere, followed by a rectangular hall, with a low arch spanned by entablatures supported on Ionic columns, and a second hall with a gallery overlooking the grand staircase. The rounded forms of Holland's section, especially the coffered dome with an oculus, recall circular Roman temples such as the Pantheon. The rich ornamentation was perhaps inspired by the discovery and subsequent excavation of Pompeii in 1748. Although this design was never executed, Holland continued his work at Carlton House, which remained incomplete at the time of his death.

MO

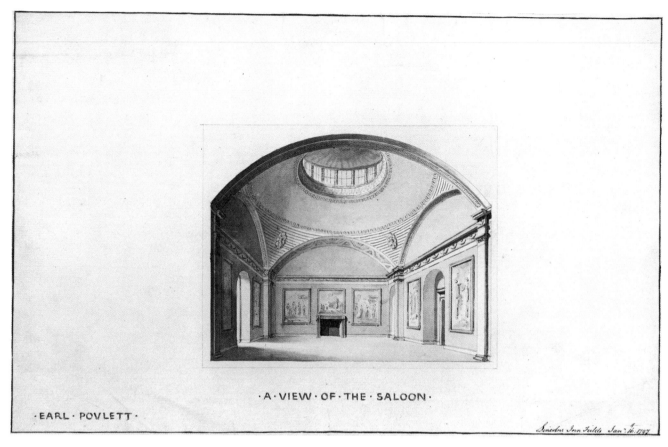

·A·VIEW·OF·THE·SALOON·

·EARL·POVLETT·

Lincoln Inn Fields Jany 16 1797

126

SIR JOHN SOANE (1753-1837)

View of the Saloon, Hinton St. George, Somerset, 1797

Watercolor over pen and graphite; 9¹⁵/₁₆ x 14¹⁵/₁₆ in. (25.2 x 37.9 cm)

Dated lower right: *Lincoln Inn Fields, Jany 16 1797;* below image at center: *A View of the Saloon;* lower left: *Earl Poulett*

PROVENANCE: ...; John Harris; from whom bt Paul Mellon, 1975

SELECTED EXHIBITIONS: YCBA, *Architectural Drawings,* 1982, no. 33

SELECTED LITERATURE: Stroud, 1961, p. 160; Bolton, 1924, p. XXXV

Paul Mellon Collection
B1975.2.420

LIKE ARCHITECTS of the previous generation such as Sir William Chambers (cats. 116-17) and Robert Adam (cats. 120-1), Soane trained in Italy. While there, he studied ancient and Renaissance architecture and met both the influential Piranesi and potential aristocratic patrons. During his sojourn, he developed his own highly individual interpretation of neoclassical forms and motifs that remained the hallmark of a style that attracted no real imitators or followers. The impact of Roman monuments such as the Pantheon is evident in Soane's design for the Saloon or Salon of Hinton St. George for the 4th Earl of Poulett. Low arches support a shallow dome, while light enters through clerestory windows in the lantern. The low vaulted space became a hallmark of Soane's style from his work as Surveyor to the Bank of England, begun in 1788, where he remodeled the structure over a period of thirty years. In contrast to Adam (cat. 121), Soane is spare in his décor and sketchier in his treatment of individual elements, such as the framed painted decoration.

Draftsmanship was an important part of Soane's architectural practice. Unlike Adam, who demonstrated his designs in two-dimensions, Soane presented the client with a perspective view. In an 1809 lecture in his capacity as Professor of Architecture at the Royal Academy, he stressed that "the real effect of a composition can only be correctly shown in perspective presentation."
MO

127

JOHN YENN (1750-1821)

Two Designs for Wall Decorations, c. 1800

Pen and watercolor on laid paper; each 10¼ x 13¾ in. (26 x 34.9 cm)

Verso of B1975.2.649, inscribed in graphite in upper right: *sketch of an architectural fragment*

PROVENANCE: ...; John Harris; bt Paul Mellon, 1975

Paul Mellon Collection B1975.2.648-9

IN 1769 JOHN YENN was one of the first students admitted to study architecture at the Royal Academy Schools, recently founded in 1768. As part of his training there, he would have studied drawing from existing structures, sciagraphy (the depiction of architectural features using light and shade), and drawing from life. A pupil of Sir William Chambers (cats. 116-17) from 1764, Yenn was later employed as a clerk in Chambers's office, eventually becoming his chief architectural draftsman. Scholars have characterized Yenn as a "faithful disciple of Chambers," and indeed Chambers himself described his pupil as "an ingenious faithful intelligent servant" as late as 1774. While his designs indicate the influence of Chambers's neoclassical style, Yenn's work is distinguished by its delicate line and color.

Color became an important aspect of late eighteenth-century architectural drawings, as the influence of French neoclassical architects who favored the practice coincided with the development of watercolor cakes, which made the medium accessible to those who did not know how to mix their own pigments. The use of color in the architectural interior received great attention in this period, when architects designed not only the exterior, but also the interior décor, the furniture, and even doorknobs. Yenn's use of light pinks and greens indicates his knowledge of color theory, as it echoes exactly the definition of "beautiful" color supplied by Edmund Burke in his *Philosophical Inquiry into the Origin of our Ideas of the Sublime and the Beautiful* of 1757: "the colours of beautiful bodies must not be dusky or muddy, but clean and fair ... those which seem most appropriate to beauty are the milder of every sort; light greens, soft blues, weak whites, pink reds, and violets." MO

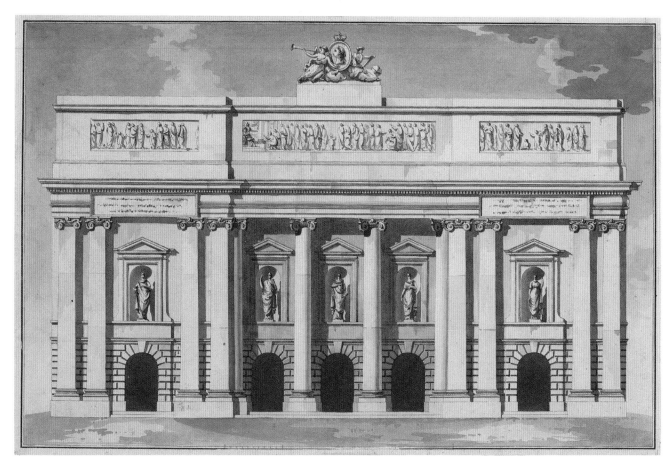

128

JAMES GANDON (1743-1823)

Elevation for the West Front of Parliament House, Dublin, c. 1787

Watercolor and pen on laid paper; 9⅞ x 15¹⁄₁₆ in. (25.1 x 38.3 cm)

PROVENANCE: ...; Iolo A. Williams to 1964; bt Colnaghi, August 1964; bt Paul Mellon, 1964

SELECTED EXHIBITIONS: YCBA, *Architectural Drawings*, 1982, no. 12

Paul Mellon Collection B1977.14.5667

AN ADMIRER AND STUDENT of Sir William Chambers (cats. 116-17), James Gandon was the foremost neoclassical architect working in Dublin in the late eighteenth century. Although his designs, such as this one for the Parliament House in Dublin, echo the forms of ancient Roman architecture, Gandon himself never traveled beyond Great Britain and Ireland. Rather, he learned classical architecture through discussions with Chambers, by looking at prints and drawings, and by studying books such as Colen Campbell's *Vitruvius Britannicus.* Admired during his lifetime as "Vitruvius Hibernicus," Gandon published a two-volume expansion of Campbell's seminal text.

Through Irish connections made at the London home of Paul Sandby, Gandon was invited to Ireland by John Dawson, 2nd Viscount Carlow (later 1st Earl of Portarlington). In Dublin by 1781, he became a prominent figure in the redesign of Dublin that marked this period. His designs for the domed Custom House (1781-91) on the River Liffey and the adjacent Four Courts building established the public face of Georgian Dublin. He also designed additions to the Irish Parliament House when Westminster renounced its right to legislate Ireland in 1783. In this design for the Ionic-columned west front, Gandon demonstrates his study of classical form as well as his interest in sculptural decoration. The project of expanding both the House of Lords and the House of Commons became the work of many architects, and Irish architect Samuel Hayes adapted Gandon's design for the west façade. MO

129

THOMAS MALTON (1748-1804)

Interior of St. Paul's Cathedral,
c. 1792

Watercolor and pen over graphite on laid
paper; 26⁵⁄₁₆ x 36⅛ in. (66.8 x 91.8 cm)

PROVENANCE: ...; The Architectural
Association; bt John Baskett; bt Paul
Mellon, 1973

SELECTED EXHIBITIONS: RA, 1792

Paul Mellon Collection
B1977.14.6220

AGITATION FOR AN ORGANIZED art
establishment and the formation of
various exhibiting societies in the
mid-eighteenth century culminated
with the foundation of the Royal
Academy in 1768. With the prominent role of architects in these proceedings and the inclusion of architecture as one of the branches of the
Academy, architectural drawings
were given increased attention, and
they were frequently shown in prox-
imity to paintings at the annual
Academy exhibitions.

As a result, a new kind of artist
arose: the architectural draftsman
whose role was to translate the plan,
section, and elevation designs of the
architect into an actual, albeit imagined, structure as well as to record
existing monuments. Thomas
Malton the Younger, like his father
the perspective specialist Thomas
Malton the Elder (1726-1801), was
one such artist. Trained as an architect in the Royal Academy schools,
Malton specialized in topographical
views and perspective drawings.
Although he showed his own
designs at Academy exhibitions, he
never executed a building. He is
best remembered for his successful
use of the newly invented method of
aquatint in his *A Picturesque Tour
through the Cities of London and
Westminster*. In this drawing he
employs the Italian convention
known as *scena per angola*, a technique used in theater design to construct perspective along one or more
diagonals rather than a central axis.
This innovation allows Malton to
convey the vast grandeur of Wren's
St. Paul's, which acts as both classical basilica and society promenade.
This drawing is one of a suite of
views of St. Paul's exhibited by
Malton at the Royal Academy in
1792. Malton took his vocation seriously, and he hoped to be elected an
Associate of the Royal Academy.
However, he was rejected as "only a
draughtsman of buildings, but no
architect." MO

The Literal Truth
TOPOGRAPHICAL ART

IN AN AGE before photography, the documentary value of the topographical drawing – providing an accurate visual record of a particular place – was incalculable. Such records were made for a variety of reasons and could serve a variety of functions. Samuel and Nathaniel Buck's association with the Society of Antiquaries and Thomas and Paul Sandby's early employment by the Board of Ordnance suggest the antiquarian and military orientation of much topographical drawing, particularly early in the eighteenth century. Indeed, Paul Sandby's production of maps for the Survey of the Highlands exemplifies the close connections between topography and cartography.

The Buck brothers in their view of Berwick upon Tweed (cat. 130) and the Sandbys in their views of Wakefield Lodge (cat. 136) and Norbury Park (cat. 137) employed the convention of the "stained" or "tinted" drawing inherited from the previous century. With its precise pen outlines and just enough modeling in gray wash (with or without the addition of pale tints of watercolor) to clarify masses, it was a convention perfectly adapted to its topographical role. Over the course of the eighteenth century the character of the topographical drawing would evolve in response to new attitudes and preoccupations.

The habits of careful and precise observation required of the topographer would suggest a concomitant attentiveness to the phenomenon of nature. As early as the 1750s, Jonathan Skelton was producing topographical drawings that reveal the sort of naturalistic concerns that come more and more to the forefront of British landscape art. In his view of the leper's hospital at Harbledown (cat. 133), from a set of views of Canterbury and its environs, Skelton seems more involved with the trees and old fences and tumbledown outbuildings than with the hospital itself, which can just be glimpsed through the trees. His note when he mounted the drawing that it

had been made after a summer shower is the sort of meteorological notation we would expect from John Constable some sixty or seventy years later.

The expressive potential of the qualities of light and weather was more fully realized by John Robert Cozens, both in his watercolors of Italy (cats. 103-4) and in home-grown views like the one from Greenwich Hill (cat. 142). He was applying to views of actual places the generalizing and abstract principles of landscape painting of his father, Alexander Cozens. In the work of a whole generation of topographical draftsmen that included Thomas Hearne and Michael "Angelo" Rooker as well as J.R. Cozens, the landscape theorizing of Alexander Cozens and William Gilpin affected the way in which topography would be presented.

Lecturing at the Royal Academy in 1801, Henry Fuseli characterized topography dismissively as "the tame delineation of a given spot." By that date the works of J.R. Cozens and the young Thomas Girtin and J.M.W. Turner had already demonstrated that topography was far from tame. Its conventional appearance and its narrow informational brief both had been outgrown. In its new expanded conception the more or less accurate representation of real places would continue to be a valid function of the topographical branch of landscape art until long after the advent of photography.

SCOTT WILCOX

THE SOUTH VIEW OF BERWICK UPON TWEED.

130

SAMUEL BUCK (1696-1779) and
NATHANIEL BUCK (d. c. 1756)

The South View of Berwick Upon Tweed, c. 1743-5

Pen and black ink with gray wash over graphite on laid paper; image: 9½ x 31⅛ in. (24.1 x 79.1 cm); sheet: 12⅜ x 31¾ in. (31.4 x 80.6 cm)

Inscribed above image in pen and black ink: THE SOUTH VIEW OF BERWICK UPON TWEED; within image landmarks numbered from 1 to 24; beneath image, lower left, key to numbered landmarks; signed in graphite beneath image, lower right: *Buck del.*; inscribed in pen and black ink, verso, with the text that appears on the engraving, an account of Berwick upon Tweed; and in graphite: *1816 | Townley's sale | lot 58th – 8-*

PROVENANCE: ...; Phillips, Son & Neale, 28 March 1983 (13), bt Fine Art Society, from whom purchased

SELECTED LITERATURE: Hyde, 1994, p. 39

Paul Mellon Fund
B1987.19

BORN IN YORKSHIRE, Samuel Buck received early encouragement and employment from the Yorkshire antiquaries Ralph Thoresby and John Warburton. It was probably Warburton who introduced Buck to the Society of Antiquaries in London. Though never a Fellow of the Society, Buck frequently attended its meetings and was certainly employed by William Stuckeley and other Fellows. These engagements led to his massive project, undertaken with his brother Nathaniel, to record sites of antiquarian interest throughout England and Wales – by far the most extensive of a number of such efforts by topographical artists in the century. Between 1721 and 1745 the Bucks produced over 423 engravings of castles, monasteries, and other ruins and an additional eighty-seven prospects of English and Welsh cities and towns. These were gathered together and reissued in three volumes by the printseller Robert Sayer in 1774 as *Buck's Antiquities or Venerable Remains of above 400 Castles, &c in England and Wales, with near to 100 Views of Cities.*

This is the finished drawing, worked up from pencil drawings made on the spot, for the engraving of Berwick upon Tweed that was published in 1745. The engraving reproduces the drawing at approximately the same size. The view of Berwick is typical of the "prospect," taken from an elevated vantage point at a sufficient distance that the town is clearly laid out for the viewer. Although related to an earlier tradition of schematic maplike representations of cities and towns seen from above, the Bucks' presentation is an actual view. SW

131

GIOVANNI ANTONIO CANAL,
called CANALETTO (1697-1768)

*The Thames Looking towards
Westminster from near York
Water Gate*, c. 1754

Pen and brown ink with gray wash on laid
paper; 15¼ x 28¼ in. (38.7 x 71.8 cm)

PROVENANCE: ... ; R.P. Roupell, sale
Christie's, 12 July 1887 (734); J.P.
Heseltine, sold Sotheby's, 28 May 1935
(136), bt Ellis & Smith; Montagu
Bernard, London; Colnaghi, 1961,
bt Paul Mellon

SELECTED EXHIBITIONS: Guildhall,
Canaletto in England, 1959, no. 53; YCBA,
English Landscape, 1977, no. 10; YCBA
Sandby, 1985, no. 9; MMA, *Canaletto*,
1989-90, no. III; Birmingham, *Canaletto
& England*, 1993-4, no. 18

SELECTED LITERATURE: Constable,
1976, no. 747

Paul Mellon Collection
B1977.14.4630

THE VENETIAN "VEDUTA" (or view)
painter Canaletto was much employed by English Grand Tourists,
keen to acquire souvenirs of their
stay in Italy. Declining business in
Venice led Canaletto in 1746 to visit
the country of so many of his patrons.
He remained in England (with two
trips back to Italy in 1750-1 and 1753)
until 1755, painting and drawing
views mostly of London. The crisp
assurance and liveliness of Canaletto's style gave an infusion of
energy to topographical art in
Britain. His bold yet elegant pen
line, evident in this elaborate drawing of the Thames, had a particularly potent legacy. Even though the
emphasis moved away from pen
outline as the century progressed,
the influence of Canaletto's line can
still be seen at the end of the century in the drawing style of Thomas
Girtin and even well into the nineteenth century in the work of
Samuel Prout.

The impact of Canaletto's English
work on the marine painter and
specialist in views of the Thames,
Samuel Scott, is frequently cited, yet
this drawing, with the subsequent
oil paintings that Canaletto made of
the same composition, appears to be
an instance of Canaletto copying
Scott. When Canaletto arrived in
London in May 1746, Westminster
Bridge was almost finished, with all
the arches completed, but Canaletto
shows only five arches in place. The
drawing seems, therefore, to be
based not on the actual view up the
Thames that Canaletto would have
seen but on a painting of the view
done by Scott in either 1742 or 1743
(Simon Dickinson Ltd.). In addition
to the unfinished bridge, the drawing shows Westminster Abbey at the
center, the water tower of the York
Buildings Waterworks company to
the right, and, immediately to the
right of the water tower, the classical
structure of the York Watergate. SW

132

JONATHAN SKELTON (d. 1759)

Views of Canterbury and Its Environs, 1757

132

The Great Gate of St. Augustine's Monastery, Canterbury

Watercolor with pen and gray ink over graphite on laid paper, on contemporary mount; 8⅛ x 15³⁄₁₆ in. (20.6 x 38.6 cm)

Inscribed in pen and brown ink, on verso: *The Great Gate of S.ᵗ Austin's Monastery | J. Skelton 1757.*; on a separate backing sheet, in pen and brown ink: *St. Augustine's Monastery. Canterbury. | J Skelton 1757;* and in a different hand, in graphite: *St. Augustines Monastery | Canterbury | J Skelton | 1757 No. 2.;* and verso in pen and brown ink: *The Great Gate of St. Austins Monastery Canterbury. | J: Skelton 1757*

PROVENANCE: ...; T. C. Blofield, to 1909; ...; George Thorn-Drury; ...; Mrs. S. M. Cowles, sold Sotheby's, 13 July 1966 (9), bt Colnaghi, from whom purchased by Paul Mellon

SELECTED EXHIBITIONS: YCBA, *Sandby*, 1985, no. 3

SELECTED LITERATURE: Pierce, 1960, no. 22

Paul Mellon Collection
B1975.4.1734

133

Harbledown, a Village near Canterbury

Watercolor with pen and gray ink over graphite on laid paper, on contemporary mount; 8 x 21 ¼ in. (20.3 x 54.0 cm)

Inscribed in pen and black ink, on verso: *Harbledown Hospital J. Skelton 1757*

PROVENANCE: ...; T.C. Blofield, to 1909; ....; George Thorn-Drury; ...; Mrs. S. M. Cowles, sold Sotheby's, 13 July 1966 (10), bt Colnaghi, from whom purchased by Paul Mellon

SELECTED EXHIBITIONS: Victoria, *British Watercolor Drawings*, 1971, no. 38; PML, *English Drawings*, 1972, no. 43; AFA, *British Watercolors*, 1985-6, no. 2

SELECTED LITERATURE: Pierce, 1960, no. 28

Paul Mellon Collection
B1975.4.1956

133

JONATHAN SKELTON seems to have belonged to a circle of talented landscape watercolorists including William Taverner (cat. 44) and the foremost landscape painter of mid-century Britain, George Lambert (1700-65). Stylistic links in the work of these three artists seem persuasive. There is, however, no documentary evidence connecting Taverner with Lambert or Skelton, and the only evidence of a connection between Lambert and Skelton is Skelton's recurring references to a "Mr. Lambert" in his letters from Rome. Apart from these letters, which provide a record of Skelton's life from his arrival in Rome in late 1757 to his premature death there in 1759, we know virtually nothing of his life. Indeed, his work was completely unknown until the rediscovery of eighty-four of his drawings in a 1909 sale.

In his earliest known watercolors, a series of views of Croydon dated 1754, Skelton's technique closely resembles that of Lambert. By 1757, the year of the series of eight views of Canterbury and its environs (four of which are in the Yale Center for British Art), Skelton had refined the style inherited from Lambert into a more expressive and atmospheric instrument. The buildings and foliage are at once more solid and more delicate, and his compositions have gained an offhand grace lacking in his earlier work. Skelton produced his Canterbury views in the manner of the "tinted" drawing standard to topographical draftsmanship of the early eighteenth century. Over a pencil outline he modeled the forms in gray wash, then added washes of color, finally strengthening the outlines with pen. Yet Skelton uses this technique with great subtlety. Because of the richness of his color and the delicate, fluttering character of his pen work, his drawings have none of the hard, linear quality that the term "tinted" drawing suggests.

The Great Gate of St. Augustine's Monastery shows the entrance gate, built by Abbot Fyndon in 1300, to the abbey founded by St. Augustine in 598. A view of the gate by J.M.W. Turner (cat. 144) is also in the exhibition. The view of Harbledown shows the buildings of the leper's hospital around which the village grew up. In both drawings the emphasis seems less on topographical detail than on the fall of light and the texture of brick and tile and old wood. Skelton's concern with light and atmosphere is further demonstrated by an inscription on the old mount (now removed) of the Harbledown drawing, which reads: "Harbledown, A village near Canterbury | J: Skelton 1757 | N:B: Drawn immediatly after a heavy Summer-Shower." SW

134

PAUL SANDBY (1730-1809)

Views of Windsor Castle, c. 1765

134

The North Terrace, Looking East

Gouache on laid paper; 15 x 21¼ in. (38.1 x 54 cm)

PROVENANCE: Sir Richard Frederick Molyneux, by whom presented to HRH the Princess Royal on her marriage to the Earl of Harewood; Christie's, 13 July 1965 (172), bt Colnaghi, from whom purchased by Paul Mellon

SELECTED EXHIBITIONS: YCBA, *Sandby*, 1985, no. 80

SELECTED LITERATURE: Borenius, 1936, no. 429; Oppé, 1947, fig. 7; Roberts, 1995, fig. 17.3

Paul Mellon Collection
B1981.25.2689

135

The Norman Gate and Deputy Governor's House

Gouache on laid paper; 15 x 21 ⅛ in. (38.1 x 53.7 cm)

PROVENANCE: Sir Richard Frederick Molyneux, by whom presented to HRH the Princess Royal on her marriage to the Earl of Harewood; Christie's, 13 July 1965 (170), bt Colnaghi, from whom purchased by Paul Mellon

SELECTED EXHIBITIONS: YCBA, *Sandby*, 1985, no. 83

SELECTED LITERATURE: Borenius, 1936, no. 427; Roberts, 1995, fig. 12.1

Paul Mellon Collection
B1981.25.2691

135

AT THE TIME OF HIS DEATH in 1809, Paul Sandby was deemed "the father of modern landscape painting in water-colours" by the *London Review and Literary Journal*. Although by that date Sandby's watercolor style seemed old-fashioned and his use of gouache outmoded, he had been very much at the center of the related development of watercolor and landscape painting over the second half of the eighteenth century. Sandby was active in the formation of the Society of Artists in 1760 and eight years later was a founding member of the Royal Academy. These organizations offered artists a new sense of status and, through annual exhibitions, provided a new public for their art. That Sandby, a watercolorist trained as a topographer, should be directly and significantly involved in these developments speaks much of his personal prestige and of the rising fortunes of watercolor.

In 1746 Paul's elder brother Thomas became the draftsman for William Augustus, the Duke of Cumberland, serving with him in the Highlands, the Netherlands, and at Windsor, where Cumberland was appointed Ranger of Windsor Great Park. In 1764 Thomas Sandby became Cumberland's Steward and the Deputy Ranger. From the 1750s Paul was a frequent visitor to his brother at Windsor, and between 1763 and 1768 he exhibited eight views of Windsor Castle at the Society of Artists. One of the two views in the exhibition here (cat. 134) was possibly shown at the Society of Artists in 1766. The two are part of a set of four Windsor views in gouache in the Yale Center for British Art (a fifth view, similar in appearance, has a different provenance). The success of the Windsor views at the Society of Artists exhibitions led Paul to repeat the compositions in gouache, in watercolors, and in oils. He exhibited further views of the castle at the Royal Academy in 1774, 1775, and 1801, and he published a set of five Windsor views in aquatint in 1776. sw

136

136

PAUL SANDBY (1730-1809)

North West View of Wakefield Lodge in Whittlebury Forest, Northamptonshire, 1767

Watercolor with pen and gray ink over graphite on laid paper, on contemporary mount; 16⅝ x 33¼ in. (42.2 x 84.5 cm)

Signed and dated in gold paint, lower left: *P. Sandby 1767*; inscribed on mount in gold paint: *North West View of WAKE-FIELD LODGE in Whittlebury Forest*

PROVENANCE: The Dowager Lady Hillingdon; Agnew 1967, bt Paul Mellon

SELECTED EXHIBITIONS: Society of Artists, 1767, no. 272; YCBA, *Sandby*, 1985, no. 77

Paul Mellon Collection
B1977.14.4648

137

THOMAS SANDBY (1721-98)

A View of Boxhill from Norbury Park, Surrey, c. 1775

Watercolor with pen and gray ink over graphite, on three joined sheets of laid paper; 12 x 39 in. (31 x 99.9 cm)

PROVENANCE: ...; Sir Edward John Poynter, PRA; Sotheran, 1930; Alfred Drayson, by descent to Mrs. A. Brown; Sotheby's, 16 July 1981 (79), bt John Morton Morris, from whom purchased, 1982

SELECTED EXHIBITIONS: YCBA, *Sandby*, 1985, no. 23

Paul Mellon Fund
B1982.7

137

WHILE THE BUCK BROTHERS created their views of British antiquities and cities for an antiquarian and civic-minded audience, and Paul Sandby's views of Windsor had broad general appeal for Englishmen, topography also had its more personal aspect. Portraits of country houses and estates, commissioned by their owners, were a staple of topographical artists of the eighteenth-century.

Cat. 136 is one of two drawings that Paul Sandby exhibited at the Society of Artists in 1767 of Wakefield Lodge, a hunting lodge built for the Duke of Grafton by William Kent (see cat. 113). The sweeping horizontal format emphasizes the extent of the property, while Sandby offsets the broad expanses of open ground with figures, horses, and deer strung out across the foreground. As so often with Sandby's figures (the foppish couple on the terrace of Windsor Castle whose lapdog is being attacked by a raven in cat. 134 is another example), a small drama or comedy is being played out – here a pair of rustics are about to be discovered purloining firewood.

Though we know little of how Thomas Sandby received his architectural training, he styled himself architect to the Duke of Cumberland and was named the first Professor of Architecture at the Royal Academy. In 1774 William Lock, father of the sitter in Lawrence's charcoal portrait (cat. 13), acquired the estate of Norbury Park and wrote to Thomas Sandby from Rome commissioning him to build a house. Sandby built the house and sent off a ground plan, elevation, and drawings of the estate from the house, one of which must have been this view towards Boxhill. sw

138

PAUL SANDBY (1730-1809)

Roslin Castle, Midlothian,
c. 1780

Gouache on laid paper mounted on
board; 18 x 24¾ in. (45.7 x 62.9 cm)

PROVENANCE: Mrs. Mew; Christie's,
7 July 1959 (152); Agnew, 1960, bt Paul
Mellon

SELECTED EXHIBITIONS: YCBA, *Sandby*,
1985, no. 109; YCBA, *Fairest Isle*, 1989,
no. 147

Paul Mellon Collection
B1975.4.1877

IN 1747 PAUL SANDBY followed his
brother Thomas in taking a position
as draftsman with the Board of
Ordnance. He was appointed chief
draftsman for the Survey of the
Highlands, ordered that autumn by
the Duke of Cumberland in the
aftermath of the Jacobite Rebellion.

Apart from the summer of 1751,
spent with his brother at Windsor,
Paul remained in Scotland until the
autumn of 1752, producing maps for
the Survey but also sketching and
etching the Scottish countryside and
people.

While there is no concrete evidence
that Paul Sandby ever returned to
Scotland, this impressive gouache of
Roslin Castle suggests that he may
have made an unrecorded trip in the
1770s. On the other hand, the view
of Roslin may be a studio concoc-
tion intended as an appropriate
landscape setting for the two fashionable Scottish ladies at the right
and based on sketches made many
years earlier. Sandby's concern
seems less topographical than naturalistic. (Roslin Castle, the ostensible subject of the painting, is barely
visible beyond the trees.) His interest is more engaged by the fall of
light on the hillside, the rickety
bridge across the River Esk, and the
two ladies, one of whom is taking
the view with a camera obscura. A

sketch by Sandby of the ladies, also
in the Yale Center for British Art,
identifies them. The woman using
the camera obscura is Lady Frances
Scott, an amateur artist and poet
who was the sister of the 3rd Duke
of Buccleuch and the wife of Lord
Douglas; her seated companion is
Lady Elliott, either the sister or the
wife of Sir Gilbert Elliott of Minto.

Sandby eschewed the more con-
sciously Picturesque view of Roslin
Castle perched dramatically over the
glen often adopted in other artists'
depictions. He does, however, allude
to the vogue for Picturesque sketching in the landscape by showing
Lady Scott with her camera obscura.
This precursor to the modern camera admitted light through a small
aperture, focusing an image on the
back of its dark chamber. An angled
mirror reflected the image onto a
glass surface where it could be
traced. The camera obscura was
used as an aid to drawing by both
amateurs such as Lady Scott and
professional artists such as Thomas
and William Daniell (see cats. 79-81).
SW

139

139

MICHAEL "ANGELO" ROOKER
(1746-1801)

*The Chapel of the Greyfriars
Monastery, Winchester*

Watercolor on wove paper, on contemporary mount; 9 x 11¼ in. (22.9 x 28.6 cm)

Signed in graphite, lower left: *MR* in monogram; inscribed in graphite on mount, lower center: *Chapel of the Grey Friars Monastery, Winchester*

PROVENANCE: ...; Charles Russell, sold Sotheby's, 30 November 1960 (81), bt Colnaghi, from whom bt Paul Mellon

SELECTED EXHIBITIONS: NGA, *English Drawings*, 1962, no. 57; PML, *English Drawings*, 1972, no. 51; YCBA, *English Landscape*, 1977, no. 51; YCBA, *Oil on Water*, 1986, no. 52

Paul Mellon Collection
B1975.4.1718

140

EDWARD DAYES (1763-1804)

Queen Square, London, 1786

Watercolor with pen and black ink over graphite on wove paper; image: 14½ x 20⅞ in. (36.8 x 53 cm); sheet: 17⅛ x 23½ in. (43.5 x 59.7 cm)

Signed and dated, in pen and black ink, lower left: *E Dayes | 1786*

PROVENANCE: Agnew, 1968, bt Paul Mellon

SELECTED EXHIBITIONS: RA, 1787, no. 582; PML, *English Drawings*, 1972, no 82; YCBA, *The Exhibition Watercolor*, 1981, no. 13; YCBA, *Presences of Nature*, 1983, no. VI.2; RA, *Great Age of British Watercolours*, 1993, no. 106

Paul Mellon Collection
B1977.14.4639

141

THOMAS HEARNE (1744-1817)

View of Bath from Spring Gardens, 1790

Watercolor with pen and gray ink over graphite on wove paper; 12⅛ x 18⅛ in. (30.8 x 46 cm)

Signed and dated, in pen and gray ink, lower right: *1790 T.H.*

PROVENANCE: Towers; Audley Gray; Sotheby's, 20 November 1963 (59); bt Colnaghi, from whom purchased by Paul Mellon, 1963

SELECTED EXHIBITIONS: YCBA, *Pursuit of Happiness*, 1977, no. 13; YCBA, *Presences of Nature*, 1983, no. VI.17

Paul Mellon Collection
B1975.3.152

142

JOHN ROBERT COZENS (1752-99)

London from Greenwich Hill, c. 1791

Watercolor over graphite on wove paper; 14¾ x 21⅛ in. (37.5 x 53.7 cm)

PROVENANCE: ...; Lt.-Col. A. E. Jelf-Reveley, sold Christie's, 6 June 1972 (98), bt Paul Mellon through John Baskett

SELECTED EXHIBITIONS: YCBA, *English Landscape*, 1977, no. 77; YCBA, *Cozens*, 1980, no. 137; YCBA, *Presences of Nature*, 1983, no. VI.16; Denver, *Glorious Nature*, 1993-4, no. 38

Paul Mellon Collection
B1977.14.4703

140

141

142

IN THE LAST DECADES of the eighteenth century, the vogue for the Picturesque reshaped the conventions of topographical drawing; new aesthetic and sensory concerns were grafted onto its longstanding informational role. The straightforward presentation of antiquities by the Bucks was replaced in the watercolors of Thomas Hearne, Michael Rooker, and Edward Dayes by images carefully calculated to enhance the sublime or picturesque qualities of the site. In place of the distant "prospects" that were a Buck specialty, these artists took the viewer right into the fashionable precincts of the city or created far-off atmospheric vistas that provided a sense of the grandeur of the metropolis without enumerating its landmarks.

From the late 1780s Michael Rooker undertook a series of autumn sketching tours through England and Wales. *The Chapel of the Greyfriars Monastery, Winchester* probably derives from one of these tours, although a painting by Rooker of a Winchester scene dated 1779 indicates an earlier visit to the city. Rooker's watercolor style, which downplays outline and emphasizes textures of stone and tile and foliage through a mosaic of touches of the brush, is quintessentially Picturesque. His inclination to situate ruins like those of the Greyfriars Monastery within a framework of everyday activities, in this case a respite from haymaking, imparts an almost cozy familiarity rather than melancholy grandeur to his watercolors of ancient monuments.

The watercolors by Thomas Hearne and Edward Dayes record new and fashionable urban developments. *Queen Square* is one of four watercolors by Dayes of the great squares that were such a striking feature of Georgian London. Dayes exhibited *Queen Square* along with *Grosvenor Square* (untraced) at the Royal Academy in 1787. These two, together with views of Bloomsbury Square (Sotheby's, 20 March 2000) and Hanover Square (British Museum), were engraved in 1787 and 1789. Hearne's *View of Bath from Spring Gardens*, exhibited at the Royal Academy in 1792, shows the view from the newly laid-out Spring Gardens, looking across the River Avon to John Wood's South Parade on the left and down the river to Robert Adam's Pulteney Bridge. Both Dayes and Hearne populate their urban views with a range of social types but give pride of place to elegant figures who help define the character of these new urban spaces.

The view of London from Greenwich Hill has been popular with artists since the seventeenth century. By choosing a vantage point in which the domes of Christopher Wren's Royal Naval Hospital are visible but the Royal Observatory and the Queen's House are not, John Robert Cozens created a composition which downplays topographical particularity in favor of an evocative association of the view with that of Rome and, in his coloring and atmosphere, imbues the view with the same melancholy grandeur that characterizes his Roman scenes. This, like *The Lake of Albano and Castel Gandolfo* (cats. 103-4), was one of Cozens's most admired compositions, as indicated by its being known in six versions, one of which (private collection) is signed and dated 1791. sw

143

143

THOMAS GIRTIN (1775-1802)

Lichfield Cathedral, Staffordshire, 1794

Watercolor over graphite on wove paper; 15⅛ x 11⅜ in. (38.4 x 28.9 cm)

Signed and dated in pen and brown ink, lower right: *T. Girtin. 1794*

PROVENANCE: Purchased from the artist by Moore-Miller at RA, London, 1795; ...; T. Girtin, 1912; Tom Girtin, bt Paul Mellon through John Baskett, 1970

SELECTED EXHIBITIONS: RA, 1795, no. 636; YCBA, *Girtin*, 1986, no. 20

SELECTED LITERATURE: Davies, 1924, pl. 13; Mayne, 1949, p. 31; Girtin and Loshak, 1954, no. 88i

Paul Mellon Collection
B1975.3.1158

144

Joseph Mallord William
Turner (1775-1851)

*St. Augustine's Gate,
Canterbury*, c. 1793

Watercolor over graphite on wove paper;
13⁹/16 x 19⁷/16 in. (34.4 x 49.4 cm)

Signed in watercolor, lower right:
W Turner

PROVENANCE: Agnew 1962, bt Paul
Mellon

SELECTED EXHIBITIONS: ?RA, 1793,
no. 316; VMFA, *Painting in England*,
1963, no. 143; Victoria, *British Watercolor
Drawings*, 1971, no. 43; YCBA, *Turner and
Printmaking*, 1993, no. 5

SELECTED LITERATURE: Wilton, 1979,
no. 33; Cormack, 1983, p. 6

Paul Mellon Collection
B1975.4.1962

BY THE END of the eighteenth century, Thomas Girtin and J.M.W. Turner had elevated landscape painting in watercolors to a new level of sophistication and laid the groundwork for the Romantic landscape painting of the new century. Although Girtin would die only two years into that new century, Turner would go on to build on those foundations one of the greatest achievements of British art.

In the early 1790s both Turner and Girtin were young topographical artists in training. Girtin was apprenticed to Edward Dayes in 1789. As part of his apprenticeship, he, along with Dayes, worked up pencil sketches made by the linen draper and antiquarian James Moore on his tours. The Yale Center for British Art has two volumes of Moore's sketches from a tour of Scotland and the north of England in 1792, as well as several watercolors by both Dayes and Girtin based on sketches in the volumes.

In the same year that Girtin was apprenticed to Dayes, Turner began working in the studio of Thomas Malton and entered the Royal Academy Schools. Turner sent his first watercolor to the Royal Academy exhibition the following year. In 1793 he exhibited a watercolor of the "Gate of St. Augustine's Monastery, Canterbury." Although the evidence is not conclusive, this would appear to be a work now untraced; however, it is possible that the work exhibited at the Royal Academy is cat. 144. Another smaller watercolor version of the composition is also in the Yale Center for British Art.

In 1794 Turner and Girtin were working together copying drawings by John Robert Cozens and Thomas Hearne at the "academy" that Dr. Thomas Monro held at his home in the Adelphi Terrace in the evenings. Monro, a specialist in mental disorders, was looking after Cozens following his mental breakdown early in 1794 and had access to Cozens's studio. That same year Girtin exhibited his watercolors for the first time at the Royal Academy, and in the autumn he accompanied James Moore on a tour of the Midlands. The watercolor of Lichfield Cathedral, deriving from that tour, was exhibited at the Royal Academy the following year and bought from the exhibition by Moore. While it is still very much indebted to the Dayes style, it has a drama, achieved largely through the play of light and shadow across the forms of the cathedral, that shows that he had learned from the example of Cozens's watercolors.

Turner too learned from Cozens. The light that plays across St. Augustine's Gate in Turner's watercolor of approximately the same date has a similar dramatic character. Indeed Girtin's *Lichfield Cathedral* and Turner's *St. Augustine's Gate* demonstrate how close stylistically these two young colleagues and rivals were at this early point in their careers. sw

The Life of the Artist

BOTH ARTISTIC PRACTICE and the concept of the professional artist underwent a profound transformation in Britain during the eighteenth century. At the beginning of the century there was little indigenous artistic tradition, and many successful practitioners were foreigners. The traditional model of training, an apprenticeship in the studio of an established artist, was increasingly perceived as inadequate, and no institutional structure existed to educate aspiring artists, or to provide them with a distinctive professional identity.

The need for formal practical and theoretical training for artists had been recognized in the seventeenth century. The first documented academy was established in London around 1673 by the portrait painter Peter Lely, apparently in response to the growing number of applications for apprenticeships in his studio, and other academies and art clubs, such as the Virtuosi of St. Luke, also came into being. Academies proliferated in the early decades of the eighteenth century. Godfrey Kneller's academy, founded in 1711, was followed by Louis Chéron and John Vanderbank's short-lived St. Martin's Lane Academy and Sir James Thornhill's Free Academy, and in 1735 Hogarth founded his own, highly influential, St. Martin's Lane Academy. Drawing, from casts of antique sculpture, écorché figures, and live models, formed the core of the curricula of these academies, which also served as forums for the discussion of theoretical and technical issues and facilitated the formation of professional relationships and friendships.

Despite the opportunities offered by these private academies, artists keenly felt the need for a more institutionalized approach. Hogarth (whose entire career can be seen as a sustained campaign to establish a British school of painting) actively promoted the notion of establishing a professional association but with characteristic independence rejected the view that it would require a royal imprimatur. Hogarth's democratic aims were seen as unrealistic, however, and artists generally welcomed the foundation in 1768 of the Royal Academy, which provided free tuition for students as well as a high-profile exhibition space and went some way to consolidating their professional status. Moreover, the profits from the annual exhibitions financed the teaching, and the Academy's fiscal independence ensured a considerable degree of freedom from political pressure.

The life of the eighteenth-century artist was almost invariably arduous and frustrating, frequently involving aesthetic compromises and/or financial hardship. History painting was seen as the most elevated category of the theoretical hierarchy, but, as Scott Wilcox has shown (see pp. 37-55), in practice the market for such works was extremely limited, and many artists were forced to work as portraitists. Aside from any considerations of artistic merit, running a successful portrait practice required a high degree of organization, excellent social skills, and sufficient capital to finance a tastefully furnished studio in a fashionable neighborhood. Portraitists frequently went unpaid by their wealthy patrons, and the tyrannical aesthetic control exerted by connoisseurs was more or less universally lamented by artists (see cat. 154). Drawing and painting also became popular activities for amateurs during the eighteenth century, and the development of this phenomenon, and its relationship with the world of the professional artist is discussed by Kim Sloan on pp. 187-90.

GILLIAN FORRESTER

145

145

SIR JAMES THORNHILL (1675-1734)

Design for Ceiling, Walls and Staircase, c. 1712-13

Pen and brown ink with gray and brown wash on laid paper; 15¼ x 19⅝ in. (38.5 x 50 cm)

Signed, bottom right below description in pencil: *Sir Ja^s Thornhill*. Inscribed top right in brown ink: *Gratitude ye Principal figure, crownd by Peace, & over, wch Providence | particularly presides | Industry, leaning on a Bee hive attended by Plenty & holding a plan or | upright Fort St George.| Fame sounding ye praise of Gratitude. & Industry*; bottom left: *Syllas Triumph, is followd by ye Citizens &c. wth loud | acclamation, in that he has redeemd them from Slavery*; bottom center: *Sylla gratefully offers ye 10th of all his Spoyls | to Hercules*; bottom right: *The Roman People, Ladys*

&c. strive to adorn y^e | ... of Sylla; along lower edge: scale in feet; bottom center below description: *Thos Pitt*; on verso in graphite and brown ink: extensive notes relating to the decorative scheme

PROVENANCE: ...; Colnaghi, 1970, bt Paul Mellon

SELECTED EXHIBITIONS: PML, *English Drawings*, 1972, no. 11; YCBA, *Fifty Beautiful Drawings*, 1977, no. 4

SELECTED LITERATURE: Jacobus, 1988, p. 154, fig. 9

Paul Mellon Collection
B1975.4.1961

AS HISTORY PAINTER IN ORDINARY to King George I, Sir James Thornhill catered to the baroque taste for large and illusionistic decorative schemes,

and he received many important commissions for the adornment of royal palaces. He also extended his services to wealthy private citizens, as indicated by this design for Thomas Pitt. Known as "Diamond Pitt" for his mercantile exploits in India, he was eventually appointed Governor of Madras at Fort St. George. He returned to England in 1710 and used his wealth to remodel his many residences, including his favorite, Swallowfield Park in Berkshire.

Thornhill devised this decorative scheme depicting events from the life of the Roman general Lucius Sulla for a stairwell in one of Pitt's homes, probably Swallowfield Park. Sulla, the victor of the first Roman civil war in the first century B.C., appointed himself dictator to enact constitutional reforms and strengthen the waning Roman republic. It is tempting to connect the figure of the victorious Sulla, here a benign victor who releases his people from slavery and distributes his wealth, with that of Pitt, as Thornhill has included a drawing of Pitt's Indian post, Fort St. George, in the hands of Industry on the ceiling. In depicting his plan, Thornhill uses the convention of architectural drawing known as "the laid out wall elevation," whereby the ceiling is depicted as above the walls, which are "ironed out" to appear as one continuous wall space. MO

146

146

SIR JAMES THORNHILL (1675-1734)

Sketch for "The Conversion of St. Paul" for the Dome of St. Paul's Cathedral, c. 1714-17

Red chalk on brown paper; 9½ x 11½ in. (24 x 29.2 cm)

Inscribed lower right in brown ink: *a first Sketch of one of the pictures | of the dome of S! Paul's;* center verso in pencil: *Sir Jas Thornhill | colls: Barnard | Lawrence | Arnal of Toulouse;* center verso, stamp in black ink: *SCIPIO,* collector's mark for H. Reitlinger (Lugt 2274a)

PROVENANCE: ...; J. Barnard; Sir Thomas Lawrence; H. Reitlinger; Mr. J. Henry; sold Colnaghi, 1962, bt Paul Mellon

Paul Mellon Collection
B1975.4.1405

THE MAJORITY OF THORNHILL'S commissions as a decorative painter were for domestic settings, although on a grand scale (see cat. 145). In 1714, however, he was awarded the prestigious public commission to decorate the cupola, lantern, and Whispering Gallery of Sir Christopher Wren's St. Paul's Cathedral (see cat. 129) with "Scripturall History taken from the Acts of the Apostles." Church decoration provided careers for Thornhill's counterparts in France and Italy but was a rare opportunity in eighteenth-century Protestant England; Thornhill's main competitors were the Italians Sebastiano Ricci and Giovanni Antonio Pellegrini.

Thornhill and his assistants concentrated on the St. Paul's project for three years, from 1714 to 1717. The cupola and drum depicted scenes from the life of St. Paul, including the saint's conversion on the road to Damascus. Thornhill's work progressed from informal studies to large cartoons and finally wall painting itself in grisaille. Working studies such as this one allowed the artist to arrange compositional groupings and experiment with the placement and expression of figures, as his attention to the fallen St. Paul demonstrates. Thornhill was committed to training younger artists in these working methods, and he was one of the twelve original directors of the earliest art academy in England, Sir Godfrey Kneller's Academy in London. He later established his own drawing school at Covent Garden, where he taught William Hogarth (see cats. 147-8). MO

147

WILLIAM HOGARTH (1697-1764)

147

Study of a Female Nude

Graphite with black chalk, heightened
with white chalk on light brown laid
paper; 10¹⁄₁₆ x 17⅛ in. (25.6 x 43.5 cm)

PROVENANCE: ...; ?J. P. Heseltine; ...;
Agnew from whom bt Paul Mellon,
1974

SELECTED EXHIBITIONS: Tate, *Hogarth*,
1971-2, no. 92; Agnew, *Master Drawings*,
1974, no. 153

Paul Mellon Collection
B1977.14.4272

148

The First Stage of Cruelty,
c. 1750

Graphite and red chalk on laid paper
with drawn borders, indented for transfer, verso reddened with chalk; 15⁷⁄₁₆ x
13³⁄₁₆ in. (39.2 x 33. cm)

PROVENANCE: Henry, Marquess of
Exeter (1754-1804); by descent to the 6th
Marquess of Exeter; Edward Speelman
from whom bt Paul Mellon, 1962

SELECTED EXHIBITIONS: VMFA,
Painting in England, 1963, no. 392;
Colnaghi-Yale, *English Drawings*, 1964-5,
no. 4; VMFA, *Hogarth*, 1967, no. 39

SELECTED LITERATURE: Oppé, 1948,
no. 70

Paul Mellon Collection
B1975.4.1543

CAT. 147 WAS ALMOST CERTAINLY
drawn by Hogarth in the early
1720s during his membership of
the St. Martin's Lane Academy
founded by Louis Chéron and John
Vanderbank, and its use of cross-
hatching for modeling is highly
characteristic of Chéron's drawing
style. Life-drawing was an important
component of the curriculum at the
Academy, which from its inception
hired female models "to make it the
more inviting to subscribers." In
the *Analysis of Beauty* Hogarth
noted that "the human frame hath
more of its parts composed of ser-
pentine-lines than any other object
in nature," and wrote at length
about the importance of studying
the human body:

> *The skin ... thus tenderly embracing*
> *and gently conforming itself to the*
> *varied shapes of every one of the*

174

outward muscles of the body, soften'd underneath by the fat ... is evidently a shell-like surface ... form'd with the utmost delicacy in nature; and therefore the most proper subject of the study of every one, who desires to imitate the works of nature, as a master should do, *or to judge of the performances of others* as a real connoisseur ought.

Although Hogarth was actively involved in the education of artists at his own St. Martin's Lane Academy during the 1730s and 1740s, he came to doubt the value of such drawing exercises. He later recorded that he had begun "copying in the usual way, and had learnt by practice to do it with tolerable exactness" until "it occur'd to me that there were many disadvantages attended going on so well continually copying Prints and Pictures. ... nay in even drawing after the life at academys ... it is possible to know no more of the original when the drawing is finish'd than before it was begun." Hogarth regarded a highly-developed visual memory as a more valuable tool for the artist than drawing from life, and his adherence to this precept is indicated by the rarity of such studies by him.

Hogarth is probably best known for the prints of "Modern Moral Subjects," which he designed and engraved, including *A Rake's Progress, Marriage A-la-Mode,* and *Industry and Idleness,* and a large proportion of his few surviving drawings are preliminary studies or cartoons for engravings. The finalized designs were transferred to a copper plate, and the engraved images appeared in reverse of the drawings. Cat. 148 is a preliminary

148

study for the first plate of *The Four Stages of Cruelty.* Hogarth subsequently produced a more highly-finished drawing for transfer to the plate. In his *Autobiographical Notes* Hogarth explained

the four stages of cruelty, were done in hopes of preventing in some degree that cruel treatment of poor Animals, which makes the streets of London more disagreeable to the human mind, than any thing ... neither great correctness of drawing or fine Engraving were at all necessary but on the contrary would set the price of them out of ... the reach of those for whome they were cheifly intended.

GF

175

149

JAMES JEFFERYS (1751–84)

Self-Portrait, c. 1771-5

Pen and brown ink on wove paper;
21¼ x 16¼ in. (54.0 x 41.3 cm)

Inscribed in artist's hand in pen and
brown ink, lower left: *rara avis in terra*
and lower center: *But <for> who can
paint this Character as it ought | Tho'
Wisdom cryeth out in the Streets yet | [...]*
and within the design area: *Hon'd Sir
July 26 | I flatter myself I have abilities for
the Art of Painting wch | I hope will
appear by the drawing I send you, but
indeed | there are so many young Persons
pursuing the same | Art, that I think it will
be a prudent Step to | drop it intirely, & get
into any kind of Business | you shall think,
proper. I make | no doubt but you will
comply | with my desire more especially |
when you inform yourself how | much the
Proffession is disgrac'd | by the Folly and
Vice of many of the Proffessors ...*

and within the design area: *To Mr
Brinchl[?ey]* and *Pride led by the | Passions
a Design from Spensers | Faery Queen*; in
a later hand in pen and brown ink,
lower right: *Pen & Ink Drawing by
Mortimer*

PROVENANCE: ...; possibly John
Newington Hughes (1776-1847); George
Hilder Libbis; by descent to Miss Nell
Hilder Libbis; sold Sotheby's, 13 March
1969 (67 as self-portrait of John
Hamilton Mortimer), bt Paul Mellon
through John Baskett

SELECTED EXHIBITIONS: PML, *English
Drawings*, 1972, no. 46; YCBA, *Fuseli
Circle*, 1979, no. 83; YCBA, *English
Portrait Drawings*, 1979-80, no. 71

SELECTED LITERATURE: Sunderland,
1970; Sunderland, 1977, pp. 279-80,
figs. 77, 78; Rogers, 1993, p. 54

Paul Mellon Collection
B1977.14.6227

150

GEORGE STUBBS (1724-1806)

Study for the Self-Portrait in Enamel, 1781

Graphite on wove paper, squared;
12 x 9 in. (30.5 x 22.9 cm), oval

Signed in graphite, in the design area
on palette: *George Stubbs*; in a later
hand, on back: *This is the portrait of
George Stubbs | the Animal Painter | and
his name is to be seen | on the palette.
5 July 1842 | Capital drawing | by whom?*

PROVENANCE: ...; H. S. Reitlinger;
Alistair Matthews; Ian Fleming-
Williams, from whom bt Paul Mellon,
1962

SELECTED EXHIBITIONS: VMFA,
Painting in England, 1963, no. 332;
PML, *English Drawings*, 1972, no. 31;
Tate, *Stubbs and Wedgwood*, 1974,
no. 29; Tate-YCBA, *Stubbs*, 1984-5,
no. 3; YCBA, *Stubbs*, 1999, no. 1

SELECTED LITERATURE: Taylor, 1965,
pp. 3-4

Paul Mellon Collection
B2001.2.1262

ARTISTS IN THE EIGHTEENTH CENTURY
often made self-portrait drawings to
explore and fashion their personal
and artistic identities. Cat. 149 is
one of a pair of self-portraits by the
little-known historical draftsman
James Jefferys and formerly attributed to John Hamilton Mortimer
(see cat. 33). The drawings depict
front and back views of the artist,
like two sides of a coin, and present
contrasting aspects of the artistic
life: disaffection and creativity.
In the Center's drawing the
Romantically disheveled Jefferys
holds a letter, apparently addressed

to his godfather and early patron John Brenchley, which renounces his chosen profession. The inscription from Juvenal in the lower margin, "Rara avis in terra", meaning "a rare bird on the earth," alludes to Jefferys's exceptional gifts and special status as a creative artist. The companion drawing, now in the National Portrait Gallery, London, shows the youthful genius with *porte-crayon* in hand, momentarily pausing from his labors on a drawing of the Massacre of the Innocents, as if receiving inspiration.

Although Jefferys's portrayal of himself as a misunderstood genius is very beguiling, there is a strong element of posturing in these self-portraits. Jefferys's career in fact began extremely well; in 1774 he was awarded prizes for historical drawings from the Society of Arts and the Royal Academy, and the following year he won one of the first traveling scholarships of the Society of Dilettanti with the support of Joshua Reynolds. Jefferys did not live to fulfill his youthful promise, however (in this respect his self-portraits seem to have been somewhat prophetic), and he died in London at the age of thirty-two.

At first sight Stubbs's self-portrait may seem to betray little about its author's personality, but this careful drawing is nonetheless revealing. Made as a study for his self-portrait in enamel (National Portrait Gallery, London), the drawing is squared up to facilitate transfer of the image to the larger ceramic plate. The high degree of finish says much about Stubbs's meticulous approach to his art, and his legendary powers of observation and extreme reticence are indicated by his composed but

150

watchful expression. In the 1770s Stubbs collaborated successfully with the master-potter Josiah Wedgwood on the production of large enamel plaques. Stubbs evidently found the smoothness and durability of the medium extremely appealing (although susceptible to cracking, their coloration remains unchanged over time), and he seems to have used enamel chiefly for his favorite subjects and for portraits of people he knew well. The inscription on the back of the finished self-portrait indicates that Stubbs made it for his friend Richard Thorold.

Cat. 150 is a rare example of a preparatory drawing by Stubbs. His 1808 posthumous studio sale included at least thirteen lots of "drawings, drawing books, studies from Nature, sketches, &c," but with the exception of the major groups of studies for the *Anatomy of the Horse* and the *Comparative Anatomy* (see cats. 64-8), only a handful of drawings by him are now known. It seems likely that Stubbs would have made careful studies for his paintings, but the mysterious disappearance of the drawings and his notorious secretiveness regarding his artistic practice have made it difficult to reconstruct his working processes conclusively.

GF

151

BENJAMIN WEST (1738-1820)

Design for a Wall of the Chapel of Revealed Religion, c. 1780

Pen and black ink and watercolor and gouache over graphite on laid paper; 11½ x 18⅜ in. (29.2 x 46.7 cm)

Inscribed, lower left, in black ink: scale in feet

PROVENANCE: By direct descent to Mrs. Claire Francis, sold Christie's 14 March 1967, bt Paul Mellon

SELECTED EXHIBITIONS: NPGUS, *West and his American Students*, 1981; San Antonio, *Revealed Religion*, 1983, no. 2; YCBA, *Crown Pictorial*, 1990-1, no. 85

SELECTED LITERATURE: Kraemer, 1975, p. 18; Erffa and Staley, 1986, p. 576; Spadafora, 1990, pp. 88-9

Paul Mellon Collection
B1977.14.4356

BENJAMIN WEST, the American-born history painter and future President of the Royal Academy, first attracted the attention of King George III with his 1768 canvas *Agrippina Landing at Brundisium with the Ashes of Germanicus* (Yale University Art Gallery, New Haven). After a decade of steady patronage, in 1780 the king commissioned what West called "the great work of my life," the Chapel of Revealed Religion for Windsor Castle. Numerous questions still remain about the program and the intended location of this important and sadly incomplete project, which the king stopped funding in 1801 for reasons that remain unclear. West continued working at his own expense until 1804.

The chapel's decorative scheme, approved by Anglican theologians, was to depict revelatory moments from the Old and the New Testaments: Patriarchal, Mosaical, and Gospel. This drawing depicts West's scheme for the north wall of the chapel, one of the earliest planned. The king's architect Sir William Chambers (see cats. 117-18) drew in the architectural background, and West added his plans for Gospel scenes in the large panels, centered around the Ascension of Christ. He places scenes from the Old Testament above, while figures from the Old Testament, such as King David with his lyre, rest atop the pilasters. Below them, caryatids display shields depicting emblems of Christianity. Highly finished designs such as this one functioned as working drawings that West could then use to present his ideas to the king. West also executed oil studies for the chapel, and he exhibited completed canvases at the Royal Academy. *The Ascension*, based on the central scene in this drawing, was shown there in 1781, labeled "For his Majesty's Chapel at Windsor." MO

152

MICHAEL (JOHANNES MICHEL)
RYSBRACK (1684-1770)

*Admiral Vernon's Monument in
Westminster Abbey*, c. 1763

Brown and black ink with brown and
gray wash over graphite on laid paper;
11³⁄16 x 9³⁄16 in. (28.5 x 17.4 cm)

Inscribed verso in ink: *Admiral Vernon s
monument | in Westminster Abby
Rysbrack sculp*! | LSD | 1.1.0

PROVENANCE: ...; Iolo Williams; his
estate; purchased by Paul Mellon,
December 1970

Paul Mellon Collection
B1977.14.5719

MICHAEL RYSBRACK arrived in
London from his native Antwerp in
1720. Almost immediately, he
formed a fruitful partnership with
the architect James Gibbs (see cat.
III) to sculpt Gibbs's designs for
funerary monuments. Rysbrack's
association with Gibbs garnered
him numerous commissions. He
soon began designing and executing
garden sculptures, including a life-
size marble figure of Palladio for
Lord Burlington, portrait busts, and
funerary monuments. This monument, completed by Rysbrack and
installed in Westminster Abbey,
commemorates Admiral Vernon,
who served in the West Indies during the reign of George II. Elaborate
funerary monuments were the pre-
serve of the wealthy, often regard-
less of rank or accomplishments,
and they earned the stern words of
moralists of the age. Joseph Addison
saw these monuments as a futile
attempt to defy "that great Day

when we shall all of us be contemporaries, and make our Appearance
together."

The monument for Admiral
Vernon takes advantage of Rysbrack's
renowned skill and innovation with
portrait busts. The winged figure of
Fame crowns an idealized bust of
the admiral in classical dress, a
mode of depiction invented by the
sculptor. Drawing occupied an

important place in the working
processes of the sculptor as well as
the painter and architect. Drawings
were part of a creative process that
also included modeling the work in
clay before executing the design in
marble. The careful draftsmanship
displayed here perhaps indicates
that this work was a presentation
drawing for the commission.
MO

179

THE LIFE OF THE ARTIST

153

ALLAN RAMSAY (1713-84)

Study for the Portrait of Sir William Guise, c. 1761

Black chalk with gouache on blue laid paper; 19³⁄₁₆ x 12¼ in. (50.3 x 31.1 cm)

Inscribed, above right: *?T. Carlson | from bottom;* and, below left, with stamp of T.E. Lowinsky (Lugt 2420a)

PROVENANCE: ...; T. E. Lowinsky; Justin Lowinsky, from whom bt Paul Mellon, 1963

SELECTED LITERATURE: Smart, 1999, p. 127, no. 220, p. 395, fig. 697

Paul Mellon Collection
B1977.14.6069

RAMSAY HABITUALLY made preparatory studies for his portraits, an unusual practice at the time, since most of his fellow portraitists preferred the more expedient method of drawing directly on the canvas. Drawing was an important element of Ramsay's training, first at the Academy of St. Luke in Edinburgh, and later in London at Hogarth's St. Martin's Lane Academy. This study is related to Ramsay's portrait of Sir William Guise of 1761. Early in his career Ramsay employed the accomplished drapery painter Joseph van Aken, who had arrived in London from Antwerp in 1720. Van Aken, or "the tailor," as he was known, was initially employed by a number of portraitists but later worked only for Ramsay and Thomas Hudson. Van Aken also made studies, and the attribution of drawings related to Ramsay's paintings can sometimes be problematic, though Ramsay was clearly the superior draftsman.

Drapery painters were customarily used by the generation of portrait painters preceding Ramsay's, and after Van Aken's death in 1749 Ramsay employed studio assistants to paint drapery and backgrounds, as did many of his contemporaries who ran busy portrait-practices. Painting drapery, particularly the elaborate "Van Dyck" fancy-dress fashionable in the eighteenth century, was a time-consuming process, and sitters' clothes and accoutrements were usually retained in the studio while the portraitist concentrated on the face during sittings. Unsurprisingly, Hogarth, with whom Ramsay enjoyed a disputatious friendship, was vociferously opposed to these practices and bitterly remarked that if an artist should "persuade the public that he had brought a new discovered method of colouring" (a palpable hit at Ramsay's technique), he need only "hire one of those painted tailors for an assistant" to be a successful portrait painter. GF

154

Thomas Rowlandson
(1756-1827)

The Connoisseurs, c. 1790

Pen and ink and watercolor over graphite on wove paper, on contemporary mount; 9⅜ x 12½ in. (23.8 x 31.8 cm)

Inscribed in ink, below at center: *The Connoisseurs*

PROVENANCE ...; L.S. Deglatigny; C.R. Rudolph; Colnaghi, from whom bt Paul Mellon, 1963

SELECTED EXHIBITIONS: Colnaghi-Yale, *English Drawings*, 1964-5, no. 26; YCBA, *Rowlandson Drawings*, 1977-8, no. 37; NGA, *Berenson*, 1979, no. 66

SELECTED LITERATURE: Paulson, 1972, pp. 83-4; Brewer, 1997, pp. 279-81

Paul Mellon Collection
B1975.3.106

CONNOISSEURSHIP was an important feature of the artist's life in eighteenth-century Britain. Hitherto confined to a limited group of wealthy amateurs, collecting, antiquarianism, and the cultivation of art-historical knowledge became more widely practiced and by the end of the century were deemed to be essential social accomplishments. Connoisseurs like the eccentric and opinionated antiquarian Richard Payne Knight wielded considerable power as self-appointed arbiters of taste, and their influence was a source of great bitterness to British artists, who felt unappreciated in a culture that privileged the Old Masters and Continental artists.

Reynolds spoke for many of his fellow-artists when he published his scorching critique of connoisseurship pseudonymously in the *Universal Chronicle* in 1759:

To those who are resolved to be criticks in spite of nature, and at the same time have no great disposition to much reading and study, I would recommend to them to assume the character of connoisseur, which may be purchased at a much cheaper rate than that of a critic in poetry. The remembrance of a few names of painters, with their general characters, with a few rules of the Academy, which they may pick up among the painters, will go a great way towards making a very notable connoisseur.

Connoisseurship was also inescapably associated with voyeurism and sexual conquest (Thomas Lawrence castigated Payne Knight's taste for being based on "sensual feeling"). The theme was, of course, irresistible to Rowlandson, whose elderly connoisseurs gaze at a painting of Susannah and the Elders with an appreciation that is clearly lascivious rather than purely aesthetic.

GF

155

155

PAUL SANDBY (1730-1809)

A Lady Copying at a Drawing Table, c. 1760-70

Graphite, red and black chalk and stump on laid paper; 7¼ x 6 in. (18.4 x 15.2 cm)

Inscribed, lower right: *F.*

PROVENANCE: William Sandby; bequeathed to Hubert Peake; ...; Agnew, from whom bt Paul Mellon, 1960

SELECTED EXHIBITIONS: YCBA, *Pursuit of Happiness,* 1977, no. 81; YCBA, *Sandby,* 1985, no. 69; YCBA, *Pleasures and Pastimes,* 1990, no. 32

SELECTED LITERATURE: Sloan, 2000, pp. 232-3

Paul Mellon Collection
B1975.4.1881

156

AMELIA LONG (1772-1837)

Kirkstall Abbey, Yorkshire

Watercolor on wove paper; 12¹³⁄₁₆ x 20¹⁵⁄₁₆ in. (32.9 x 51.9 cm)

Inscribed on verso: *Kirkstall Abbey Yorkshire | by Girtin*

PROVENANCE: ...; Appleby Brothers, from whom bt Paul Mellon, 1967

Paul Mellon Collection
B1993.30.106

As DRAWING GAINED in popularity as an amateur pastime throughout the eighteenth century, the demand for drawing-masters and -mistresses increased. Although some artists, including J.M.W. Turner, regarded such work as servile and irrecoverably damaging to their careers, teaching was for many others an important aspect of their artistic practice. Artists gave lessons in homes and private academies and also produced practical and theoretical manuals that were published and widely circulated. The social phenomenon of the "polite and useful art" of drawing and the role of such pedagogic literature in its development are discussed by Kim Sloan on pp. 187-90.

The topographical draftsman Paul Sandby was appointed chief drawing-master at the Royal Military Academy at Woolwich in 1768, and he also built up a clientele of amateur pupils, including Earl Harcourt, his son Lord Nuneham, and Lady Frances Scott, whom he depicted drawing outdoors with the aid of a camera obscura in his

156

watercolor of Roslin Castle (cat. 138). The unidentified sitter of cat. 155, who was presumably one of Sandby's pupils, is depicted copying with a *porte-crayon* a drawing of a head pinned to the wall. A drawer with disks of watercolor is visible, and a palette, shown pulled out in a very similar watercolor in the Royal Collection, is folded under the left-hand corner of the table. Copying was a key component of the teaching of drawing, and, as Kim Sloan has shown, many surviving works by Sandby's pupils are copies of imaginary Italianate landscapes rather than studies from nature.

Amelia Long, later Lady Farnborough, was the daughter of Sir Abraham Hume, an amateur artist and distinguished connoisseur. Nothing is known of her early education, but her cultivated parents took her on an extended tour of Italy when she was fourteen, and she demonstrated considerable artistic talent from a young age. Long's earliest known works, accomplished small-scale watercolor copies of oil paintings, are close in style to the work of Bernard Lens (see cats. 26-7 and 43), and suggest that she was taught by a traditional drawing-master. A keen and knowledgeable collector, Long was particularly interested in Dutch painting; her husband Charles, whom she married in 1793, supported contemporary British artists. After her marriage Long was taught by Thomas Girtin and Henry Edridge and was said to be Girtin's favorite pupil. The nature of her training is unrecorded, but it evidently involved copying. Cat. 156 is an accurate copy of Girtin's watercolor of Kirkstall Abbey in Yorkshire (Victoria & Albert Museum), one of his most celebrated subjects. GF

157

JOHN SINGLETON COPLEY
(1738-1815)

157

*Study for the Central Group in
"The Death of the Earl of
Chatham,"* 1778

Black and white chalk on blue wove
paper; 10⅜ x 12⁹⁄16 in. (26.4 x 31.9 cm)

Inscribed top left in graphite in later
hand: *Study for principal | Group in
Picture of the | Death of Lord Chatham |
J.S. Copley R.A.*; verso in pencil: figure
study for a different compositional
group.

PROVENANCE: ...; Elizabeth Richardson
Simmons; sold Christie's, 12 November
1968 (28), bt John Baskett, purchased
by Paul Mellon, 1968

SELECTED EXHIBITIONS: YCBA, *Painters
and Engraving*, 1980, no. 105

SELECTED LITERATURE: Prown, 1966,
pp. 275-91

Paul Mellon Collection
B1975.4.1077

158

*Study for Captain William
George Fairfax for the Painting
"The Victory of Lord Duncan,"*
c. 1798

Black and white chalk squared in red
chalk on blue wove paper; 12⁷⁄16 x 7⁵⁄16 in
(31.6 x 18.6 cm)

Inscribed in pencil in artist's hand on
upper left verso: *Sketch for picture | of
Lord Duncan*; lower right verso: *G/L*

PROVENANCE: By direct descent from
the artist to Lord Aberdare, Agnew,
December 1967, bt Paul Mellon

SELECTED LITERATURE: Prown, 1966,
pp. 353-9

Paul Mellon Collection
B1975.4.1075

LIKE HIS COMPATRIOT Benjamin
West (cat. 151), John Singleton
Copley went to England to become
a history painter. Although successful as a portraitist working in
Boston, Copley yearned to expose
his talents to a European audience.
Uncomfortable with Revolutionary
politics, he left Boston in 1774 and
spent a year in Italy studying the
work of both ancient and modern
masters before his arrival in
London. In 1778 he exhibited
Watson and the Shark (Museum of
Fine Arts, Boston) at the Royal
Academy, and in the following year
was elected a member of the
Academy. Copley shared West's
interest in furthering a new kind of
history painting that recognized the
heroic quality of current events and
portrayed this "history" in its contemporary guise.

Copley's *Death of the Earl of
Chatham* (1779-81; Tate, London),
continued his exploration of history
painting; it depicts the sudden col-
lapse of William Pitt, Earl of
Chatham, as he rose to speak in
the House of Lords on 7 April
1778 about the war with colonial
America. Chatham had suffered a
stroke and died a few weeks later.
As Jules Prown has indicated, this
subject matter allowed Copley to
combine history painting with portraiture, as the painting portrays
fifty-five prominent nobles. This
early drawing shows Copley ignor-
ing the rigors of portraiture to focus
on the arrangement of the central
group in the composition, with the
Earl cradled in the arms of his family and peers. The artist has reworked
the placement of the heads, as well
as the location of the Earl's left arm.

Copley continued to play with the arrangement, and, typically, this study is just one of many that exist for this canvas.

Copley held a special exhibition of the finished canvas at the Great Room, Spring Gardens, a popular London venue that hosted both art exhibitions and more commercial ventures until the 1820s. It was reported that more than 20,000 came to view the work.

Copley continued his exploration of contemporary history in numerous canvases. By the time he painted *The Victory of Lord Duncan (Surrender of the Dutch Admiral DeWinter to Admiral Duncan, 11 October 1797)* (Dundee Art Gallery, Scotland) in 1798-9, however, it had been fifteen years since his last historical composition. Captain William George Fairfax, depicted in this study, formed part of the central compositional group, positioned between Admiral DeWinter and the victorious Lord Duncan on the deck of Duncan's flagship *Venerable.* Thus, his dramatic gesture and elegant pose seem appropriate to this momentous occasion. This study, more advanced than the one for the *Death of the Earl of Chatham,* accurately depicts the features of the captain, and the artist has drawn a grid over it to facilitate the translation of the figure from compositional drawing to large-scale canvas. With typical dramatic flair Copley first exhibited this picture on the decks of the *Venerable.* MO

158

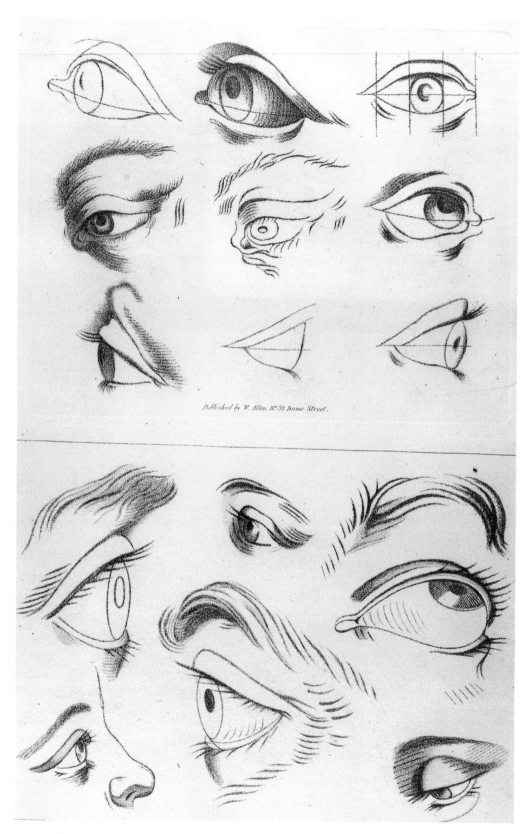

FIG. 1: Plate 2 from William Allen, *The Student's Treasure: A New Drawing Book*, Dublin, 1789, stipple engraving

"The Draughtsman's Assistant"

EIGHTEENTH-CENTURY DRAWING MANUALS

THE EARLIEST ENGLISH DRAWING MANUALS were written not, as one might expect, by and for artists, but rather by men like Henry Peacham, gentleman and tutor to the Earl of Arundel's son, whose *The Art of Drawing with the Pen, and Limning in Water Colours* in 1606 was intended "for the behoofe of all Younge Gentlemen, or Any Els that are Desirous for to Become Practitioners in This Excellent, and Most Ingenious Art." Throughout the seventeenth century, to demonstrate an interest in the practice of drawing and painting, to 'limn' (to paint in watercolor and gouache, often on a small scale), and to mix and even invent pigments were the signs of a *virtuoso*, a gentleman who collected and admired objects of *vertu*. Many gentlemen and women at the Stuart court received lessons in drawing and painting and presented the King with their own jewel-like limned copies of larger oils (see cats. 26-8).

Professional artists seldom relied upon manuals to learn their trade. Instead, they learned to draw and paint through long apprenticeships in the studio of an artist, where they copied from the master's collection of Old Master drawings and prints, drew from plaster casts of antique sculpture, and assisted with the laborious grinding and mixing of pigments. Among the prints might be some of the better-known collections published by seventeenth-century Italian and Dutch masters for other professional artists. These were books of prints of eyes, ears, mouths, heads, and parts of the body, without any text. Written material was mainly confined to recipes collected in manuscript and handed down through generations.

The studio might have translations of treatises by the most respected members of the artists' Academies at Paris, Bologna or Rome, such as Giovanni Paolo Lomazzo's *Trattato dell'arte de la pittura* (1584), or one of the many publications like *Albert Durer Revived*, which incorporated Albrecht Dürer's treatise on proportions with excerpts from other writers into more general treatises on the art of drawing. These continued to be published in successive editions throughout the eighteenth century, when they were joined by translations of Gérard de Lairesse's *Principles of Drawing*, Charles Le Brun's

Passions, and Charles Dufresnoy's *De Arte Graphica*. Such texts were cited on the title pages of hundreds of more general drawing manuals like Bernard Lens's *New and Compleat Drawing Book* (1750) or *The Compleat Drawing Master* (from 1766). Directed more towards amateurs than professional artists, successive editions of the last two titles and later *The Draughtsman's Assistant*, published by printsellers such as Carington Bowles or Robert Sayer, were little more than compilations of their stock of prints. This helps to explain why so few copies of these manuals contain exactly the same plates in the same order. They were prefaced by excerpts from the texts of the earlier treatises by Lairesse or Le Brun, which lent them academic and professional credibility.

The early eighteenth century was the age of the Earl of Shaftesbury's advocation of "civic humanism," when the definition of a virtuous gentleman was one who equated beauty with truth and was expected to lead the country by moral example. It was also the period when a newly emergent consumer society enabled growing numbers of men from the middle classes, who were "gentle" by wealth if not by birth, to participate with them in the "polite" culture of the eighteenth-century Enlightenment. But it was the educational philosophy of Shaftesbury's own tutor, John Locke, which was to have the greatest impact on the activity of learning to draw and the production of drawing manuals in the eighteenth century.

Locke's fundamental belief that knowledge was acquired through experience and reflection meant that one did not have to be born with a natural ability to draw in order to do well at it or even to excel. Instead, he argued that it was possible to achieve skill in the arts or indeed to master any other subject through practice and experiment and through reflection upon or even questioning authority or received opinion. Thus, both men and women who were gentle by birth and those who were not, might through education and industry achieve their goal of "politeness"; and, with the assistance of a drawing-master or such self-help tools as drawing manuals, they could learn to draw and paint as well as they might wish.

Locke promoted reason in education, arguing that children should be educated to be of benefit to society and should be taught subjects which would be useful in promoting virtue, not just pleasure. The resulting educational revolution was a gradual one; the curricula at established English grammar and public schools such as Eton were almost completely confined to the classics by the end of the seventeenth century. Parents who followed Locke's arguments for the inclusion of more useful subjects such as mathematics, modern languages, natural philosophy, and the arts (he specifically recommended drawing for those who would travel and in order to help express ideas of objects) employed tutors to teach their children privately at home or sought private academies where these subjects were taught. The many Dissenting academies were among the first to provide this type of liberal education to large numbers of children of the merchant middle classes all over the country.

Intimately connected with these developments, drawing-masters and drawing manuals began to flourish and then proliferate. The first establishment to employ a drawing-master was the Royal Mathematical School at Christ's Hospital, where the more promising orphans of the city guilds who had already received the basics of reading, writing, Latin, and arithmetic were taught by the Mathematics master and his assistant all the various subjects necessary for navigation, such as geometry, trigonometry, astronomy, and reading and making maps and charts. Near the end of the seventeenth century, the Hospital began to employ masters to teach drawing to the "Mathemats" and later to the boys in the Writing and Grammar Schools as well. One of the first was Bernard Lens II, father of the well-known miniaturist of the same name (cats. 16, 26-7, 43), who was succeeded in his position by his other son, Edward (from 1725 to 1749), who in turn was succeeded by Alexander Cozens (1750 to 1754, cats. 45, 105), and later by Benjamin Green. All produced drawings and watercolors for the boys to copy, which were later printed as popular drawing manuals. The boys produced magnificent exercise books illustrated with beautifully drawn and colored maps, prospects, ships, and munitions, along with topographical as well as ideal landscapes, indicating that their models were not only their masters' published drawing manuals, but that they also copied some of their more finished landscapes of the type intended for sale or exhibition. John Hipwell's

Elements of Navigation, produced in 1759 while he was a student at Christ's Hospital, has drawings in the style of both Lens and Cozens, whose drawing manuals and original examples for the students to copy were clearly still in use at the school.

The example set by Christ's Hospital was soon followed by the private Academy at Greenwich, where George Bickham taught drawing, and at Portsmouth Naval Academy, where young gentlemen like Edmund Rice submitted exercises titled *A Plan of Mathematical Learning* for admission to the navy. At Woolwich Military Academy Paul Sandby with a number of assistant drawing-masters taught the drawing of figures, landscape, surveying, and perspective for nearly thirty years. Sandby and his brother Thomas, whose copy of Debreuil's *The Practice of Perspective* (1743) is in the exhibition, were both products of the Drawing Room of the Board of Ordnance in the Tower of London. There young men were taught surveying, perspective, and the drawing of munitions as preparation for joining the new Military Survey being conducted by the army in Scotland or for similar chart- and map-making service in the colonies.

Private academies and a number of public schools, including Eton and Rugby, all followed suit before the middle of the century by providing the services of drawing-masters. In every county town in the country, particularly Bath, Brighton, and other spas during "the season," masters advertised private lessons in the clients' homes or in rented rooms. William Austin, the original author and engraver of Locatelli's *Specimen of Sketching Landscapes*, appended to his 1760s advertisements a list of 400 "Nobility and Gentry, &c" who were his pupils, and many others boasted long lists of illustrious subscribers to their publications, such as that found in J.T. Smith's *Remarks on Rural Scenery* (1797).

Except at Woolwich, where each of the drawing-masters' duties were spelled out in the orders for the Academy published in the 1780s, the format of the lessons must be garnered from the manuals the drawing-masters produced for their pupils. Through the first half of the century, the methods for learning to draw remained the same as those found in drawing books produced by and for professional artists from the Renaissance through the seventeenth century, when man was the measure of all things. Sometimes prefaced by a brief text setting out rules for drawing outlines and shading, for drawing heads, figures, portraits, and landscapes, or rules of perspective or lists of materials required, they invariably contained a series of plates to be copied. The plates occasionally began with a series of lines but more normally consisted of sets of eyes, then noses, mouths and ears, and entire heads, of old and young men and women and children, then limbs, hands and feet, and entire figures, partly draped then fully clothed, followed by groups of figures for more elaborate compositions, often based on antique sculpture or Old Master paintings, and finally, increasingly through the century, by images of animals, then sea and landscapes. The first statement of any text always confirmed the historical importance of drawing and painting, and the first instruction after listing materials usually concerned how to copy, emphasizing the need to carry on until one had "accustomed the hand." Repetition and practice at copying were the only ways to achieve this, underlining the close ties with the almost identical methods used for teaching writing, as demonstrated in John Langton's writing copy book of 1723. In 1665 Samuel Pepys described his wife's first lessons in limning, when she began by copying eyes, and over fifty years later Margaret Knight's copy of Clark's *A New Drawing Book of Outlines, &c.* bears two plates of eyes next to the title page. Nearly every manual through the century began in a similar fashion, even to 1789 when William Allen's *The Student's Treasure* started with a large stipple engraving of eyes in imitation of red-chalk examples provided by such artists as Angelica Kauffmann and Benjamin West (fig. 1).

In the seventeenth century, if a gentleman wanted to learn to draw or paint, he bought and studied the theoretical treatises, visited an artist in his studio, or had him attend his house for private lessons for himself, his wife, or children. By the beginning of the eighteenth century, however, gentlemen were encouraged to become members of the various artists' clubs and societies that were springing up in London, as professional artists sought the imprimatur and patronage of gentlemen who were not only collectors, but also often amateur artists themselves. Thus the portrait painter Jonathan Richardson's first publication, *An Essay on the Theory of Painting* was in the form of a treatise on the practical aspects of drawing and painting, while his second, *Two Discourses*, followed Lockean philosophy, argu-

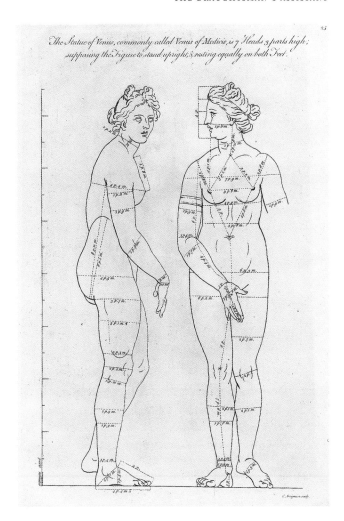

FIG. 2: Plate 25, *The Statue of Venus*, from Charles Grignion, *Triumph of Painting*, London, 1794, engraving and etching

ing that all Englishmen should have an informed interest in painting. His third publication was a combination of both.

Gentlemen not only attended the convivial artists' gatherings but sat alongside them in the life classes they set up for members and frequently accompanied them on sketching expeditions and tours. As the practice of studio apprenticeship slowly died out, it was replaced by a growth in more formal establishments for professional training, such as Thornhill's Academy at Great Queen Street where Richardson (cats. 1-2) was a director and the successive Academies in St. Martin's Lane. Gentlemen were still welcome to attend and frequently did so, and the concurrent rise in the status of professional artists contributed to the foundation of the Society for the Encouragement of Arts and Manufactures and eventually to the creation of the Royal Academy in 1768, for which John Gwynn and others had been arguing for decades. Gentlemen, and women, were even welcome to show their paintings alongside the works of professionals in the annual exhibitions.

However, although the venue for learning to draw for professional artists gradually moved from the studio to the academy through the century, the lessons themselves hardly changed at all. In the Cast Room at New Somerset House, young artists still learned, just as they had at Old Somerset House, by copying from prints and from casts which exemplified ideal classical proportions (fig. 2), while in the Life Room they drew from carefully-posed live models – the two traditional foundations of draftsmanship. There were some innovations: Dr. William Hunter was appointed to lecture on and give demonstrations as Professor of Anatomy; a Professor of Perspective (see fig. 3) was also appointed, and Reynolds's *Discourses* were published annually, providing an underpinning of aesthetic theory.

With the foundation of the Royal Academy, the status of professional artists rose, and they became anxious to be perceived as distinct from non-professional amateurs, who were gradually excluded from the Royal Academy's drawing classes and became more reliant on the type of drawing lessons provided in schools, privately in homes, and by drawing manuals. The latter began to reflect the change in the market and became much more directed towards providing every gentleman or lady with his or "her own drawing-master." With growing numbers of women wishing to learn to draw and a general rise in interest in landscape accompanied by a new national passion for picturesque travel, the new genre of the landscape drawing manual was born. These focused on providing easy to follow instructions and examples to copy, which, just as earlier drawing manuals had done with faces and figures, broke landscape down into easy to master component parts: leaves and branches and shapes of trees; birds, animals, and rural figures to populate the landscape; and suitable forms of architecture – ruined, rustic, or refined.

In the second half of the eighteenth century, there had been further revolutionary changes in education after the ideas promoted by a French admirer of Locke, Jean-Jacques Rousseau, in his pedagogical novel *Emile* (trans-

lated into English shortly after its publication in France in 1762), began to take root in the minds of more liberal British parents. His strong advocacy of learning by experience and his encouragement of subjects that promoted imagination and creativity had a considerable effect on the manner in which drawing was taught, which was clearly reflected in the manuals of the final two decades of the century particularly. By then it was no longer a prerequisite for amateurs to master drawing by repetitive copying before being allowed to progress to landscape. William Gilpin, William Marshall Craig, and the printseller Rudolph Ackermann reflect this through the absence of figure drawing in most of their landscape manuals. By this time composition, light and shade, and truthfulness to nature through imitation rather than slavish copying had replaced correct outline as the most desirable elements in a landscape drawing or watercolor. Through a sequence of steps with examples to copy, they enabled amateurs to produce their own landscapes by mixing elements provided in their pages and those of other special publications such as Sayer's *Introduction to Drawing Ships*, Smith's *Rural Scenery*, with its various rustic cottages, or Orme's *Pocket Sketch Book* and similar sewn booklets with rustic figures. The age of specialization, when drawing manuals reflected the specific audience to which they were addressed, amateur or professional, had begun to develop in parallel with drawing becoming a universal activity – one that was a world away from gentlemen and artists' clubs and societies, studio apprenticeships, and repetitive copying of eyes, ears, and mouths.

KIM SLOAN

FIG. 3: Frontispiece from Thomas Malton, *A Compleat Treatise on Perspective, in Theory and Practice*, London, 1776, engraving

THE
ANALYSIS
OF
BEAUTY.

Written with a view of fixing the fluctuating IDEAS of
TASTE.

BY *WILLIAM HOGARTH.*

So vary'd he, and of his tortuous train
Curl'd many a wanton wreath, in sight of Eve,
To lure her eye.-------- Milton.

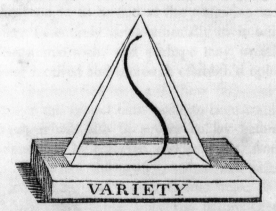

LONDON:

Printed by *J. REEVES* for the *AUTHOR,*
And Sold by him at his House in LEICESTER-FIELDS.

MDCCLIII.

Title page from William Hogarth, *The Analysis of Beauty*, London, 1753

DM I

Rudolph Ackermann, 1764-1834. *Flower Groups*. London,
R. Ackermann, 1798.

DM 2

Rudolph Ackermann, 1764-1834. *Lessons for Beginners in the
Fine Art*. London, R. Ackermann, 1796.

DM 3

William Allen. *The Student's Treasure: A New Drawing Book*.
Dublin, W. Allen, 1789.

DM 4

*The Artist's Vade Mecum: Being the Whole Art of Drawing Taught
in a New Work Elegantly Engraved on One Hundred Folio Copper
Plates, Containing Great Variety of Examples in Every Branch of
that Noble Art*. 2nd ed. London, Robert Sayer, 1766.

DM 5

William Austin, 1721-1820. *Specimen of Sketching Landscapes,
in a Free and Masterly Manner; Exemplified in Thirty-eight
Etchings, from the Original Drawings of Lucatelli, after Nature,
in and about Rome*. London, Printed for T. Simpson, 1781.

DM 6

George Bickham, (Jr.?), 1704?-1771. *An Introduction to the Art
of Drawing*. London, R. Sayer, c. 1745.

DM 7

George Bickham, Sr., 1683/4-1758. *The Museum of Arts, or,
The Curious Repository*. London, G. Bickham, 1745?

DM 8

Carington Bowles, 1724-93. *The Draughtsman's Assistant, or,
Drawing Made Easy, Wherein the Principles of that Art are Rendered Familiar in Instructive Lessons ... With a Suitable Introduction on the Utility of this Noble Art and Observations on Design as
Well in Regard to Theory as Practice*. London, R. Sayer, 1794.

DM 9

Petrus Camper, 1722-89. *The Works of the Late Professor Camper,
on the Connexion Between the Science of Anatomy and the Art of
Drawing, Painting, Statuary*. London, C. Dilly, 1794.

DM 10

Chinese Landskips. London, R. Sayer, 1752?

DM II

Sebastian Clark. *A New Drawing-Book of Out-Lines*. London,
Bakewell, 1722.

DM 12

*The Compleat Drawing-Master, Containing a Curious Collection
of Examples, Consisting of Parts of the Human Body, Academy
Figures, and Le Brun's Passions of the Soul, As They are Expressed
in the Human Countenance*. London, R. Sayer, 1766.

DM 13

William Marshall Craig, 1765-1834. *Essay on the Study
of Nature in Drawing Landscape*. London, W. Bulmer, 1793.

DM 14

Humphry Ditton, 1675-1715. *A Treatise of Perspective,
Demonstrative and Practical*. London, B. Tooke and
D. Midwinter, 1712.

DM 15

Jean Dubreuil, 1602-70. *Perspective Practical, or, A Plain and
Easie Method of True and Lively Representing All Things to the Eye
at a Distance, By the Exact Rules of Art. Set Forth in English by
Robert Pricke*. London, S. Sprint, 1698.

DM 16

Jean Dubreuil, 1602-70. *The Practice of Perspective, or, An Easy
Method of Representing Natural Objects According to the Rules of
Art*. 3rd ed. London, Thomas Bowles and John Bowles, 1743.

DM 17

*The Excellency of the Pen and Pencil, Exemplifying the Uses of
Them in the Most Exquisite and Mysterious Arts of Drawing,
Etching, Engraving, Limning, Painting in Oyl, Washing of Maps
& Pictures*. London, Dorman Newman, 1688.

DM 18

*The Florist, Containing Sixty Plates of the Most Beautiful Flowers
Regularly Dispos'd in Their Succession of Blowing, To Which is
Added an Accurate Description of their Colours, with Instructions
for Drawing & Painting Them According to Nature. Being a New
Work Intended for the Use and Amusement of Gentlemen and
Ladies Delighting in that Art*. London, R. Sayer, T. Bowles, &
J. Bowles & Son, 1760.

DM 19

William Gilpin, 1724-1804. *Observations on the River Wye, and
Several Parts of South Wales, &c. Relative Chiefly to Picturesque
Beauty, Made in the Summer of the Year 1770*. 3rd ed. London,
R. Blamire, 1792.

DM 20

Willem Goeree, 1635-1711. *The Art of Limning, in ... Which the
True Grounds and Perfect Use of Water-Colours with All Their
Properties, are Clearly and Perfectly Taught*. London, Robert
Pricke, 1674.

DM 21
Charles Grignion, 1717-1810. *Triumph of Painting*. London, Laurie & Whittle, 1794.

DM 22
John Gwynn, d. 1786. *An Essay on Design, Including Proposals for Erecting a Public Academy to be Supported by Voluntary Subscription (Till a Royal Foundation can be Obtain'd) for Educating the British Youth in Drawing, and the Several Arts Depending Thereon*. London, I. Brindley, 1749.

DM 23
John Hipwell. *Elements of Navigation, 1759*. Manuscript.

DM 24
William Hogarth, 1697-1764. *The Analysis of Beauty. Written with a View of Fixing the Fluctuating Ideas of Taste*. London, Printed by J. Reeves for the author, 1753.

DM 25
Thomas Jenner, fl. 1631-56. *Albert Durer Revived, or, A Book of Drawing, Limning, Washing, or Colouring of Maps and Prints and the Art of Painting, with the Names and Mixtures of Colours Used by the Picture-Drawers, with Directions How to Lay and Paint Pictures upon Glass, or, The Young-Man's Time Well Spent*. London, Printed by F. Collins for John Garrett, 1698.

DM 26
Franciscus Junius, 1589-1677. *The Painting of the Ancients, in Three Bookes, Declaring by Historicall Observations and Examples, the Beginning, Progresse, and Consvmmation of That Most Noble Art*. London, Printed by R. Hodgkinsonne, and sold by Daniel Frere, 1638.

DM 27
John Joshua Kirby, 1716-74. *Dr. Brook Taylor's Method of Perspective Made Easy, Both in Theory and Practice ... Being an Attempt to Make the Art of Perspective Easy and Familiar, to Adapt It Intirely to the Arts of Design, and to Make It an Entertaining Study to Any Gentleman Who Shall Chuse So Polite an Amusement*. Ipswich, Printed by W. Craighton for the author, 1754.

DM 28
Gérard de Lairesse, 1640-1711. *The Principles of Drawing, or, An Easy and Familiar Method Whereby Youth Are Directed in the Practice of That Useful Art ... Improved with Abstracts by C.A. Du Fresnoy*. 5th ed. London, Thomas Bowles and John Bowles and Son, 1752.

DM 29
Batty Langley, 1696-1751. *The City and Country Builder's and Workman's Treasury of Designs, or, The Art of Drawing, and Working the Ornamental Parts of Architecture*. London, Printed by J. Ilive for Thomas Langley, 1740.

DM 30
John Langton, fl. 1720-1727. *A New Copy-Book of the Italian Hand*. Stamford, 1723.

DM 31
Johann Casper Lavater, 1741-1801. *Essays on Physiognomy, Calculated to Extend the Knowledge and the Love of Mankind*. London, John Murray, 1788-99.

DM 32
Charles Le Brun, 1619-90. *Bowles's Passions of the Soul, Represented in Several Heads, Engraved in the Manner of Drawing in Chalk, from the Designs of the Late Celebrated Monsieur Le Brun*. London, Bowles and Carver, 1800?

DM 33
Charles Le Brun, 1619-90. *A Method to Learn to Design the Passions, Proposed in a Conference on Their General and Particular Expression, Written in French and Illustrated with a Great Many Figures Excellently Designed by Mr. Le Brun. Translated into English and All the Designs Engraved on Copper by John Williams*. London, F. Huggonson and Mr. Croyton, 1734.

DM 34
Bernard Lens II, 1659-1725, and Edward Lens, c. 1685-1749. *For the Curious Young Gentlemen and Ladies That Study and Practice the Commendable Art of Drawing, Colouring, etc., a New and Compleat Drawing Book ... Being the Close Study ... of the Late Mr. Lens ... in Sixty-Two Copper-Plates, to Which is Prefixed an Introduction to Drawing ... Translated from the French of Monsieur Gerrard de Lairesse, and Improved with Extracts from C. A. Du Fresnoy*. London, B. Dickinson, 1751.

DM 35
James Malton, d. 1803. *Young Painter's Maulstick*. London, Printed by J. Barfield for Carpenter & Co., 1800.

DM 36
Thomas Malton, 1726-1801. *A Compleat Treatise on Perspective, in Theory and Practice, on the True Principles of Dr. Brook Taylor. Made Clear, in Theory, by Various Moveable Schemes, and Diagrams, and Reduced to Practice ... Containing Diagrams, Views, and Original Designs, in Architecture, &c*. London, Printed for the author and sold by Messrs. Robson, 1776.

DM 37
A New Drawing Book of Heads, from Castiglione. Very Useful for Youth to Draw After. London, R. Sayer, 1760.

DM 38
Edward Orme. *Orme's Pocket Sketch Book*. London : E. Orme, 1799.

DM 39
Henry Overton, fl. 1706-1764. *View's of All the Cathedrall Church's of England and Wales &c. Neatly Engrav'd*. London, H. Overton, 1724.

DM 40
Henry Peacham, 1576?-1643? *The Art of Dravving Vvith the pen, and Limming in Water Colovrs, More Exactlie then Heretofore Tavght and Enlarged.* London, Printed by Richard Braddock for William Jones, 1607.

DM 41
The Principles of Drawing, Design, and Engraving, by Rules Formed from Nature and Truth, with the Late Various Improvements, and Some New Discoveries, Never Before Published, Being Entirely the Result of Practical Experience and Self-Observation. London, Printed by J. Roach for J. Vandrant, 1800.

DM 42
Edward Noyle Rice. *Plan of Mathematical Learning Taught in the Royal Academy,* Portsmouth, 1770. Manuscript.

DM 43
Jonathan Richardson, 1665-1745. *An Essay on the Theory of Painting.* London, W. Bowyer for John Churchill, 1715.

DM 44
Cesare Ripa, fl. 1600. *Iconologia, or, Moral Emblems, Wherein are Express'd Various Images of Virtues, Vices, Passions, Arts, Humours, Elements and Celestial Bodies, Illustrated with Figures, with their Explanations.* London, Printed by Benjamin Motte, 1709.

DM 45
John Russell, 1745-1806. *Elements of Painting with Crayons.* London, J. Wilkie and J. Walter, 1772.

DM 46
Paul Sandby, 1730-1809. *A Collection of Landskips and Figures, &c. ... They Merit a Place in the Cabinets of the Curious, and Are Useful Studies to Those Who Would Draw Landskips with Taste and Effect.* London, R. Sayer, 1773.

DM 47
Robert Sayer, 1725-94. *Introduction to Drawing Ships.* London, R. Sayer, 1788.

DM 48
John Thomas Smith, 1766-1833. *Remarks on Rural Scenery.* London, Nathaniel Smith, 1797.

DM 49
George Stubbs, 1724-1806. *The Anatomy of the Horse, Including a Particular Description of the Bones, Cartilages, Muscles, Fascias, Ligaments, Nerves, Arteries, Veins and Glands, in Eighteen Tables, All Done from Nature.* London, Printed by J. Purser for the author, 1766.

BIOGRAPHIES OF ARTISTS

ADAM, ROBERT (1728-92)

After attending the High School in Edinburgh and Edinburgh University, Robert Adam trained under his father, an architect and builder. In 1754 he embarked on a Grand Tour with his younger brother James. In Italy he met painters and architects, including Piranesi and the French neoclassical architect Charles-Louis Clérisseau, who taught him "all those Knacks so necessary to us architects." In these years Adam concentrated on his painting and drawing while he developed his knowledge of antiquity. In 1758 he settled in London where he established an architectural practice; his brothers James and William joined him in 1763. Adam became a member of the Society of Arts, a forum for meeting new clients, and in 1761 he was elected a member of the Royal Society. Benefiting from the boom in country-house building in the 1760s, Adam designed or remodeled country houses in the neoclassical style, combining the forms of Roman monuments with more traditional Palladian designs, as at Kedleston Hall (1760-71). He also designed elaborate interior schemes, from ceiling painting to carpeting, such as those at Headfort House. Adam also developed an interest in urban planning, participating in London developments such as Adelphi (1768-82) and Fitzroy Square (1790-94). He received official recognition when he was appointed, with Sir William Chambers, as Architect of the King's Works, a position he resigned in 1765 when he became MP for Kinross-shire. See cats. 120-1.
SELECTED LITERATURE: Bryant, 1992; Parissien, 1992; Tait, 1993.
MO

ALEXANDER, WILLIAM (1767-1816)

Born in Maidstone, Kent, William Alexander was apprenticed to Julius Caesar Ibbetson and entered the Royal Academy Schools in 1784. When Ibbetson turned down the position of official draftsman with Lord Macartney's embassy to China, Alexander took up the post, traveling with Macartney between 1792 and 1794. After his return to England, Alexander's Chinese sketches provided subjects for finished watercolors and illustrations for a number of publications, beginning with Sir George Staunton's *An Authentic Account of the Earl of Macartney's Embassy from the King of Great Britain to the Emperor of China* in 1797. In 1802 Alexander became the first Master of Landscape Drawing at the Royal Military College, Great Marlow, and in 1808 he was appointed Assistant Keeper of Prints and Drawings at the British Museum. See cat. 82.
SELECTED LITERATURE: Legouix, 1980; Legouix and Conner, 1981.
SW

ANDERSON, WILLIAM (1757-1837)

Born in Scotland, William Anderson worked as a shipwright before going south to London and becoming a marine painter. He first exhibited at the Royal Academy in 1787 and at the British Institution in 1810. In addition to marine subjects he also painted battle scenes and topographical views. He was a friend of Julius Caesar Ibbetson, with whom he collaborated on some paintings. See cat. 70.
SW

BALUGANI, LUIGI ANTONIO MELCHIORRE (1737-C. 1777)

Born in Bologna, Balugani demonstrated an aptitude for drawing from an early age and was apprenticed to Giuseppe Civoli, the professor of architecture at the Accademia Clementina, the Bolognese academy of art. Balugani proved an able architectural draftsman; he won a gold medal in an open competition organized by the R. Accademia di Belle Arti of Parma in 1759 and was elected as an academician of the Accademia Clementina at the unusually young age of twenty-two. Balugani traveled to Rome in 1761 to further his architectural studies. Four years later he was hired by the British explorer James Bruce to be his assistant on a private expedition to document classical remains in North Africa. After achieving his initial objective, Bruce continued toward Ethiopia. Balugani remained with Bruce after the expedition left North Africa, and he made a remarkable series of annotated field sketches and highly finished drawings of the flora and fauna. Although he does not seem to have been trained as a professional botanical artist, Balugani's drawings are very accomplished, and his records of new species made an important contribution to the study of natural science. Balugani died in Ethiopia, and after Bruce returned to Britain he claimed the draftsman's work as his own. The authorship was not systematically investigated until the 1980s, but the majority of the drawings are now firmly attributed to Balugani. See cats. 60-3.
SELECTED LITERATURE: Hulton, Hepper and Friis, 1991.
GF

BLAKE, WILLIAM (1757-1827)

Sent to drawing school at the age of ten, Blake learned to draw from casts of antiquities. During his subsequent apprenticeship with the engraver James Basire, Blake continued to use classical models, while also turning towards Gothic and more exotic ancient material. In 1779 he entered the Royal Academy Schools as an engraver and trained under George Moser. By late 1780 he was working as a professional engraver and also began exhibiting drawings and watercolors of historical and biblical subjects at the Royal Academy. From 1787 to 1789

Blake developed a unique method of printing called relief etching, which enabled him to combine text and image on one plate. It became his hallmark, and he employed it throughout the rest of his life in his "illuminated books," beginning with *Songs of Innocence* (1789), a series of poems addressed to children. From 1793 to 1795, he produced a series of "prophetic" books, including *America: A Prophecy* (1793) and *Europe: A Prophecy* (1794), in which he used mythological figures of his own creation to discuss current politics, especially the revolutions in America and France. Blake continued in a similar vein with his later illuminated books *Milton* (1804) and *Jerusalem* (1804-27). See cats. 36-7.
SELECTED LITERATURE: Gilchrist, 1863; Bindman, 1977; Noon, 1997, Hamlyn and Phillips, 2000.
RO

BORRA, GIOVANNI BATTISTA (1713-70)

Borra was born in Dogliani in the Piedmont region of Italy. Little is known about his early life, although by 1737 he was a pupil of the architect Bernardo Antonio Vittone. He studied with Vittone for three years, producing plates for the elder architect's treatise on civil architecture. In 1748 Borra published his own treatise on the stability of buildings, indicating a knowledge of engineering as well as architecture. By 1748 he was in Rome, where he met traveler Robert Wood and agreed to accompany him on his expedition to Asia Minor in 1750-51. Upon their return in 1751 Borra's drawings were used to illustrate Wood's travel volumes, and he began to accept architectural commissions from English patrons. He designed interiors in the rococo style, and in 1756 executed designs done by Robert Adam at Stowe, the home of Richard Grenville, 2nd Earl Temple. It is not known why Borra left England, but in 1756 he was established in an architectural practice in Piedmont. He continued to work as an architect and civil engineer in Italy until his death. See cats. 59, 97, 118.
SELECTED LITERATURE: Zoller, 1996.
MO

BROWN, JOHN (1749-87)

An Edinburgh native, John Brown began his training at the Edinburgh School of Art under the direction of William Delacour. In 1771 he traveled to Rome, where he was befriended by Henry Fuseli, who shared his admiration for Michelangelo. Brown lived for ten years in Italy, spending part of his time working for the antiquarian Scotsmen Charles Townley and Sir William Young, who were then engaged in studying Sicilian antiquities; he exhibited some of these works at the Royal Academy in 1774. In 1781 Brown returned to Edinburgh, where he exercised his talent as a portraitist before journeying to London in 1786. Although he exhibited at the Royal Academy that year, his health failed him soon after. See cat. 58.
SELECTED LITERATURE: Pressly, 1979.
MO

BUCK, SAMUEL (1696-1779) and BUCK, NATHANIEL (D. C. 1756)

Born in Yorkshire, Samuel Buck received early employment as a topographical draftsman from the Yorkshire antiquary John Warburton. When Samuel Buck moved to London in the early 1720s, it was probably Warburton who introduced him to the Society of Antiquaries, whose Fellows provided him with commissions. Working with his brother Nathaniel Buck and employing other engravers and draftsmen, Samuel Buck produced over 423 engravings of castles, monasteries, and other ruins and an additional 87 prospects of English and Welsh cities and towns. These were gathered together and reissued in three volumes by the printseller Robert Sayer in 1774 as *Buck's Antiquities or Venerable Remains of above 400 Castles, &c in England and Wales, with near to 100 Views Of Cities*. In the 1750s Samuel Buck gave up printmaking and set up as a drawing-master. See cat. 130.
SELECTED LITERATURE: Hyde, 1994.
SW

CAMPBELL, COLEN (1676-1729)

The Scottish architect Campbell began his professional career as a lawyer in Edinburgh. By 1708, however, he had abandoned the law and Scotland to become an architect in London. It is thought that a period of travel abroad, including two years in Italy, influenced this decision, as well as his friendship with architect James Smith, Master of the Royal Works in Scotland. Smith directed Campbell's attention to the work of the Italian architect Andrea Palladio (1508-80), and Campbell achieved his greatest measure of fame as a proponent of the Palladian style with the publication of *Vitruvius Britannicus*. With this work, Campbell joined Lord Burlington's circle of Neo-Palladians, which included the architect and painter William Kent. Although he never attained his goal of becoming Master of the Royal Works for Scotland, Campbell's work did find official recognition. In 1718 he became the Chief Clerk and Deputy Surveyor of the Royal Works, and in 1719 was appointed Architect to the Prince of Wales. Although he did not design for the Prince himself, the post introduced him to new clients among the courtiers. In 1728 Campbell published an English translation of Palladio's *First Book of Architecture*. He died in 1729, and was buried in an unmarked grave in Westminster Abbey. See cat. 112.
MO

CANALETTO [CANAL, GIOVANNI ANTONIO] (1697-1768)

Born in Venice to a theatrical-set painter, Canaletto worked as his father's assistant for several years, and this training established the skills in perspective and draftsmanship that would define the cityscapes and capriccios which he began to paint in the 1720s. He gradually turned towards realistic views of Venetian townscapes and from 1725 to 1740 worked almost exclusively in this mode. Canaletto was most productive and commercially successful during the 1730s. Most of his paintings were made for wealthy British Grand Tourists, with the connoisseur Joseph Smith acting as an intermediary. Encouraged by his pictures' popularity with the British, Canaletto moved to London in 1746 and quickly established a thriving practice there, depicting many of the city's best known sites, including Whitehall, the Horse Guards, Westminster Bridge, and the Thames. He returned to Venice in 1755. See cat. 131.

SELECTED LITERATURE: Constable, 1976; Baetjer and Links, 1989; Liversidge and Farrington, 1993.

RO

CHAMBERS, SIR WILLIAM (1723-96)

The son of a Scottish merchant with business interests in Sweden, Chambers was educated at an English grammar school and then sent to train as a merchant in the Swedish East India Company. During the long journeys to foreign locales such as China that the post required, Chambers devoted himself to learning "the fine arts, chiefly civil architecture." By 1749 he was in France studying at Jacques-François Blondel's Ecole des Arts, an architectural training-ground devoted to neoclassicism. Chambers was in Rome by 1750, where he lived in the same house as Giovanni Battista Piranesi. He befriended visiting English noblemen and earned a reputation as, according to fellow architect Robert Adam, "a Prodigy for Genius, for Sense & good taste." He returned to England in 1755 and, almost immediately after he established his practice, executed a series of important commissions, such as the redesign of Kew Gardens, and in 1757 published the first of many architectural treatises, *Designs of Chinese Buildings.* Chambers exhibited his designs publicly throughout his career, and he was instrumental in founding the Royal Academy in 1768, acting as its first treasurer. He brought some of the French practices of architectural drawing, such as the use of watercolor and the perspective depiction of the structure, to English architecture. Chambers's greatest public work is Somerset House, begun in 1776 and not completed until after his death in 1796. His successful architectural practice trained some of the notable architects of the succeeding generation, such as James Gandon and John Yenn. See cats. 116-17.

SELECTED LITERATURE: Harris, 1970; Harris and Snodin, 1996.

MO

CHATELAIN, JEAN-BAPTISTE-CLAUDE (C. 1710-C. 1758)

Chatelain was of French Huguenot ancestry, and little else is known about his family background or his early life. In 1737 he produced a drawing manual, *A New Book of Landskips,* and he soon gained a reputation as one of the most skilled engravers of landscape then working in London. He assisted Arthur Pond with his *44 Italian Landscapes* (1741-43), and worked with topographical artist William Bellers on his *Six Views in the North of England* (1754). Although he was admired by his contemporaries, he did not achieve great fame or wealth during his lifetime. See cat. 114.

SELECTED LITERATURE: Murdoch, 1985, pp. 166-7.

MO

CHIPPENDALE, THOMAS (BAP. 1718-79)

The son of a joiner, Chippendale probably received his earliest training from his father and from Richard Wood, a cabinetmaker in York. Around 1740 Chippendale moved to London, where he probably took drawing lessons, possibly from Matthias Darly, with whom he shared lodgings. In 1754 he formed a partnership with the Scottish merchant James Rannie, whose death in 1766 forced Chippendale to auction his goods and his tools and begin anew, a situation exacerbated by the difficulty in obtaining payments from clients. Chippendale achieved his greatest measure of fame with the publication in 1754 of the *Gentleman and Cabinet-makers Director,* illustrated with engravings done for the most part by Darly. This work made the name Chippendale synonymous with English rococo style furniture and spread his influence abroad, to North America and Russia, where Catherine the Great obtained a copy. He later worked in the neoclassical style, a shift evident in the second edition of the *Director* from 1762. Chippendale specialized in architectural interiors and fittings such as furniture, often working with the architect or the client in planning his designs. At times he was commissioned to execute the designs of others, such as Robert Adam. See cat. 123.

SELECTED LITERATURE: Gilbert, 1978.

MO

CLEVELEY, ROBERT (1747-1809)

Robert Cleveley was the son of John Cleveley Senior, a carpenter in the Royal Dockyards in Deptford who from the late 1740s worked as a marine painter as well. Like his father and his twin brother, John Cleveley Junior, Robert began working in the Deptford dockyards before turning to art. A specialist in depicting naval battles, Robert was appointed marine draftsman to William, 4th Duke of Clarence in 1791 and later became marine painter to the Prince Regent. See cat. 69.

SW

COPLEY, JOHN SINGLETON (1738-1815)

A son of Irish immigrants to Boston, John Singleton Copley's career was divided between Boston and London and straddled the American Revolution. His strongest early influences were likely his stepfather, the engraver and mezzotint portraitist Peter Pelham, and the painter John Smibert, who possessed a rare colonial collection of copies of Old Master paintings and casts after antique sculpture. Having become an established and fashionable Boston portraitist, in 1766 Copley sent *Boy with a Squirrel* to the Society of Artists' exhibition in London. Joshua Reynolds and Benjamin West responded favorably but not uncritically and urged Copley to come to England to perfect his art. Unwilling to leave his prosperous Boston portrait practice, Copley declined the invitation until the Boston Tea Party (1773) left him torn between political factions, unable to reconcile the growing rift between his Tory and Patriot friends, family, and clients. He studied in Italy from 1774 to 1775 and then moved to London, where he lived for the remainder of his life. Copley's style changed in response to British influences, his

brushwork becoming looser, more painterly, and flamboyant, like that of Reynolds and Romney. He also began to paint history pictures with present-day subjects, in the tradition of Benjamin West. In the 1790s, Copley attempted history paintings with seventeenth-century themes, but these did not achieve the success of his modern history paintings. See cats. 157-8.
SELECTED LITERATURE: Prown, 1966; Neff, 1995; Rebora, 1995.
ES

COSWAY, RICHARD (1742-1821)

From his humble beginnings as the son of a Devonshire schoolmaster, Richard "Dapper" Cosway became one of the most fashionable miniature painters of Regency society, as well as a dealer and collector of Old Master works. He demonstrated his skills as a draftsman at the age of twelve, winning prizes while at Shipley's School in London and studying under Thomas Hudson. Cosway's career progressed quickly as he exhibited publicly at a variety of venues and continued to win awards throughout the 1760s; he entered the Royal Academy Schools in 1769 and was elected an Academician in 1771. Cosway established himself in this period as a portrait painter specializing in miniatures. He won the favor of the Prince of Wales, and in 1785 he began to sign his works "Principal Painter of His Most Serene Prince of Wales." This success and Cosway's arrogance made him an easy target for ridicule from colleagues such as Richard Wilson and William Hogarth, who lampooned him as a dandy in the guise of the trained monkey that Cosway kept as a pet. In 1781 he married the Anglo-Florentine artist Maria Hadfield, and they settled in stylish Pall Mall, where they became known for their glittering social gatherings. Cosway continued to execute and exhibit large oil paintings as well as miniatures throughout his career, but his miniatures, noted for their delicate modeling and characteristic blue "sky" backgrounds, secured his reputation. See cats. 19-20, 40.
SELECTED LITERATURE: Williamson, 1905; Lloyd, 1995.
MO

COZENS, ALEXANDER (1717-86)

The son of an English master shipbuilder to Peter the Great, Alexander Cozens was born in Russia. He was sent to England for schooling at the age of ten, and when he was sixteen he began to learn etching, soon followed by drawing and painting. In 1746 he journeyed to Italy to study oil painting with Claude-Joseph Vernet. When Cozens returned to London he held a variety of teaching positions, giving drawing lessons at Eton College and working as a private drawing-master to royal and aristocratic pupils. As an artist and teacher, Cozens was concerned with combining the study of nature with the depiction of ideal landscapes. To this end he published treatises on painting that advocated various methods or systems to assist in the creation of ideal landscape. The most famous of these, *New Method of Assisting in Invention in Drawing Original Compositions in Landscape* (1786) described the "blot" method: "a blot is not a drawing, but an assemblage of accidental shapes, from which a drawing may be made." This method and other sys-

tems devised by Cozens not only proved to be an important influence on the work of his son John Robert Cozens, but were also studied by a number of other artists, such as Joseph Wright of Derby, J.M.W. Turner, Thomas Girtin, and John Constable. See cats. 45, 105.
SELECTED LITERATURE: Oppé, 1946; Wilton, 1980; Sloan, 1986.
MO

COZENS, JOHN ROBERT (1752-97)

The son of Alexander Cozens, John Robert Cozens was trained from an early age in both his father's methods of landscape "invention" and the direct study of nature. He began exhibiting at the Society of Artists in 1767, submitting monochromatic ink and pencil landscapes in the manner of his father. In 1776 he exhibited an oil work at the Royal Academy depicting Hannibal marching through an Alpine landscape, a work that J.M.W. Turner cited as an important influence. Later that year Cozens traveled through the Alps with Richard Payne Knight, an antiquarian and connoisseur. He returned to Italy a few years later with another wealthy patron, William Beckford, for whom he produced more than ninety watercolors. The malaria Cozens contracted in Italy in 1782 worsened the ill health, both mental and physical, that plagued him throughout his life. When he returned to England, he continued producing watercolors of foreign and native locales for patrons. In 1794, however, Cozens suffered a mental breakdown and became the ward of Dr. Thomas Monro of Bethlehem (Bedlam) Hospital. He was supported in his last years by gifts from friends, pupils, and the Royal Academy. See cats. 96, 103-4, 142.
SELECTED LITERATURE: Wilton, 1980; Sloan, 1986.
MO

DANCE, GEORGE (THE YOUNGER) (1741-1825)

George Dance the Younger was the son of George Dance the Elder, the architect of Mansion House in London and long-time "Architect to the Corporation of London." Dance the Younger succeeded his father in that position in 1769 and established his own reputation as the architect of Newgate Prison (1770-78) and the Royal College of Surgeons (1806-13). With his brother, the painter Nathaniel Dance, he spent five years in Italy studying and drawing, concentrating chiefly on architectural remains. The younger Dance's accomplishments as an architect and his role as mentor and teacher to Sir John Soane have overshadowed his achievements in drawing. In addition to executing numerous architectural drawings, he drew portraits of his friends and family in his spare time. A member of the Royal Academy as an architect, Dance produced portraits of fifty-three of his fellow-Academicians between 1793 and 1800. These portraits were eventually engraved and published in 1809. He is buried in St. Paul's Cathedral, where his inscription memorializes him as "the last surviving Member of the Original Forty Royal Academicians." See cat. 14.
SELECTED LITERATURE: Stroud, 1971; Geffrye Museum, 1972.
MO

DANIELL, THOMAS (1749-1840) and DANIELL, WILLIAM (1769-1837)

After being apprenticed to a coach-painter, Thomas Daniell entered the Royal Academy Schools in 1773, and between 1774 and 1784 he exhibited topographical views and flower paintings at the Royal Academy. Between 1786 and 1794 Thomas and his orphaned nephew William Daniell traveled extensively in India, sketching the country and its architecture, often with the aid of a camera obscura. One hundred and seventy-six of their working drawings are in the Yale Center for British Art. Back in England in 1794, they worked up their sketches into finished watercolors, which they published as colored aquatints in the six-volume *Oriental Scenery* (1795-1808). In 1812 and 1813 William Daniell traveled around the entire British coastline. The 308 colored aquatints with which he documented the undertaking were published in eight parts between 1814 and 1825 as a *Voyage Round Great Britain*. Having exhibited at the Royal Academy since 1795, William Daniell became a Royal Academician in 1822. See cats. 79-81.
SELECTED LITERATURE: Sutton, 1954; Archer, 1980.
SW

DAVIS, SAMUEL (1757-1819)

Samuel Davis traveled to India in 1780. In 1783 he was named the "draughtsman and surveyor" to Samuel Turner's mission to Tibet. Nine of his drawings from the expedition were engraved as illustrations to Turner's *An Account of an Embassy to the Court of Teshoo Lama in Tibet; Containing a Narrative Journey through Bhutan, and Part of Tibet* in 1800. Four of his drawings had already appeared in Thomas Pennant's *The View of Hindustan* in 1798. William Daniell, who with his uncle Thomas, had spent twelve months with Davis in India in 1790-91, published another six of his drawings as aquatints under the title *Views in Bootan* in 1813. Davis remained in India until 1806, holding a succession of civil-service positions and pursuing an interest in Indian astronomy. He published two papers on the subject in *Asiatick Researches* (1790, 1792) and was elected a fellow of the Royal Society in 1792. His journal of the mission to Tibet was published by his son in the *Transactions of the Royal Asiatic Society of Great Britain and Ireland* in 1830. See cat. 78.
SELECTED LITERATURE: Aris, 1982.
SW

DAY, WILLIAM (1764-1807)

Born in London to a prosperous linen-draper, William Day followed his father's profession but took a keen amateur interest in geology, mineralogy, and painting. He formed one of the earliest private collections of minerals in England. Presumably self-taught as an artist, he was from the age of eighteen a regular "Honorary Exhibitor" at the Royal Academy. By 1787 he had become the friend of John Webber, with whom he toured Derbyshire in 1789 and Wales in 1791. In 1801 Day's father inherited his brother's Sussex estate, which passed to William Day and his brother on his father's death in 1803. William Day died of consumption four years later. See cat. 55.
SELECTED LITERATURE: Egerton, 1970.
SW

DAYES, EDWARD (1763-1804)

Dayes began his artistic career studying mezzotint engraving under William Pether. He entered the Royal Academy Schools at the age of seventeen and exhibited his first picture there six years later. He continued to exhibit miniatures, landscapes, and genre works at the Royal Academy and the Society of Artists throughout his career. Dayes is chiefly remembered today as the teacher of his more famous pupil Thomas Girtin. During his own lifetime, however, he was highly regarded as a topographical painter, and was appointed draftsman to the Duke of York. Throughout the 1790s he worked up drawings for topographical publications and published records of his own picturesque tour, *An Excursion through Derbyshire and Yorkshire*. Towards the end of his life, Dayes exhibited, without success, large-scale oil works with biblical or classical subjects. He committed suicide in 1804. See cats. 52, 140.
SELECTED LITERATURE: Long, 1929; Dayes, 1971.
MO

DIGHTON, ROBERT (1752-1814)

The son of the printseller John Dighton, Robert Dighton was the head of a family of graphic artists and painters that included his sons Robert, Denis, and Richard and his grandsons Richard, Joshua, and Robert. Robert Dighton began exhibiting drawings at the Society of Artists and the Free Society at the age of seventeen, and three years later entered the Royal Academy Schools. By the 1790s Dighton had earned a reputation for making watercolors and colored engravings, as well as for acting and singing at Sadler's Wells. He added to his income by giving drawing lessons and by opening a print shop like his father's in the Charing Cross section of London. Overwhelmed by financial problems, Dighton came up with the unscrupulous solution of stealing prints from the British Museum. In 1806 Dighton was discovered to have stolen a Rembrandt landscape. He left London in disgrace, moving between Oxford, Cambridge, Bath, Cheltenham, and Brighton, and during his exile began producing caricatures of eminent British figures. In 1810 Dighton returned to London, where he managed a printing press with his sons for the last four years of his life. See cat. 39.
SELECTED LITERATURE: Calthorp, 1906; Rose, 1981.
RO

DONALDSON, JOHN (1737-1801)

John Donaldson was born in Edinburgh in 1737 to a glovemaker and his wife. Displaying a talent for drawing at an early age, he sold copies of engravings and miniature portraits done in India ink to support himself and assist his family. When he was twenty, the Edinburgh Society of Artists awarded him a stipend to continue his study of art. With that support, he journeyed to London where he was awarded a premium by the Society of Arts in 1764. At this time Donaldson began to specialize in painting on Worcester porcelain and enamel and also in executing miniatures. He won an award in Newcastle in 1768 for an historical subject on enamel, as well as numerous

awards from the Society of Arts for his work in that medium. Donaldson exhibited at the Royal Academy throughout his career. See cat. 5.
SELECTED LITERATURE: Long, 1929.
MO

DOWNMAN, JOHN (1750-1824)

Following his training under Benjamin West (1768) and in the Royal Academy Schools (1769), John Downman rapidly consolidated his reputation as a painter and draftsman. He exhibited portraits at the Royal Academy from 1770 to 1773, and his first subject picture was shown there in 1773. In the same year, Downman went to Italy to study, and after his return exhibited regularly at the Royal Academy from 1777. Despite the occasional production of subject pictures based on themes from poetry, theater, mythology, and classical history Downman was primarily known for his portrait drawings and paintings. See cat. 8.
SELECTED LITERATURE: Williamson, 1907; Croft-Murray, 1939.
ES

DUCROS, ABRAHAM-LOUIS-RODOLPHE (1748-1810)

The Swiss-born painter Louis Ducros studied in Geneva at the private academy of Nicolas Henri Joseph Fassin from 1769 to 1771. He sketched and made watercolors of the Swiss countryside until 1776, when he traveled to Rome. In 1778 he accompanied a Dutch antiquary named Nicholas ten Howe through southern Italy, Sicily, and Malta as a topographical draftsman. Ducros returned to Rome in 1779, and for the next ten years he worked in partnership with Giovanni Battista Volpato, producing views for tourists in watercolor, which Vopato would then engrave. By 1782 Ducros was working independently on private commissions for oil paintings, but he was best known for his large-scale watercolors. Between 1786 and 1793 Sir Richard Colt Hoare, his most important patron, bought thirteen watercolor landscapes from him. In 1793 Ducros moved from Rome to Naples, and in 1800 he went to Malta. Ducros finally returned in 1807 to Switzerland, where he spent the last three years of his life. Ducros's work inspired a younger generation of British watercolor artists, especially J.M.W. Turner, who was familiar with his work through Colt Hoare's collection of watercolors. See cat. 102.
SELECTED LITERATURE: Chessex, 1985.
RO

ENGLEHEART, GEORGE (1753-1829)

George Engleheart was born in Kew, one of eight sons of a German father and an English mother. In 1769 he entered the Royal Academy Schools and became the pupil of Joshua Reynolds and the landscape painter George Barrett. Living and working in London, Engleheart associated with a diverse group of artists, including George Romney and William Blake. He concentrated on miniature painting on ivory and exhibited his work at the Royal Academy from 1773 to 1822. Acknowledged for both his coloring and draftsmanship, Engleheart was a

sought-after portraitist of the aristocracy and royalty. In 1790 he was appointed "Miniature-Painter to His Majesty the King." In 1813 he retired to a country house at Belfort, near Hounslow but died at Blackheath, where he had lived with his son for the last ten years of his life. See cats. 21-3.
SELECTED LITERATURE: Williamson and Engleheart, 1902.
MO

FLAXMAN, JOHN (1755-1826)

The son of a plaster-cast maker, Flaxman took to sculpture early in life and exhibited at the Royal Academy from 1771. In 1775 he was commissioned by Josiah Wedgwood to make designs for ceramic medallions and plaques, and he had established himself as a monumental sculptor by the mid-1780s. Flaxman studied and worked in Rome between 1778 and 1794, and after his return to England his large monument to William Murray, 1st Earl of Mansfield, for Westminster Abbey (erected 1801) established him as the foremost monumental sculptor in England at the time. Flaxman was also celebrated for his draftsmanship. During his time in Rome, he received several commissions to illustrate literary texts, and he produced designs for Dante's *Divine Comedy*, the works of Aeschlyus, and Homer's *Iliad* and *Odyssey*, which were engraved and published. Flaxman's distinctive outline illustrations were widely disseminated as engravings throughout Europe, often in pirated versions, and had a considerable impact on the visual and decorative arts of the period. Flaxman's designs were praised particularly for their "authenticity" (George Romney noted that they looked "as if they had been made in the age, when Homer wrote"), but Flaxman claimed that his models were Roman sarcophagi and that they were not complete works but rather designs for future relief sculptures. See cats. 34-5, 109.
SELECTED LITERATURE: Essick and Belle, 1977; Irwin, 1979; Symmons, 1984.
RO

GAINSBOROUGH, THOMAS (1727-88)

Born in Suffolk, the landscape and portrait painter Thomas Gainsborough came to London at the age of thirteen to study with the French artist Hubert-François Gravelot. While in London, he visited the St. Martin's Lane Academy and became familiar with the work of William Hogarth. Gainsborough returned to Suffolk in 1748, where he painted landscapes and portraits, and in 1752 he moved to Ipswich. In 1759 Gainsborough established his practice in the fashionable spa-town of Bath, where he was in demand as a portraitist. He exhibited at the Royal Academy from 1769, and he returned to London in 1774. At this time Gainsborough assumed his place among the social and cultural elite, receiving royal commissions and rivaling Sir Joshua Reynolds. Despite his considerable success as a portraitist, Gainsborough aspired to dedicate himself to landscapes, but was unable to make a living from his chosen *métier*. Gainsborough was an inveterate draughtsman, and produced numerous chalk and charcoal drawings, which he used both as studies for paintings and sold as independent works. In 1784

he quarreled with the Royal Academy. From then until his death in 1788, he exhibited his work at his own home. After Gainsborough's death Reynolds devoted a lecture to him (published as the fourteenth *Discourse*), in which he hailed him as the first great English painter, the beginning of "the honorable distinction of an English school." See cats. 47-9.
SELECTED LITERATURE: Waterhouse, 1958; Hayes, 1971; Hayes, 1983.
MO

GANDON, JAMES (1741-1823)

In 1757 James Gandon began his training in the office of Sir William Chambers, where he developed his style of conservative classicism. Gandon never traveled to Italy but gleaned his knowledge of classical architecture from books, prints, and drawings. After seven years with Chambers, Gandon set up his own practice in London, although he achieved little success until 1781. That year he refused an invitation to work for the Empress Catherine the Great in St. Petersburg and instead moved to Dublin to become the city's leading architect. Through numerous important public commissions, such as the Four Courts and the Custom House as well as for streets and bridges such as Carlisle (now O'Connell) Bridge, Gandon became the style-maker in Irish architecture. He retired in 1808 at the peak of his profession, having exerted formidable influence on younger Irish architects such as Francis Johnston and Richard Morrison. See cat. 128.
SELECTED LITERATURE: McParland, 1985.
MO

GARDNER, DANIEL (1750-1805)

A pupil of George Romney in his native town of Kendal from 1762, Gardner went to London in 1767. He entered the Royal Academy Schools in 1770 and won his first award, a silver medal, in 1771. Gardner worked as a studio assistant to Sir Joshua Reynolds from 1773 and established himself as a portraitist with a predominantly middle-class clientele. Although he executed works in oil, Gardner particularly favored pastel for his portraits. He used his chosen medium in an unconventional and innovative manner, grinding his crayons to fine dust and mixing them with other media; the distinctive drawings produced by this method have the appearance of brilliantly-colored oil paintings. See cat. 9.
SELECTED LITERATURE: Williamson, 1921; Kapp, 1972.
MO

GIBBS, JAMES (1682-1754)

A Catholic Scotsman, Gibbs journeyed to Rome in 1703 with the intention of becoming a priest. In 1704 he entered the studio of the Italian baroque master Carlo Fontana, the most important architect then working in the city. While in Rome, Gibbs supported himself by guiding Grand Tourists throughout the city and making drawings for them. When he arrived in London in 1708, he was able to use these connections to

launch his career in architecture. Although his religious faith was an impediment to receiving important public commissions, Gibbs's Scottish supporters in Parliament, such as John Erskine, 11th Earl of Mar, ensured that his career advanced. In 1713 Gibbs succeeded William Dickinson on the Commission for Building Fifty New Churches in London. His first public building, the Church of St. Mary-le-Strand garnered him praise and attention. Just as Vanbrugh was the architect of the Whig aristocracy, Gibbs became the architect of the Tory aristocracy after he was dismissed from the Commission in 1716. He also achieved great popularity as the author of architectural treatises such as the 1732 *Rules for Drawing the Several Parts of Architecture*. See cat. III.
SELECTED LITERATURE: Little, 1955; Friedman, 1984.
MO

GILPIN, THE REVEREND WILLIAM (1724-1804)

The clergyman and schoolmaster William Gilpin was also an amateur artist and print collector, and one of the most influential theorists of the Picturesque movement. In his *Essay on Prints* (1768) Gilpin published his first definition of the Picturesque, "that peculiar kind of beauty, which is agreeable in a picture," which he argued was distinct from the Sublime and Beautiful, and he went on to explore his aesthetic theories on a series of excursions taken in different parts of England. His manuscript records and drawings of his travels were circulated among his friends, and with their encouragement he published his tours, beginning with his *Observations on the River Wye* in 1782. His publications were intended not as guidebooks, but as picturesque itineraries "in which the writing and illustrations complement one another to sing the praises of nature," and the drawings were generalized rather than topographical views. Gilpin graded scenery according to his aesthetic precepts, and deemed the northern end of Lake Windermere in the Lake District "rather amusing than picturesque," and the Firth of Forth in Scotland "exceedingly grand and amusing [but] not indeed picturesque." Gilpin's methodology for studying and depicting landscape may now seem eccentric, but his publications were extremely influential in the late eighteenth and early nineteenth centuries. See cat. 46.
SELECTED LITERATURE: Barbier, 1963; Sloan, 2000.
GF

GIRTIN, THOMAS (1775-1802)

Along with his contemporary, friend, and rival J.M.W. Turner, Thomas Girtin is credited with expanding the possibilities of watercolor as a medium and transcending the tradition of topographical painting to create a more expressive form of landscape art. A pupil of the topographical painter Edward Dayes, Girtin exhibited his first work at the Royal Academy in 1794, while continuing his training at the Monro "Academy," an informal gathering of artists in the home of Dr. Thomas Monro, a staunch supporter and collector of British artists. At the Monro Academy Girtin and Turner copied drawings by John

Robert Cozens, whose work was an important formative influence on both artists. Following the traditional pattern of the topographical artist, Girtin, like Turner, regularly went on sketching tours in Britain between 1795 and 1801 and used the material he gathered on his travels for the finished watercolors which he exhibited at the Royal Academy. Girtin died in 1802 from tuberculosis. See cat. 143.

SELECTED LITERATURE: Girtin and Loshak, 1954; Morris, 1986; Hill, 1999.

MO

GOUPY, JOSEPH (1686-C. 1770)

Born in Nièvre, France, the painter, printmaker, and collector Joseph Goupy was the nephew of the portrait painter Louis Goupy. He began his career as an artist in Malta, where he painted four panoramic views of the port of Valetta. In 1711 Goupy moved to London, where he was an early subscriber to Godfrey Kneller's Academy. Goupy specialized in small copies of Old Master paintings in pastel and gouache, which were much in demand, and acquired some distinguished patrons. For George I, Goupy restored Andrea Mantegna's *Triumphs of Caesar,* and he was hired by Frederick, Prince of Wales, as a curator of his collection and a drawing-master to his family. Goupy continued to produce some original works, including portraits and set designs for the Royal Academy of Music, and he painted sets for several operas by George Frideric Handel. See cat. 28.

SELECTED LITERATURE: Grundy, 1921; Croft-Murray, 1962-70, vol. II, pp. 211-12; Simon, 1985.

RO

GRAVELOT, HUBERT-FRANÇOIS (1699-1773)

Born Hubert-François Bourguignon, this son of a Parisian tailor later took the name of his godfather, Gravelot. When his early attempt at a career in overseas trade failed, Gravelot turned to art. He trained in France, first under Jean Restout II and then under François Boucher, and became a highly accomplished draftsman, engraver, and painter. In 1732 or 1733 he traveled to London to assist the engraver Claude du Bosc with the engraving of illustrations for an English translation of Bernard Picart's *Cérémonies et coutumes religieuses de tous les peuple et de tous les temps.* Gravelot's refined and accomplished engravings brought him great fame in England, and he received numerous commissions for book illustrations. He became friendly with William Hogarth and Francis Hayman and taught at St. Martin's Lane Academy, where he exerted considerable influence on young British painters, including Thomas Gainsborough. Gravelot also collaborated with Hayman on the designs for the decorative scheme at Vauxhall Gardens. Through his illustrations, his teaching activities, and his collaborations with British artists, Gravelot played a significant role in the introduction of the French rococo style into England. In 1745, uncomfortable in an increasingly Francophobic atmosphere, Gravelot returned to France, where he continued his career as a book illustrator.

See cat. 29.

SELECTED LITERATURE: Salomons, 1911; Hammelmann and Boase, 1975; Victoria & Albert Museum, 1984.

RO

GRIMM, SAMUEL HIERONYMOUS (1733-94)

A native of Burgdorf, Switzerland, Grimm began his artistic training in Bern under the direction of Johann Ludwig Alberli, specializing in topographical landscapes in both oil and watercolor, and book illustrations. In 1764 Grimm abandoned oil painting to devote his energy exclusively to watercolor. A year later he traveled to France, and in 1768 he settled in England, where he was best known for his satirical drawings and illustrations to Shakespeare. He also continued to produce topographical watercolors. Grimm worked for a variety of patrons, including Gilbert White, Richard Kaye, and Sir William Burrell. See cats 83-5.

SELECTED LITERATURE: Clay, 1941.

MO

HAMILTON, GAVIN (1723-98)

Educated at Glasgow University, the Scottish artist Gavin Hamilton went to Rome in 1748 and spent most of the remainder of his life there, only leaving for short visits to Britain. Hamilton initially studied portrait painting with Agostino Masucci, and his portraits were quite successful in London. He later shifted to history painting, inspired by the recently rediscovered classical antiquities in Herculaneum and Pompeii. Hamilton became a leading excavator himself and developed a neoclassical style of history painting, which was inaugurated by his *Andromache Mourning the Death of Hector* in 1760. Hamilton turned to Homer for his subject matter and to antique sculptural reliefs for composition, dress, and accessories. This approach, unique at the time, was praised by Johann Joachim Winckelmann. Hamilton considered as his greatest accomplishment a series of six scenes from Homer's *Iliad,* executed between 1760 and 1775. He also made important paintings based on Roman history, such as *Brutus Promising to Avenge the Death of Lucretia.* For over thirty years Hamilton was an important mentor for artists in Rome, including the sculptor Antonio Canova whom he persuaded to abandon the rococo in favor of a neoclassical style. Through exhibiting at the Society of Artists and the Royal Academy, Hamilton also had an impact upon artists in Great Britain, and engravings after his paintings extended his influence throughout the Continent. See cats. 31-2.

SELECTED LITERATURE: Irwin, 1962; Irwin, 1975; Stainton, 1975.

RO

HAMILTON, HUGH DOUGLAS (C. 1740-1808)

Born in Dublin, Hamilton began his artistic training at the Dublin Society's Drawing School before moving to London in the 1760s. While in London, he won awards from the Society of Artists and obtained numerous commissions for portraits, mostly in pastel, from the Irish and the English aristocracy, including the royal family. Hoping to move beyond portraiture to history painting, Hamilton left for Rome in 1779. He spent thirteen years there, painting canvases on mythological subjects while he supported himself by executing portraits of Grand Tourists. Impoverished and disillusioned by his lack of success as a history painter, Hamilton returned in 1792 to Dublin, where he resumed his portrait practice, working mostly in oils. Hamilton enjoyed considerable success in this phase of his career, but disliked Dublin, which he described "exile for one who truly loves art." See cat. 11.
SELECTED LITERATURE: Crookshank, 1978; Cullen, 1982.
MO

HARRIS, JOHN, THE ELDER (1767-1832)

The son of Moses Harris, a natural history painter and draftsman, John Harris grew up in the neighborhood of the Royal Dockyards at Deptford. Both his father's naturalist interests and his boyhood surroundings were reflected in his art. Often employed as an illustrator by publishers and booksellers, he painted and drew insects, fruit, flowers, sea pieces, and rustic genre subjects. He exhibited at the Royal Academy from 1797 to 1814. His son, John Harris the Younger, was also an artist, who made a specialty of creating facsimile leaves for the repair of rare books. See cat. 71.
SW

HEALY, ROBERT (1743-71)

The son of a successful architect and decorator, Healy studied at the Dublin Society's Drawing Schools under the pastellist Robert West. Like many of his Irish contemporaries, Healy specialized in pastel and chalk drawings but seems to have eschewed the use of color, since all his few surviving works are in grisaille. He exhibited portrait drawings at the Society of Artists in Dublin between 1766 and 1770 and was awarded a silver palette by the Society in 1770 for "the best exhibited drawing of a group of figures." Healy's friend John O'Keefe recalled that the artist "excelled at drawing in chalks, portraits, etc., but his chief forte was horses which he delineated so admirably that he got plenty of employment from those who had hunters, mares, or Ladies palfreys." The only known examples of Healy's equestrian subjects, however, are eight drawings made for the Conollys of Castletown in the late 1760s. Healy's promising career was cut short when he died at the age of twenty-eight in 1771, reputedly from a cold brought on while sketching cattle in Lord Mornington's park at Dangan, County Meath. See cat. 92.
SELECTED LITERATURE: Guinness, 1982, pp. 80-5; Crookshank, 1994, pp. 62-5.
GF

HEARNE, THOMAS (1744-1817)

Known during his lifetime as an artist of carefully drawn and colored watercolors, Hearne was sought after by government officials and antiquarians to provide accurate records of their travels and discoveries. Born in Wiltshire, Hearne was in London by 1763, when he earned a premium from the Society of Artists. In 1765 he began a six-year apprenticeship with landscape engraver William Woollett. During this period, he continued to execute watercolors, which he exhibited at the Society of Artists. After his apprenticeship ended, Hearne accompanied the new governor of the Leeward Islands, Sir Ralph Payne, to the West Indies to produce topographical studies of the landscape. Upon his return to London in 1775, he turned his attention to British topography. His *Antiquities of Great Britain* produced in collaboration with the engraver William Byrne was an important picturesque successor to the antiquarian print series of the Buck brothers. Although Hearne exhibited at the Royal Academy, he relied on loyal collectors such as Richard Payne Knight and Dr. Thomas Monro, who thought him "superior to everybody drawing." See cats. 51, 77, 141.
SELECTED LITERATURE: Morris and Milner, 1985; Morris, 1989.
MO

HOARE, PRINCE THE YOUNGER (1755-1834)

Prince Hoare the Younger was born into an artistic family; his father William Hoare was a painter and printmaker, while his uncle Prince Hoare the Elder was a fashionable sculptor working in Bath. William Hoare encouraged his son's artistic talents, and in 1772 Prince Hoare the Younger won a prize from the Society of Arts; the following year he entered the Royal Academy Schools. Like other artists of his generation, Hoare continued his training in Italy. In Rome he became a member of the circle of artists gathered around the Swiss painter Henry Fuseli, who shared his interest in exploring the emotional range of the neoclassical. After a productive period in Rome, Hoare returned to England in 1780. Although he exhibited at the Royal Academy until 1785, Hoare's artistic output declined, and he abandoned painting in 1788, when he began a new career as a playwright. He maintained his connections with the art world, however, acting as Secretary for Foreign Correspondence at the Royal Academy and publishing a book of art criticism, *Epoch of the Arts* in 1813. See cat. 4.
SELECTED LITERATURE: Pressley, 1979.
MO

HOGARTH, WILLIAM (1697-1764)

Hogarth was apprenticed to Ellis Gamble, a London silver-plate engraver, in 1713, and by early 1720 had opened up his own business as an engraver, executing both metalwork and prints. In October 1720, he enrolled as one of the first subscribers to a drawing academy in St. Martin's Lane. In 1721, with *The South Sea Scheme*, he began engraving satires inspired by Dutch models. In the early 1730s Hogarth embarked on his "Modern Moral Subjects," a series of narrative paintings that he later

engraved. *A Harlot's Progress* was the first work in this vein, followed by *A Rake's Progress*, and *Marriage A-la-Mode* in 1743. Hogarth also painted conversation pieces, large-scale history paintings, and portraits. Through his career, Hogarth worked to improve the status of British artists. In 1735 he lobbied for an engraver's copyright act and established a new drawing academy in St. Martin's Lane. He was instrumental in creating showcases for his own paintings and those of his contemporaries at the Foundling Hospital and Vauxhall Gardens. Hogarth was, however, opposed to the founding of a formal academy of art under government control. In 1753 he published *The Analysis of Beauty*, which set out to undermine the authority of connoisseurs and provide a commonsense approach to aesthetics. See cats. 147-8.
SELECTED LITERATURE: Oppé, 1948; Paulson, 1992-3; Bindman, 1997; Uglow, 1997.
RO

HOLLAND, HENRY (1745-1806)

Although he was the son of a builder, little is known about Holland's early education in architecture. By 1767 he was assisting his father with different projects, and in 1770 he was offered a partnership with Capability Brown, the landscape gardener and architect. Holland successfully collaborated with Brown on a number of commissions, in which he was responsible chiefly for the interior decoration. He married Brown's daughter in 1773. A contemporary of architects such as Sir John Soane and George Dance the Younger, who were known for their large professional practices, Holland preferred to focus on relatively few commissions, each undertaken as a complete design project, including the structure and interior fittings. Holland's interest in French design helped secure him the commission to redecorate Carlton House of the Prince of Wales, who admired the French style. His other major commissions in the 1780s included Althorp House for George, 2nd Earl Spencer, and Woburn Abbey for Francis Russell, 5th Duke of Bedford. In 1790 Holland was named Surveyor of the East India Company and designed their headquarters and warehouse. Throughout his career Holland participated in profitable building projects, including the design of Sloane Street and Sloane Square in London. See cat. 125.
SELECTED LITERATURE: Stroud, 1966.
MO

IBBETSON, JULIUS CAESAR (1759-1817)

The painter, printmaker, and watercolorist was apprenticed to a ship-painter in Hull and became a theatrical scene-painter. He moved to London in 1777 and exhibited portraits, genre scenes, and landscapes from 1785 at the Royal Academy. Ibbetson accompanied Colonel Charles Cathcart as his personal draftsman on the first British Mission to Bejiing and, after Cathcart's death, returned to London, where he concentrated mainly on landscapes derived from his frequent travels. Despite the considerable charm of Ibbetson's work, it appears not to have been commercially successful, and the artist left London for Liverpool in straitened circumstances in 1798, eventually settling in 1805 in Yorkshire. In 1803 he published his manual-cum-autobiography, *An Accidence, or Gamut, of Painting in Oils and Watercolours*. Ibbetson is now best known from his atmospheric and delicate watercolors, which are clearly indebted to seventeenth-century Dutch models. See cat. 93
SELECTED LITERATURE: Clay, 1948; Mitchell, 1999.
GF

JEFFERYS, JAMES (1751-1784)

The son of a portraitist and coach painter, James Jefferys was educated in his native Maidstone, Kent. In 1771 he began an apprenticeship to the engraver William Woollett in London, where he met fellow-artist and engraver John Hamilton Mortimer, who was to be a strong influence on his work. Jefferys also attended classes at the Royal Academy schools from 1772 to 1775, and he exhibited drawings of historical subjects there and at the Society of Arts. In 1774 he was awarded a gold medal from both institutions, an honor that helped him secure the support of the Society of Dilettanti, who sponsored a period of study in Rome from 1775 to 1778. While in Rome, he entered into the circle of the Swiss artist Henry Fuseli and became acquainted with George Romney. His activities between 1778 and 1782 are undocumented, but in 1783 he exhibited an ambitious history painting at the Royal Academy. He died the following year. See cat. 149.
SELECTED LITERATURE: Clifford and Legouix, 1976; Noon, 1979.
MO

JONES, THOMAS (1742-1803)

The son of a Welsh landowner, after matriculating from Jesus College, Oxford, Jones studied at William Shipley's drawing school and then became a pupil of Richard Wilson. Following the example of Wilson, he pursued Grand Manner historical landscape painting. The figures in his landscapes were sometimes provided by his friend John Hamilton Mortimer. Jones set out for Italy in the autumn of 1776, and remained in Italy until 1783, dividing his stay mostly between Rome and Naples. He was part of a community of British artists including William Pars, Francis Towne, and John "Warwick" Smith. His memoirs, written later from diaries he kept at the time, provide a lively and detailed account of the group. On his return to Britain, he lived in London until he inherited the family home at Pencerrig in 1789 and moved back to Wales. Though from the 1780s he did not make his living as a professional artist, he continued to exhibit at the Royal Academy until 1798. See cat. 101.
SELECTED LITERATURE: Oppé, 1951; Edwards, 1970; Gowing, 1985; Hawcroft, 1988.
SW

KENT, WILLIAM (BAP. 1685-1748)

Nothing is known of Kent until his apprenticeship to a coach-painter in Hull at the age of fifteen. Kent went to Italy in 1709, sponsored by a group of fellow-Yorkshiremen. After spending time in Livorno, Pisa, and Lucca, he remained in Florence for five months before leaving for Rome in 1710. He is thought to have attended classes at the Academy of San Luca, where he won second prize at their 1713 exhibition for students of painting with his drawing of a religious subject. The following year he was elected an associate member of the Florentine Accademia del Disegno. Kent focused on his painting throughout the decade, supporting himself through patrons and his work as an art dealer. One of his clients, Thomas Coke introduced Kent to Richard Boyle, 3rd Earl of Burlington and an admirer of Palladio. In 1720 Kent returned to England, where he immediately found work as an interior decorator for Kensington Palace. He was later appointed Master Mason and Deputy Surveyor in the Office of the Royal Works, and in this capacity he designed structures such as the Royal Mews, Treasury Buildings, and Horse Guards in London. Kent also produced numerous designs for private commissions in the Palladian and Gothick style, as well as working as a garden designer who championed informal layouts at Boyle's Chiswick House and at Stowe. See cat. 113.
SELECTED LITERATURE: Wilson, 1984; Wilton-Ely, 1985.
MO

LANGENDIJK, DIRK (1748-1805)

The Dutch draftsman, painter, and etcher Dirk Langendijk was born and died in Rotterdam. The pupil of Dirck Anthonie Bisschop, Langendijk specialized in battle pieces and in landscapes with scenes of military life. In the late 1780s and 1790s his work frequently depicted events in his country's civil war between the Patriots and Orangeists and the French and Anglo-Russian invasions. See cat. 76.
SW

LAWRENCE, THOMAS (1769-1830)

Though he had little formal art education, Lawrence showed great talent as a draftsman from an early age, and after meeting Sir Joshua Reynolds in 1787 Lawrence decided to devote himself to portraiture. The portraits he exhibited at the Royal Academy from 1787 established his reputation and quickly led to other successes, including receiving the title of Painter-in-Ordinary to George III, following his 1792 portrait of the king. As the Napoleonic wars drew to a close, he received a royal commission for a series of military portraits of the Allied leaders and traveled around Europe completing them. On his return to England in 1820 he was elected President of the Royal Academy. At his death he left behind one of the largest private collections of Old Master drawings and prints in England, which was offered to the nation for £18,000 but refused. The collection was eventually dispersed; some works are in the Ashmolean Museum, Oxford, and the British Museum. See cat. 13.
SELECTED LITERATURE: Levey, 1979; Garlick, 1989; Garlick, 1993.
ES

LENS, BERNARD III (1682-1740)

Bernard Lens III was the most successful member of a family of artists. Primarily a painter of portrait miniatures, he adopted the practice of painting in watercolor and gouache on an ivory support introduced by the Venetian artist Rosalba Carriera. Lens also copied Old Master paintings in miniature and worked as a topographical draftsman. He was the official limner to George I and George II. His sons Peter Paul Lens and Andrew Benjamin Lens followed their father's example, becoming painters in miniature and topographical artists, while a third son, John Lens, was active as a printmaker and drawing instructor. See cats. 16, 26-7, 43.
SELECTED LITERATURE: Fleming-Williams, 1968; Murdoch, Murrell and Noon, 1981; Sloan, 2000.
ES

LONG, AMELIA (1772-1837)

Amelia Long (née Hume) was a talented watercolorist and garden designer respected by her professional male peers. Nothing is known of her early education, but she demonstrated considerable artistic talent from a young age and may have been taught by a traditional drawing-master. Long's earliest known works are accomplished small-scale watercolor copies of oil paintings, close in style to the work of Bernard Lens III. Long became a pupil of Thomas Girtin and Henry Edridge in the 1790s, and was said to have been Girtin's favorite pupil. She painted in oil and watercolor, made soft-ground etchings, and experimented with lithography but was most accomplished as a draftsman. A keen and knowledgeable collector, Long was particularly interested in Dutch painting, and her husband Charles Long, whom she married in 1793, supported contemporary British artists. She was granted honorary status at the Royal Academy in 1807 and at the British Institution in 1825. See cat. 156.
SELECTED LITERATURE: Sidey, 1980; Sloan, 2000.
ES

LOUTHERBOURG, PHILIPPE JACQUES DE (1740-1812)

A native of Alsace, Loutherbourg trained with the Academic artist Carl Vanloo and attended the engraving academy of Jean-George Wille in Paris. Loutherbourg was influenced by seventeenth-century Dutch landscapes, and he was a frequent exhibitor of landscape scenes at the Paris Salon from 1762 to 1771; in 1766 he was elected as a member of the French Academy. In search of clients, Loutherbourg traveled to England after sojourns in Italy, Germany, and Switzerland. He was introduced to the actor-manager David Garrick upon his arrival in 1771, and he soon became the head stage-set designer at the Drury Lane theater, where he introduced many innovations such as the painted act-drop between scenes. Loutherbourg also continued his practice as a landscape painter, traveling throughout England and Wales in search of subject matter and exhibiting these works at the Royal Academy. After a period as a faith healer, he turned to subject pictures, exhibiting works at Macklin's Poet's Gallery and Boydell's Shakespeare Gallery, as well as history paintings at the Royal Academy and the Paris Salon. See cat. 50.

SELECTED LITERATURE: Joppien, 1973.

MO

MALTON, THOMAS (1748-1804)

The son of Thomas Malton the Elder (1726-1801), a cabinet-maker, professor of perspective, and architectural draftsman, and the brother of architect and architectural draftsman James Malton, Thomas Malton the Younger received his earliest instruction from his father. In 1773 Malton entered the Royal Academy schools as an architecture student, winning a premium from the Society of Arts in 1774 and a Royal Academy Gold Medal in 1782 for theater design. While he worked as a scenery painter for Covent Garden theater, he continued to exhibit architectural drawings and designs, chiefly at the Royal Academy, between 1773 and 1803. A master of perspective, he became a drawing-master in 1783, and his pupils included J. M. W. Turner, who praised his teacher in his 1811 lectures as the Royal Academy Professor of Perspective. Malton was known for his topographical views of London, which combined architectural accuracy with a sense of grandeur, traits evident in his 1791 volume of etchings with aquatint *A Picturesque Tour Through the Cities of London and Westminster*. Malton's designs for buildings were never executed, and he was never made a member of the Royal Academy. See cat. 129.

SELECTED LITERATURE: Wilton, 1977.

MO

MARLOW, WILLIAM (1740-1813)

William Marlow began his artistic training with the well-known marine and topographical painter Samuel Scott. Marlow studied with the older artist from 1756 to 1761, during which time he also attended classes at the St. Martin's Lane Academy in London. In 1765 he traveled throughout France and Italy to further his education and sketch landscapes and the ruins of antiquity. These sketches then provided the basis for oil paintings, many of which were exhibited at the Society of Artists and the Royal Academy. Marlow's work appealed to Grand Tourists, who purchased his views of Italy and at times commissioned landscape paintings of their own property. He also specialized in views of London. See cat. 95.

SELECTED LITERATURE: Howgego, 1956.

MO

MORTIMER, JOHN HAMILTON (1740-79)

Born in Eastbourne, Sussex, John Mortimer Hamilton moved to London in 1757, where he studied with the portraitist Thomas Hudson, the sculptor Cipriani, and the portrait and history painter Robert Edge Pine. In the 1760s Mortimer mostly exhibited portraits and conventional conversation pieces in the style of Johan Zoffany. Yet he was also developing as a history painter, frequently turning to themes from British history. During the 1770s he became known for his *banditti* scenes inspired by the seventeenth-century Italian painter Salvator Rosa. Mortimer was a prolific and accomplished draftsman as well as a painter, and most of his *banditti* scenes survive in the form of drawings rather than as oil paintings. Rosa was Mortimer's model, not only in his romantic subject matter, but also in his bohemian lifestyle. At the same time, Mortimer was entrenched in the art establishment. In 1765 he was elected a Fellow of the Society of Artists of Great Britain, becoming vice-president in 1770 and president in 1774. See cat. 33.

SELECTED LITERATURE: Nicholson, 1968 (1); Sunderland, 1988.

RO

NIXON, JOHN (1760-1818)

A merchant by trade, John Nixon was a prolific amateur artist, who is best known for his considerable output of caricatures and humorous drawings, which were strongly influenced by the work of his friend Thomas Rowlandson. Nixon traveled extensively in Britain and on the Continent, and his tours and wide-ranging interests, which included the visual arts, music, opera, and theater, provided subjects for his drawings. Nixon showed regularly at the Royal Academy, as an Honorary Exhibitor. See cat. 94.

SELECTED LITERATURE: Brown, 1994; Crown, 1998.

GF

OTTLEY, WILLIAM YOUNG (1771-1836)

Ottley first studied drawing with George Cuitt the Elder near Richmond, Yorkshire, and then entered the Royal Academy Schools in London, where he was taught by John Brown in 1787. After Brown's death in the same year, Ottley purchased the contents of his studio, which contained 219 drawings. From 1791 to 1799, Ottley traveled in Italy, studying, drawing, and building up what was to be a renowned collection of Italian Old Master drawings. Ottley was a skilled draftsman, but he remained an amateur, only exhibiting one work at the Royal Academy, *The Battle of the Angels* in 1833. When he returned to London in 1799, he began a career as an art dealer and writer. Ottley sold many of his prints and drawings in three important sales in 1804, 1807, and 1814, He wrote a number of books which reflect his interest in Italian art and the history and techniques of printmaking. In 1833 Ottley became the Keeper of Prints and Drawings at the British Museum and remained at this post until his death. See cat. 42.

SELECTED LITERATURE: Gere, 1958; Waterhouse, 1962.

RO

PARS, WILLIAM (1742-82)

Nothing is known of Pars's early training, although he was active as an artist in London as early as 1760, when he exhibited works at the Society of Artists and the Free Society of Artists. In 1764 he was awarded a prize from the Royal Society of Arts and was

chosen by the Society of Dilettanti to accompany Richard Chandler and Nicholas Revett on their journey to Asia Minor and Greece. Pars acted as draftsman on the expedition, and his views were published in 1769 as *Ionian Antiquities*. Some of Pars's work also appeared in the second volume of James "Athenian" Stuart's 1777 *Antiquities of Athens*. Pars exhibited some of his watercolor studies of Greece and Asia Minor at the Royal Academy in 1769, and in 1770 he was elected ARA. He traveled to Switzerland with Henry Temple, 2nd Viscount Palmerston in 1770, and produced views of Horace Walpole's Strawberry Hill in 1772. In 1775 the Society of Dilettanti sponsored Pars's trip to Rome, and he re-mained there until his death. See cat. 100.
MO

PATCH, THOMAS (1725-82)

The painter, engraver, and antiquarian Thomas Patch traveled to Rome in 1747, where he met Joshua Reynolds. He worked in Joseph Vernet's studio but was banished from the Papal States in 1755, apparently for a homosexual indiscretion, and settled in Florence, where he remained until his death. Through his friend and neighbor Sir Horace Mann (who noted, "though he does not live in my house, he is never out of it a whole day"), Patch was introduced to English Grand Tourists, for whom he painted views of Florence and copies of Old Masters. In the 1760s Patch etched and painted caricatures of well-known personalities in Anglo-Florentine society, which not only reflect his incisively satirical outlook, but are also the results of his extensive researches into physiognomy. See cat. 107.
SELECTED LITERATURE: Watson, 1940; Watson, 1967
GF

PLIMER, ANDREW (1763-1837)

Rebelling against apprenticeship in their father's Wellington clock-making shop, Andrew Plimer and his brothers left home to join a band of gypsies. Arriving in London in 1781, Andrew obtained a position as a personal servant to miniaturist Richard Cosway, who had been impressed by his copying abilities. In 1785 Plimer set up his own miniature portraiture studio in Hanover Square but moved his shop to the highly fashionable Golden Square only a year later. In 1801 he and his family left London, first traveling through Devon and Cornwall and settling for three years in Exeter in around 1815. The family returned to London after three years, but Plimer departed on an extensive tour throughout the British Isles soon thereafter. During his travels he painted numerous miniature portraits of the families in whose homes he stayed. The artist died in 1837, two years after a final relocation to the fashionable "Western Cottages" district of Brighton. See cat. 18.
SELECTED LITERATURE: Williamson, 1903.
ES

RAMBERG, JOHANN HEINRICH (1763-1840)

Although he lived in Germany for much of his life, Ramberg's studies under Benjamin West at the Royal Academy of Arts in London between 1781 and 1788 were a formative experience for his artistic career. It was in London that he first developed an interest in etchings and drawings in the English satiric tradition. Upon returning to Hannover in 1788, Ramberg received a major commission for the design of the Theater Leineschloss's stage curtain, which launched his reputation in Germany. After a tour of Italy in the early 1790s, during which he made drawings and watercolors of everyday life, he was appointed Hof und Cabinetsmaler in Hannover. Although Ramberg's satirical works were not well-received in Germany, his book illustrations were extremely popular there, and he illustrated the works of virtually every German contemporary writer. Late in life, he produced and published drawings of three narrative cycles and *Anweisung zum Zeichnen der menschlichen Gestalt*, an instruction manual on drawing the human form. See cat. 10.
SELECTED LITERATURE: Stuttmann, 1929; Rohr, 1998.
ES

RAMSAY, ALLAN (1713-84)

Born in Edinburgh, the eldest son of the Scottish poet of the same name, Allan Ramsay became the preeminent portrait painter in London in the mid-eighteenth century. Ramsay studied at the Academy of St. Luke in Edinburgh between 1729 and 1732 and moved to London where he worked under the acclaimed portrait painter Hans Hysing. After a period of further study in Rome, he returned to London and commenced a highly successful career as a portraitist. Ramsay also secured a place in intellectual circles in both London and Edinburgh; he established with David Hume and Adam Smith the Edinburgh debating club in 1754 and formed a friendship with William Hogarth who promoted Ramsay's treatise *Dialogue on Taste* (1755). A well-received portrait of George William Frederick, Prince of Wales, was followed by an invitation to become the Principal Painter-in-Ordinary of His Majesty, after the Prince's accession as George II in 1761. In 1773 Ramsay suffered a crippling accident to his left arm which forced his retirement from active involvement in his large and very productive studio. He made further visits to Italy, from 1775 to 1777, and again in 1782 when he worked on a treatise on Horace's Sabine villa. Ramsay died on his return to England in 1784. See cats. 3, 153.
SELECTED LITERATURE: Smart, 1992 (1); Smart, 1992 (2); Smart, 1999.
ES

REPTON, HUMPHRY (1752-1818)

Repton attended Norwich Grammar School, and after three years in the Netherlands returned to Norwich, where he was apprenticed to a local textile merchant. After a brief stint in business with his father, he moved to Norfolk to become a "gentleman farmer." Repton traveled to Ireland as William Windham's secretary and served as his election manager upon

his entry into Parliament in 1784. During this time Repton educated himself about estate management and arboriculture, the cultivation of trees. In 1788 he become a landscape gardener, a term he actually coined. Repton's skill as a watercolorist was an important means of attracting clients, and as part of the commission he would present them with beautifully drawn volumes of his designs for their parks known as "Red Books." In 1794 he published his treatise *Sketches and Hints on Landscape Gardening*, which advocated the importance of utility in garden design. In the 1790s Repton formed an important partnership with the architect John Nash that was dissolved in 1800 due to financial disagreements. His most profitable partnership was with his son John Adey Repton (1775-1860); together they popularized the "Queen Elizabeth Gothic" and the picturesque cottage. After an accident in 1811 Repton was confined to a wheelchair for the remainder of his life, and he concentrated on smaller domestic designs until his death. See cat. 115.
SELECTED LITERATURE: Daniels, 1999.
MO

RICHARDSON, GEORGE (C. 1736-1813)

Richardson began his career as an apprentice in the office of Robert and James Adam, where he trained as a draftsman. He accompanied James Adam on his Grand Tour to Italy from 1760 to 1763 and studied ancient architecture. Upon his return to England Richardson continued to work with the Adam brothers. He exhibited drawings at the Royal Academy and at the Society of Artists in London under his own name, and he was awarded a premium in 1765. Richardson designed few buildings, working instead as an interior decorator and drawing-master. He also published numerous treatises on architecture and design, such as *A Treatise of the Five Orders of Architecture* (1787) and *The New Vitruvius Britannicus* in two volumes (1802-08) to illustrate "the taste and science of the English nation in its style of Architecture at the close of the eighteenth century." See cat. 122.
SELECTED LITERATURE: Fleming, 1962.
MO

RICHARDSON, JONATHAN (THE ELDER) (1665-1745)

An apprentice in the portrait painter John Riley's studio, Richardson lived in his master's house and married his niece. Although his early work was much in Riley's manner, by the second decade of the eighteenth century Richardson had evolved his own style, and in the early 1730s was considered by George Vertue one of the three foremost portraitists of the day. In 1715 he published his highly influential *Essay on the Theory of Painting*, which was the first significant work of artistic theory by an English author. Richardson was an inveterate draftsman and devoted his retirement to drawing portraits of himself, his family, and friends. He also amassed an important collection of Old Master drawings. Successful both as an artist and writer, Richardson died, a wealthy man, in 1745. See cats. 1-2.
SELECTED LITERATURE: Gibson-Wood, 2000.
ES

RIOU, STEPHEN (1720-80)

The son of a London merchant of French Huguenot ancestry, Riou was an English citizen who served in the army as Captain in the 2nd Troop of Horse Grenadier Guards. In 1743 he was studying architecture at the University of Geneva, and in 1746 he published *The Elements of Fortification*. In the late 1740s and early 1750s he acted as a tour guide in Italy and Greece. He met with James "Athenian" Stuart and Charles Revett during their celebrated expedition and accompanied them to Athens. By 1760 Riou had returned to England, where he competed in buildings competitions without success. In fact, no building by Riou is known to exist, although he was a prolific draftsman who produced many proposed designs for royal palaces, country villas, and London streets. Riou played a leading role in the promotion of the Greek Revival in Britain. In 1768 he published with a dedication to James Stuart *The Grecian Orders of Architecture Delineated and Explained from the Antiquities of Athens*, an architectural treatise which demonstrated how elements of Greek architecture could be incorporated into Palladian designs. See cat. 119.
SELECTED LITERATURE: Harris, 1990.
MO

ROOKER, MICHAEL "ANGELO" (1746-1801)

Michael Rooker learned engraving from his father Edward Rooker, an engraver and pantomime actor, before becoming a pupil of Paul Sandby. It was Sandby who nicknamed him "Michael Angelo." Rooker entered the Royal Academy Schools in 1769 and became one of the first Associates of the Royal Academy in 1770, exhibiting regularly at the Academy between 1769 and 1800. From 1779 he worked as a scene painter at the Theatre Royal, Haymarket. Beginning in the late 1780s, he made annual autumnal walking tours through England and Wales, which provided material for his topographical watercolors. See cats. 90, 139.
SELECTED LITERATURE: Conner, 1984.
SW

ROMNEY, GEORGE (1734-1802)

Apprenticed to the itinerant painter Christopher Steele in 1755, Romney set up his own portrait practice in Kendal in 1757 and moved to London in 1762. Portrait painting was a lucrative profession for Romney, yet throughout his life he aspired to be a history painter. Due to the constraints of patronage, however, Romney's passion for historical subject matter was generally expressed only in his fluent drawings, which he produced in great numbers. In 1773 he went to Rome, where he was closely associated with Henry Fuseli's circle and developed a drawing style characterized by simplified forms, histrionic gestures, and broadly applied wash. Romney returned to London two years later to resume his portrait practice. His portraits were in great demand through most of the 1780s, but during the 1790s his health declined and he produced little. See cats. 38, 108.
SELECTED LITERATURE: Ward and Roberts, 1904; Chamberlain, 1910; Wark, 1970.
RO

ROWLANDSON, THOMAS (1756-1827)

The accomplished caricaturist, draftsman, and engraver Thomas Rowlandson was a highly perceptive chronicler of late eighteenth- and early nineteenth-century British life, whose output of drawings and prints was prodigious. Raised by a wealthy aunt in London, Rowlandson studied at the Royal Academy Schools for two years and in 1775 first exhibited at the Royal Academy. In 1784 he made the first of several sketching tours, traveling from Salisbury to Portsmouth; in the same year he exhibited three works at the Royal Academy, but by 1787 he had ceased to exhibit. Rowlandson inherited a considerable fortune from his aunt Jane, but he rapidly squandered his inheritance by gambling and was virtually destitute by 1797 when Rudolph Ackermann employed him as an illustrator. In the following twenty years Rowlandson was extraordinarily prolific, producing drawings for publications including *The Microcosm of London* (1808) in collaboration with Augustus Charles Pugin, *The Tour of Dr. Syntax* (1809), and *The English Dance of Death* (1814-16). See cats. 7, 75, 86-9, 154.
SELECTED LITERATURE: Wark, 1975; Baskett and Snelgrove, 1977; Riely, 1978; Hayes, 1990.
ES

RUSSELL, JOHN (1745-1806)

Born in Guildford, Surrey, John Russell was the son of a bookseller, printseller, and amateur artist. After winning premiums for his drawings from the Society of Artists in 1759 and 1760, Russell was apprenticed to the portraitist Francis Cotes. By 1767 he had established his London studio, catering to a fashionable clientele, and he exhibited at the Society of Artists in 1768 and at the Royal Academy between 1769 and 1806. He entered the Royal Academy Schools in 1770 and was elected Associate of the Royal Academy in 1772 and Royal Academician in 1788. In the same year he was named Crayon Painter to George III and to George, Prince of Wales. Russell's interests and talents, however, were not limited to the portrait studio, and he was a dedicated amateur lunar astronomer whose work was highly regarded by his scientific contemporaries. Russell also published a manual on pastel techniques, *Elements of Painting with Crayons* (1772). See cats. 15, 57.
SELECTED LITERATURE: Williamson, 1894.
ES

RYSBRACK, MICHAEL (1684-1770)

Baptized Johannes Michel Rysbrack in Antwerp in 1684, the sculptor Michael Rysbrack was the most accomplished member of an artistic Antwerp family. It is likely that he trained from 1706 to 1712 under Michiel van der Voort I in Antwerp. In 1720 he moved to London with his brother Pieter Andreas Rysbrack, who was a still-life and landscape painter, and remained there for the rest of his life. Rysbrack was England's foremost monumental, architectural, and portrait sculptor in England in the 1720s and 1730s. Rysbrack worked for the preeminent architects of his age, including James Gibbs, William

Kent, and Robert Adam. He popularized the two distinctive types of portrait bust: the informal presentation of the sitter *en négligé* (in contemporary indoor dress) and the formal presentation of the sitter *all'antica* (in the guise of a Roman senator or general). Like many other Flemish sculptors, including his teacher, Michiel van der Voort I, Rysbrack was a distinguished draftsman. See cats. 30, 152.
SELECTED LITERATURE: Webb, 1954; Eustace, 1982.
RO

SANDBY, PAUL (1730-1809)

The son of a Nottingham textile worker and the younger brother of the architect and topographical draftsman Thomas Sandby, Paul Sandby followed his brother in taking a position as a military draftsman for the Board of Ordinance at the Tower of London in 1747. Soon thereafter, he was appointed official draftsman to the Military Survey in Scotland, making maps of the Highlands and topographical drawings. He returned to London in about 1751, establishing himself as a drawing-master, printmaker, and painter of topographical landscapes. He was a founding member of the Royal Academy in 1768, and from 1768 to 1796 he was chief drawing-master at the Royal Military Academy at Woolwich. His *XII Views in South Wales* (1776), made pioneering use of the medium of aquatint. See cats. 56, 134-6, 138, 155.
SELECTED LITERATURE: Oppé, 1947; Robertson, 1985; Herrmann, 1986.
ES

SANDBY, THOMAS (1721-98)

The architect and topographical draftsman Thomas Sandby described himself as self-taught, but in his youth he was apprenticed to land surveyors in his home county of Nottingham. In 1741 he was appointed to the Board of Ordnance's drawing office in the Tower of London, where he was responsible for maps, surveys, and topographical records. In 1743 he became draftsman to William Augustus, Duke of Cumberland, the Chief Engineer of Scotland, and accompanied him on his military campaigns. Three years later Cumberland named him the Deputy Ranger of Windsor Great Park, a position that Sandby was to hold for the rest of his life. The most important project he executed as Deputy Ranger was the creation of Virginia Water, a landscape garden that contained what was then the largest artificial lake in Britain. In 1752 Sandby moved to London, becoming active in societies to promote and teach the fine arts. He was a founder-member of the Royal Academy, established in 1768, as well as its first Professor of Architecture. Sandby's most important architectural work was Freemasons' Hall, on Great Queen Street in London (1775-76; destroyed 1932). Although Sandby was neither an outstanding designer nor a profound theorist, he played an important role in promoting the profession of architect in eighteenth-century England. See cat. 137.
SELECTED LITERATURE: Oppé, 1947; Herrmann, 1986.
RO

SERRES, JOHN THOMAS (1759-1825)

John Thomas Serres was the son and pupil of the marine painter Dominic Serres. He also studied at the Royal Academy Schools from 1776 and from 1780 exhibited seascapes at the Royal Academy and later at the British Institution. On his father's death in 1793, he succeeded him as marine painter to King George III. He became marine draftsman to the Admiralty in 1800, and in that capacity produced coastal profiles of France and Spain, a selection of which were published in 1801 with the title *The Little Sea Torch*. Serres taught drawing at the Chelsea Naval School and in 1805 published the *Liber Nauticus, and Instructor in the Art of Marine Drawing*. An unfortunate marriage led to financial difficulties and a loss of royal favor, and Serres died in debtor's prison. See cats. 72-3.

SW

SKELTON, JONATHAN (D. 1759)

Apart from a group of watercolors of Croydon, London, Rochester, and Canterbury bearing dates between 1754 and 1757, little of Skelton's life is known prior to his journey to Italy in 1757. An inscription on a drawing of the Archbishop's Palace in Croydon indicates that Skelton was a footman in the employ of the Archbishop Thomas Herring. He seems to have been a pupil of the landscape painter George Lambert. In contrast to the scanty evidence for his life in England, his period in Italy is well documented through a series of letters he wrote to William Herring, a cousin of the Archbishop. In September 1757 Skelton sailed from Portsmouth to Leghorn, arriving in Rome in December of that year. In Rome, studying the works of Claude and Gaspard Dughet and painting from nature (his letters report that he painted outdoors both in watercolors and oils), he sought to transcend the topographical limitations of his English work and become a landscape painter; however, he found it difficult to sell his landscapes and lived in conditions of personal deprivation. He died of a fever in Rome in early 1759. See cats. 132-3.

SELECTED LITERATURE: Ford, 1960; Pierce, 1960.

SW

SMART, JOHN (1742/3-1811)

At the age of twelve, John Smart began to exhibit at the Society of Arts, winning prizes for his chalk drawings in three consecutive children's competitions. Around 1760 he dedicated himself to miniature portraiture, evolving a distinctive style characterized by its meticulous attention to detail and brilliance of color. He continued to exhibit his work at the Society of Arts until 1783 and in 1778 became the Society's President. In 1785 he obtained permission from the East India Company to travel to Madras, attracted by the notion that English artists could make large sums of money on the subcontinent. Smart was extremely successful in Madras, and worked as miniature painter to Muhammad Ali, the Nawab of Arcot, and his family, and also received commissions from government officials, army officers, and English residents. A decade later he re-

turned to London where he remarried and resided in Fitzroy Square. In 1809 Smart went back to Madras, but died shortly after his arrival there. See cats. 24-5.

SELECTED LITERATURE: Foskett, 1964.

ES

SMITH, JOHN "WARWICK" (1749-1831)

John "Warwick" Smith first studied under the animal painter Sawrey Gilpin. While traveling to Derbyshire with Gilpin, Smith came into contact with George Greville, 2nd Earl of Warwick. The Earl funded Smith's stay in Italy from 1776 to 1781, where Smith explored Rome and Southern Italy while sketching with William Pars and Francis Towne. Upon his return to England, Smith settled in Warwick, although he took frequent sketching trips throughout England and Wales and produced volumes such as *Twenty Views of the Lake District* (1791-5). Although Turner described Smith's views as "mechanically systematic," he achieved great success in his lifetime, eventually becoming President of the Society of Painters in Water-Colours in 1814. See cat. 74.

MO

SOANE, SIR JOHN (1753-1837)

The son of a bricklayer, Soane trained in the office of George Dance the Younger from 1768 to 1772. In 1771 he entered the Royal Academy Schools and in 1776 won a gold medal for the design of a bridge. With the intervention of Sir William Chambers, Soane secured the Academy's traveling scholarship to Rome, where he met Piranesi and potential clients such as William Pitt. He returned to London in 1780, where he built up his practice through commissions for small country houses. Soane's practice grew throughout the following decades, and he began to employ draftsmen and take on pupils. When William Pitt became Prime Minister, he appointed Soane as Surveyor of the Bank of England in 1788. He was responsible for the expansion and renovation of the structure, a project that occupied him for the rest of his life. Soane built his own house, at No. 13, Lincoln's Inn Fields, which housed his extraordinary collection of architectural fragments and casts, paintings and drawings, architectural drawings and books; he also designed the first public picture gallery in Europe, the Dulwich College Picture Gallery. In 1806 Soane was appointed Professor of Architecture at the Royal Academy, and in 1832 he was knighted upon his retirement from the Office of Works. See cats. 124, 126.

SELECTED LITERATURE: Stroud, 1984; Watkin, 1996; Richardson and Stevens, 1999.

MO

Stubbs, George (1724-1806)

A largely self-taught artist from Liverpool, George Stubbs began his career in the service of a provincial artist, copying pictures in the collection of Edward Stanley, the 11th Earl of Derby. In about 1745 Stubbs moved to York to study anatomy, and in 1751 he designed and engraved the illustrations for John Burton's *Essay Towards a Complete New System of Midwifery*. In 1756 Stubbs began an intensive study of equine anatomy that culminated in his 1766 publication, *The Anatomy of the Horse*. By the end of the 1750s, Stubbs had established himself in London, attracting the patronage of noblemen with a penchant for breeding and racing horses. Noted for his portraits of horses and dogs, Stubbs also painted exotic animals, animals in conflict, scenes of rural life, and historical subjects. Between 1761 and 1774 Stubbs exhibited with the Society of Artists, serving as its President in 1772-3. In collaboration with Sir Josiah Wedgwood, Stubbs devised a method of painting in enamel on ceramic plaques. He was also a highly accomplished and innovative printmaker, and his few surviving drawings demonstrate his extraordinary skills as a draftsman. In 1795 Stubbs embarked on a major project, a comparative anatomical exposition of the structure of the human body with that of a tiger and a common fowl, which was uncompleted at his death. See cats. 64-8, 150.

SELECTED LITERATURE: Doherty, 1974; Egerton, 1984 (2); Lennox-Boyd, Dixon and Clayton, 1989.
ES

Taverner, William (1700-72)

A lawyer by profession, William Taverner was a highly gifted and pioneering amateur artist. Taverner became well-known in artistic circles by 1733, and George Vertue noted that he had "a wonderful genius to drawing of Landskap in an excellent manner ... adorned with figures in a stile above the common ... & paints in oil in a very commendable & masterly manner." None of Taverner's oil paintings are now known, and his reputation is based on his surviving watercolors. Taverner was influenced by seventeenth-century classical landscape painters, such as Claude Lorrain, Gaspard Dughet, Nicolas Poussin, and Cornelis van Poelenbergh, to whom his *Nymphs Bathing in a Glade* (Yale Center for British Art; cat. 44) is clearly indebted. His use of the watercolor medium for historical landscapes was highly innovative in England at the period, and his work seems to have been influential for professional artists. Paul Sandby owned at least twenty landscapes by Taverner. See cat. 44.
SELECTED LITERATURE: Hardie, 1967-8, vol. III; Sloan, 2000.
GF

Thornhill, Sir James (1675-1734)

The celebrated English baroque decorative painter James Thornhill began his career working as an apprentice to Thomas Highmore, who specialized in decorative painting. Although Thornhill received little formal training, working with Highmore on commissions in large houses gave him the opportunity to see the work of foreign decorative painters such as Louis Chéron, Antonio Verrio, and Louis Laguerre, and these artists were important formative influences. By the early 1700s Thornhill was working on his own and was the only English painter to compete successfully with foreign artists for the few large-scale decorative commissions in England in the early eighteenth century. Thornhill's most important commissions were the upper and lower halls and vestibule at the Royal Naval Hospital in Greenwich (1705-27) and the interior of the dome of St. Paul's Cathedral, London (1714-17). In 1718 Thornhill was made History Painter in Ordinary to the King, and in 1720 Sergeant-Painter to the King. He was also the first English-born artist to be knighted. See cats. 145-6.
SELECTED LITERATURE: Osmun, 1950; Croft-Murray, 1962-70.
ES

Towne, Francis (1739-1816)

Francis Towne was apprenticed to a coach painter in London in 1752. He attended the St. Martin's Lane Academy and, after he moved to Exeter in the 1760s, he set himself up as a drawing-master and began painting landscape views and portraits of country houses. In 1777 Towne toured Wales with his patron James White and produced a number of watercolors based on drawings made on the tour. Towne traveled to Rome in 1780, where he excelled in the depiction of architecture and began the practice of carefully noting the date and time that he executed his watercolor studies. He also toured Switzerland, where he became interested in the Sublime effects of the mountainous landscape. Although Towne tried unsuccessfully to gain entry into the Royal Academy and establish a clientele in London, his work for the most part was focused in his native Devon. See cat. 52.
SELECTED LITERATURE: Oppé, 1920.
MO

Turner, Joseph Mallord William (1775-1851)

The painter, watercolorist, and printmaker J.M.W. Turner is the most famous British artist of the Romantic period, celebrated both for his extraordinary technical virtuosity and "wonderful range of mind," as John Constable noted so memorably. Born in London, Turner demonstrated considerable artistic talent from a young age, and after working as an architectural draftsman in the offices of Thomas Hardwick and Thomas Malton, he entered the Royal Academy Schools at the age of fourteen. Turner's earliest exhibited works were watercolors of architectural subjects, and he continued to produce topographical subjects throughout his career. Turner became familiar with the watercolors of John Robert Cozens and Edward Dayes through copying them at the "academy" of Thomas Monro, which he attended with his friend Thomas Girtin, and these artistic predecessors were important influences on his early topographical drawings. An extraordinarily accomplished and innovative watercolorist, Turner constantly experimented with the medium, and there is a close and reciprocal relationship between his watercolor and oil techniques. His output of watercolors, including presentation drawings, models for prints, and working sketches, was prodigious; in addition to the numerous drawings Turner sold in his lifetime, some 20,000 sheets of watercolor studies remained in his studio at his death, and are now part of the Turner Bequest at the Tate Gallery, London. See cat. 144.

SELECTED LITERATURE: Wilton, 1979; Gage, 1987; Townsend, 1996.

GF

VANBRUGH, SIR JOHN (1664-1726)

Born in London to a Dutch father and an English mother, John Vanbrugh worked briefly in the wine trade, before accepting the first of what would be many military commissions. He became a highly successful playwright, acclaimed for such late Restoration comedies as *The Provok'd Wife* (1697), and finally settled on a career as an architect in 1699. Even though he was, according to Jonathan Swift, "without thought or lecture" in architectural training, Vanbrugh became one of the leading architects of the English baroque style. He launched his architectural career spectacularly by designing one of the most renowned estates in Great Britain, Castle Howard for Charles Howard, 3rd Earl of Carlisle, and then proceeded to work on Blenheim Palace for John Churchill, 1st Duke of Marlborough. Vanbrugh reached the pinnacle of the architectural profession in the eighteenth century as Comptroller of His Majesty's Works, becoming the colleague of Sir Christopher Wren. In 1711 he formed part of the Commission for building Fifty New Churches throughout London and its suburbs. He became the favored architect of the Whig aristocracy, and he was subsequently removed from his post under a Tory government in 1713. See cat. 110.

SELECTED LITERATURE: Downes, 1987.

MO

VISPRÉ, FRANÇOIS-XAVIER (FL. 1730-90)

François-Xavier Vispré began his career in Paris as an engraver of portraits in mezzotint. It is not known when he came to England, but by 1760 he had established himself in London as a painter and draftsman specializing in miniatures, portraits, and small genre scenes. Vispré exhibited regularly until 1783 at the Society of Artists and was elected a Fellow of the Society in 1771. Vispré experimented with painting on glass and in 1774 produced some of the earliest aquatints made in England. In 1776 he moved to Dublin but returned to London by the end of the decade. See cat. 6.

SELECTED LITERATURE: Noon, 1979.

ES

WEBBER, JOHN (1751-93)

Born in London to the Swiss sculptor Abrahm Wäber, John Webber was sent to Berne for schooling in 1757. He was later apprenticed to the Swiss landscape painter Johann Ludwig Aberli and studied at the Académie Royale in Paris before returning to London in 1775 and entering the Royal Academy Schools. From 1776 to 1780 he served as the official artist for Captain James Cook's third Pacific voyage. Back in London he supervised the engraving of his drawings of the voyage for the official account published as *A Voyage to the Pacific Ocean* in 1784. A proof set of soft-ground etchings of South Sea views, on which he worked between 1788 and 1792, is in the Yale Center for British Art. These were aquatinted and published as *Views in the South Seas* in 1808. From 1786 Webber made a number of sketching tours in the west of England, Wales, Derbyshire, the Lake District, and the Isle of Wight. Having been elected Associate of the Royal Academy in 1785, he became a full Academician in 1791. See cat. 54.

SELECTED LITERATURE: Joppien and Smith, 1985-8, vol. 3; Hauptman, 1996.

SW

WEST, BENJAMIN (1738-1820)

Born to a Quaker family in Pennsylvania, West began painting portraits in 1752. In 1756 he moved to Philadelphia where he received art lessons from William Williams and John Valentine Heidt. Thanks to the financial support of two leading Philadelphia families, the Allens and the Shippens, West took a study-trip in Italy from 1760 to 1763, during which he studied with Anton Raphael Mengs and Gavin Hamilton. After Italy, West went to England where he remained for the rest of his life. West soon became the foremost history painter in England and was perhaps the greatest promoter of the neoclassical style in all of Europe. West brought a new realism to history painting with works such as *The Death of General Wolfe* (exhibited 1771), which depicted a contemporary subject with figures wearing modern dress. West helped found the Royal Academy in 1768 and became its second president. He was a leading figure in British art, as well as a mentor for American artists who came to London to study with him, including Gilbert Stuart, Charles Wilson Peale, and John Trumbull. Although West was American, he was able to retain George III's favor during the American Revolution, but in the 1790s he was criticized as a French sympathizer, and a visit to France in 1802 ended the king's patronage. By 1805 West had found a new wealthy patron, William Beckford. See cat. 151.

SELECTED LITERATURE: Erffa and Staley, 1986; Staley, 1989.

RO

WESTALL, RICHARD (1765-1836)

Westall was apprenticed to a silver engraver named John Thompson from 1779 to 1784, but the miniaturist John Alefounder convinced him to become a painter instead, and in 1785 he entered the Royal Academy Schools. Westall became an ARA in 1792 and an RA in 1794. He exhibited over three hundred works at the Royal Academy between 1784 and 1836. His first entries were chalk portrait drawings, but he soon became known for his watercolors of figural subjects. Westall also produced many small oil paintings of domestic subjects and some large history paintings, several of which were commissioned by Boydell's Shakespeare Gallery and Bowyer and Macklin's historic and poetic galleries. Westall's greatest accomplishments, however, were his book illustrations, such as those for Milton's poetical works (1794-7). Towards the end of his career, Westall experienced financial difficulties, and worked as a drawing-master to Princess Victoria. See cat. 41.
SELECTED LITERATURE: Warner, 1979-80; Westall, 1984.
RO

WHEATLEY, FRANCIS (1747-1801)

Francis Wheatley received his first training at William Shipley's school in London, and from 1769 he attended the Royal Academy Schools. He won numerous prizes throughout the 1760s from the Society of Artists for his portraits and conversation pieces on a small scale, as well as landscape subjects. Wheatley enjoyed a fashionable lifestyle, but lived beyond his means, and in 1779 he moved to Dublin to escape his creditors. Upon his return to London in 1783, he formed a lucrative association with publisher and impresario John Boydell; in addition to producing pictures for Boydell's Shakespeare Gallery, Wheatley was commissioned to illustrate novels and produce genre subjects for popular engraving. It was Boydell who commissioned his *Cries of London* to record the itinerant street merchants of the city, a work that secured his popularity and reputation. During this period he continued to produce oil paintings, and he was elected RA in 1791. See cat. 91.
SELECTED LITERATURE: Webster, 1970.
MO

WILSON, RICHARD (C. 1713/1714-82)

Richard Wilson, the foremost landscape painter of his generation and chief proponent of the classical landscape in England, began his career as a portrait painter. The son of a prominent clergyman in Wales, Wilson received an extensive classical education before studying with the portrait painter Thomas Wright in London in 1729. By the 1740s Wilson was established as a portraitist, but he left his London practice in 1750 for Italy, where he devoted himself to landscape painting. Wilson returned to London in 1757, where he established a studio and exhibition rooms for himself in fashionable Covent Garden. He was a founding member of the Royal Academy in 1768 and served as its librarian in 1776. His fortunes declined in the 1770s, and he returned to Wales in about 1780.

See cats. 98-9, 106.
SELECTED LITERATURE: Ford, 1951; Constable, 1953; Solkin, 1982.
MO

WRIGHT, JOSEPH (OF DERBY) (1734-97)

After training in the London studio of the portrait painter Thomas Hudson from 1751 to 1753, Joseph Wright returned to his native Derby to set up a successful portrait practice with a clientele drawn both from the landed gentry and the middle classes. Wright also specialized in painting atmospheric artificially lit, figure subjects, such as *A Philosopher Lecturing on an Orrery* (1766) and *Experiment on a Bird in the Air Pump* (1768), which explore philosophical and scientific themes, and reflect Wright's close personal association with the scientific community. In 1773 and 1774 Wright traveled in Italy, where he made studies from the Sistine Chapel, drew classical sculpture and architecture, and sketched scenes in the Campagna and Kingdom of Naples. His travels also inspired him to produce thirty paintings depicting the eruption of Mount Vesuvius, which he witnessed in 1774. On his return Wright set up a portrait practice in Bath, but returned to Derby in 1777. See cat. 12.
SELECTED LITERATURE: Nicolson, 1968 (2); Egerton, 1990.
ES

YENN, JOHN (1750-1821)

In 1764 Yenn became a pupil in the office of Sir William Chambers, the foremost architect then working in London. While with Chambers, he attended the newly established Royal Academy Schools, where he was awarded a gold medal in 1771 for his design of an aristocratic villa. Yenn was the chief architectural draftsman and perspective artist in Chambers's practice, and he assisted Chambers with the Somerset House project throughout the 1770s. Yenn was elected an associate of the Royal Academy in 1774 and became a full Academician in 1791. Although he maintained a small practice as a architect, he achieved his greatest measure of recognition as an architectural draftsman. From 1781 Yenn occupied various government architectural positions or clerkships, first at Richmond Park and then at Buckingham Palace and Kensington Palace. In 1791 he was a founding member of the Architect's Club, a group of Royal Academy architects who hoped to focus great attention on the education of the architect within the Academy. Yenn succeeded Chambers as Treasurer of the Royal Academy in 1796. His important collection of architectural drawings is now in the Royal Academy's collection. See cat. 127.
MO

AFA, *British Watercolors, 1985-6*: *British Watercolors: Drawings of the 18th and 19th Centuries from the Yale Center for British Art,* American Federation of Arts tour, 1985-6, catalogue by Scott Wilcox.

AIA, *Architect and the British Country House, 1985. The Architect and the British Country House, 1620-1920,* The Octagon (The American Institute of Architects), Washington, DC, 1985, catalogue by John Harris.

Agnew, *Master Drawings, 1974*: *Master Drawings and Prints,* Thomas Agnew and Sons, London, 1974.

AGO, *Cozens, 1986-7*: *Alexander and John Robert Cozens: The Poetry of Landscape,* Art Gallery of Ontario and Victoria & Albert Museum, London, 1986-7, catalogue by Kim Sloan.

Arts Council, *Gainsborough Drawings, 1960-1*: *Gainsborough Drawings,* Arts Council, London, tour, 1960-1.

Arts Council, *Stubbs, 1958*: *George Stubbs: Rediscovered Anatomical Drawings from the Worcester Free Library, Worcester, Massachusetts,* Arts Council. London, 1958.

Beinecke, *Grand Tour, 1998*: *The Grand Tour,* Beinecke Rare Book and Manuscript Library, Yale University, New Haven, 1998, catalogue by John Marciari.

Bern, *Webber, 1996*: *John Webber, 1751-1793, Pacific Voyager and Landscape Artist,* Kunstmuseum, Bern, and Whitworth Art Gallery, Manchester, 1996, catalogue by William Hauptman.

Birmingham, *Canaletto & England, 1993-4*: *Canaletto & England,* Birmingham Museums and Art Gallery, 1993-4, catalogue edited by Michael Liversidge and Jane Farrington.

Birmingham, *Wilson, 1948-9*: *Richard Wilson and his Circle,* Birmingham City Museum and Art Gallery, and Tate Gallery, London, 1948-9.

Colnaghi-Yale, *English Drawings, 1964-5*: P. & D. Colnaghi & Co. Ltd., London, and Yale University Art Gallery, New Haven, *English Drawings and Watercolours from the Collection of Mr. and Mrs. Paul Mellon, 1964-5.*

Cooper-Hewitt, *Adam and His Style, 1982*: *City Dwellings and Country Houses: Robert Adam and His Style,* Cooper-Hewitt Museum, New York, 1982.

Courtauld, *Chambers, 1996. Sir William Chambers: Architect to George III,* Courtauld Gallery, London, 1996, and National Museum, Stockholm, 1997, catalogue edited by John Harris and Michael Snodin.

Denver, *Glorious Nature, 1993-4*: *Glorious Nature: British Landscape Painting, 1750-1850,* Denver Art Museum, 1993-4, catalogue by Katharine Baetjer *et al.*

Dublin, *Irish Portraits, 1969*: *Irish Portraits, 1660-1860,* National Gallery of Art, Dublin, 1969, catalogue by Anne Crookshank and the Knight of Glin.

Eastbourne, *Mortimer, 1968*: *John Hamilton Mortimer ARA 1740-1779,* Towner Art Gallery, Eastbourne, and Iveagh Bequest, Kenwood, London, 1968, catalogue by Benedict Nicolson.

Frick, *Rowlandson, 1990*: *The Art of Thomas Rowlandson,* The Frick Collection, New York, The Frick Art Museum, Pittsburgh, PA, and Baltimore Museum of Art, MD, 1990, catalogue by John Hayes.

Grand Palais, *Gainsborough, 1981*: *Gainsborough, 1727-1788,* Grand Palais, Paris, 1981.

Guildhall, *Canaletto in England, 1959*: *Canaletto in England,* Guildhall Art Gallery, London, 1959.

Guildhall, *Marlow, 1956*: *William Marlow, 1740-1813,* Guildhall Art Gallery, London, 1956.

Hall & Knight, *Stubbs, 2000*: *Fearful Symmetry: The Art of George Stubbs, Painter of the Enlightenment,* Hall & Knight (USA) Ltd., New York, 2000.

IEF, *Gainsborough Drawings, 1983-4*: *Gainsborough Drawings,* International Exhibition Foundation tour, 1983-4, catalogue by John Hayes and Lindsay Stainton.

Kenwood, *Gardner, 1972*: *Daniel Gardner 1750-1805,* Iveagh Bequest, Kenwood, London, 1972, catalogue by Helen Kapp.

Kenwood, *Gilpin, 1959*: *William Gilpin and the Picturesque,* Iveagh Bequest, Kenwood, London, 1959.

LACMA, *Visions of Antiquity, 1993-4*: *Visions of Antiquity: Neoclassical Figure Drawings,* Los Angeles County Museum of Art, 1993, Phila-delphia Museum of Art, 1993-4, and Minneapolis Institute of Arts, 1994, catalogue by Richard J. Campbell and Victor Carlson.

Marble Hill, *Jones, 1970*: *Thomas Jones (1742-1803),* Marble Hill House, Twickenham, and National Museum of Wales, Cardiff, 1970.

MC, *Collections Parisiennes, 1950*: *Chefs d'oeuvre des collections Parisiennes,* Musée Carnavalet, Paris, 1950.

MMA, *Canaletto, 1989-90*: *Canaletto,* Metropolitan Museum of Art, New York, 1989-90, catalogue by Katharine Baetjer and J.G. Links.

Munich, *Englische Malerei, 1979-80*: *Zwei Jahrhunderte Englische Malerei: Britische Kunst und Europa 1680 bis 1880,* Haus der Kunst, Munich, 1979-80.

Museum of London, *Quiet Conquest, 1985*: *The Quiet Conquest: The Huguenots 1685 to 1985,* Museum of London, 1985, catalogue by Tessa Murdoch.

NGA, *Berenson, 1979*: *Berenson and the Connoisseurship of Italian Painting,* National Gallery of Art, Washington, DC, 1979, handbook by David Alan Brown.

NGA, *English Drawings, 1962: An Exhibition of English Drawings and Watercolours from the Collection of Mr. and Mrs. Paul Mellon*, National Gallery of Art, Washington, DC, 1962.

NGA, *Jefferson, 1977: The Eye of Thomas Jefferson*, National Gallery of Art, Washington, DC, 1977, catalogue edited by William Howard Adams.

NGA, *Wright of Derby, 1969-70: Joseph Wright of Derby: A Selection of Paintings from the Collection of Mr. and Mrs. Paul Mellon*, National Gallery of Art, Washington, DC, 1969-70, catalogue by R. Watson.

NPG, *Master Drawings, 1993: Master Drawings from the National Portrait Gallery*, National Portrait Gallery, London, 1993 and tour, catalogue by Malcolm Rogers.

NPGUS, *West and His American Students, 1980: Benjamin West and His American Students*, National Portrait Gallery, Smithsonian Institution, Washington, DC, 1980, catalogue by Dorinda Evans.

NYPL, *Wordsworth, 1987-8: William Wordsworth and the Age of English Romanticism*, New York Public Library, Indiana University Art Museum, Bloomington, and Chicago Historical Society, 1987-8, catalogue by Jonathan Wordsworth, Michael C. Jaye, and Robert Woof.

PML, *English Drawings, 1972: English Drawings and Watercolors 1550-1850: in the Collection of Mr. and Mrs. Paul Mellon*, Pierpont Morgan Library, New York and Royal Academy, London, 1972, catalogue by John Baskett and Dudley Snelgrove.

PP, *Peinture Romantique, 1972: La Peinture Romantique anglais et les preraphaelites*, Petit Palais, Paris, 1972, catalogue introduction by Kenneth Clark.

RA, *The Great Age of British Watercolors, 1993: The Great Age of British Watercolors 1750-1880*, Royal Academy of Arts, London, and National Gallery of Art, Washington, DC, 1993, catalogue by Andrew Wilton and Anne Lyles.

RA, *Sir Thomas Lawrence, 1961: Sir Thomas Lawrence, PRA, 1769-1830*, Royal Academy of Arts, London, 1961.

RIBA, *Headfort House, 1973: Headfort House and Robert Adam: Drawings from the Collection of Mr. and Mrs. Paul Mellon*, Royal Institute of British Architects, London, 1973, catalogue by John Harris.

San Antonio, *Revealed Religion, 1983. Revealed Religion: Benjamin West's Commissions for Windsor Castle and Fonthill Abbey*, San Antonio Museum of Art, TX, 1983, catalogue by Nancy L. Pressly.

Smith College, *Romney, 1962: The Drawings of George Romney*, Smith College Museum of Art, Northampton, MA, 1962.

SNPG, *Cosway, 1995: Richard and Maria Cosway: Regency Artists of Taste and Fashion*, Scottish National Portrait Gallery, Edinburgh, and National Portrait Gallery, London, 1995, catalogue by Stephen Lloyd.

Tate, *Gainsborough, 1980-1: Thomas Gainsborough*, Tate Gallery, London, 1980-1, catalogue by John Hayes.

Tate, *Hogarth, 1971-2: Hogarth*, Tate Gallery, London, 1971-2, catalogue by Lawrence Gowing.

Tate, *Stubbs, 1976: George Stubbs, Anatomist and Animal Painter*, Tate Gallery, London, 1976, catalogue by Judy Egerton.

Tate, *Stubbs and Wedgwood, 1974: Stubbs and Wedgwood*, Tate Gallery, London, 1974, catalogue by Bruce Tattershall.

Tate, *Towne, 1997-8: Francis Towne*, Tate Gallery, London, and Leeds City Art Gallery, 1997-8, catalogue by Timothy Wilcox.

Tate, *William Blake, 1978: William Blake*, Tate Gallery, London, 1978, catalogue by Martin Butlin.

Tate-YCBA, *Stubbs, 1984-5: George Stubbs 1724-1806*, Tate Gallery, London, 1984-5, and Yale Center for British Art, New Haven, 1985, catalogue by Judy Egerton.

University of Missouri-Columbia, *British Comic Art, 1988: British Comic Art from the Yale Center for British Art*, Museum of Art and Archaeology, University of Missouri-Columbia, 1988, catalogue by Patricia Crown.

Victoria, *British Watercolour Drawings, 1971: British Watercolour Drawings in the Collection of Mr. and Mrs. Paul Mellon*, The Art Gallery of Greater Victoria, Canada, 1971.

VMFA, *Hogarth, 1967: William Hogarth*, Virginia Museum of Fine Arts, Richmond, 1967, catalogue edited by William Francis.

VMFA, *Painting in England, 1963: Painting in England 1700-1850: Collection of Mr. and Mrs. Paul Mellon*, Virginia Museum of Fine Arts, Richmond, 1963, catalogue by Basil Taylor.

Wash U, *Spirit of Antiquity, 1984: The Spirit of Antiquity: Giovanni Battista Piranesi, Robert Adam, and Charles-Louis Clérisseau*, Washington University Art Gallery, St. Louis, 1984, catalogue by Joni Kinsey, Laura Meyer, Michal Voligny, and Lucinda Wyeth.

YCBA, *Architectural Drawings, 1982. British Architectural Drawings*, Yale Center for British Art, New Haven, 1982, catalogue by Eric R. Wolterstorff.

YCBA, *Blake, 1982-3: William Blake: His Art and Times*, Yale Center for British Art, New Haven, and Art Gallery of Ontario, Toronto, 1982-3, catalogue by David Bindman.

YCBA, *Classic Ground, 1981: Classic Ground: British Artists and the Landscape of Italy, 1740-1830*, Yale Center for British Art, New Haven, 1981, catalogue by Duncan Bull, Linda Cabe and Peter Nisbet.

YCBA, *Country Houses, 1979: Country Houses in Great Britain*, Yale Center for British Art, New Haven, 1979, catalogue by Joy Breslauer, Ellen D'Oench, and Mary Spivy.

YCBA, *Cozens, 1980: The Art of Alexander and John Robert Cozens*, Yale Center for British Art, New Haven, 1980, catalogue by Andrew Wilton.

YCBA, *Crown Pictorial, 1990-1: Crown Pictorial: Art and the British Monarchy*, Yale Center for British Art, New Haven, 1990-1, catalogue by Duncan Robinson *et al.*

YCBA, *Devis*, 1980: *The Conversation Piece: Arthur Devis and His Contemporaries*, Yale Center for British Art, New Haven, 1980, catalogue by Ellen D'Oench.

YCBA, *English Caricature*, 1984: *English Caricature 1620 to the Present: Caricaturists and Satirists, their Art, their Purpose and Influence*, Yale Center for British Art, New Haven, Library of Congress, Washington DC, Victoria & Albert Museum, London, and National Gallery of Canada, Ottawa, 1984, catalogue by Richard T. Godfrey.

YCBA, *English Landscape*, 1977: *English Landscape 1630-1850: Drawings, Prints and Books from the Paul Mellon Collection*, Yale Center for British Art, New Haven, 1977, catalogue by Christopher White.

YCBA, *English Portrait Drawings*, 1979-80: *English Portrait Drawings and Miniatures*, Yale Center for British Art, New Haven, 1979, catalogue by Patrick Noon.

YCBA, *The Exhibition Watercolor*, 1981: *Works of Splendor and Imagination: The Exhibition Watercolor, 1770-1870*, Yale Center for British Art, New Haven, 1981, catalogue by Jane Bayard.

YCBA, *Fairest Isle*, 1989: *Fairest Isle: The Appreciation of British Scenery, 1750-1850*, Yale Center for British Art, New Haven, 1989.

YCBA, *Fifty Beautiful Drawings*, 1977: *Exhibition of Fifty Beautiful Drawings*, Yale Center for British Art, New Haven, 1977.

YCBA, *First Decade*, 1986: *Acquisitions: The First Decade, 1977-1986*, Yale Center for British Art, New Haven, 1986.

YCBA, *Fuseli Circle*, 1979: *The Fuseli Circle in Rome: Early Romantic Art of the 1770s*, Yale Center for British Art, New Haven, 1979, catalogue by Nancy L. Pressly.

YCBA, *Georgian Landscape Garden*, 1983. *The Early Georgian Landscape Garden*, Yale Center for British Art, New Haven, 1983, catalogue by Kimberly Rorschach.

YCBA, *Girtin*, 1986. *Thomas Girtin, 1775-1802*, Yale Center for British Art, New Haven, 1986, catalogue by Susan Morris.

YCBA, *Human Form Divine*, 1997: *The Human Form Divine: William Blake from the Paul Mellon Collection*, Yale Center for British Art, New Haven, 1997, catalogue by Patrick Noon.

YCBA, *Masters of the Sea*, 1987: *Masters of the Sea: British Marine Watercolours*, Yale Center for British Art, New Haven, and National Maritime Museum, Greenwich, 1987, catalogue by Roger Quarm and Scott Wilcox.

YCBA, *Oil on Water*, 1986: *Oil on Water: Oil Sketches by British Watercolorists*, Yale Center for British Art, New Haven, 1986, atalogue by Malcolm Cormack.

YCBA, *Painters and Engraving*, 1980: *Painters and Engraving: The Reproductive Print from Hogarth to Wilkie*, Yale Center for British Art, New Haven, 1980, catalogue by David Alexander and Richard T. Godfrey.

YCBA, *Pleasures and Pastimes*, 1990: *Pleasures and Pastimes*, Yale Center for British Art, New Haven, 1990, catalogue by Elisabeth Fairman.

YCBA, *Pope*, 1988. *The World of Alexander Pope*, Yale Center for British Art, 1988, catalogue by Maynard Mack.

YCBA, *Presences of Nature*, 1983: *Presences of Nature: British Landscape 1780-1830*, Yale Center for British Art, New Haven, 1983, catalogue by Louis Hawes.

YCBA, *Pursuit of Happiness*, 1977: *The Pursuit of Happiness: A View of Life in Georgian England*, Yale Center for British Art, New Haven, 1977, catalogue by J.H. Plumb, Edward J. Nygren and Nancy L. Pressly.

YCBA, *Romantic Vision*, 1995-6: *Romantic Vision: Responses to Change*, Yale Center for British Art, New Haven, 1995-6.

YCBA, *Rowlandson Drawings*, 1977-8: *Rowlandson Drawings from the Paul Mellon Collection*, Yale Center for British Art, New Haven, 1977, and Royal Academy of Arts, London, 1978, catalogue by John Riely.

YCBA, *Sandby*, 1985: *The Art of Paul Sandby*, Yale Center for British Art, New Haven, 1985, catalogue by Bruce Robertson.

YCBA, *Selections*, 1977: *Selected Paintings, Drawings, and Books*, Yale Center for British Art, New Haven, 1977.

YCBA, *Stubbs*, 1999; *George Stubbs in the Collection of Paul Mellon*, Yale Center for British Art, New Haven, 1999, and Virginia Museum of Fine Arts, Richmond, 2000.

YCBA, *Turner and Printmaking*, 1993: *Translations: Turner and Printmaking*, Yale Center for British Art, New Haven, 1993, catalogue by Eric M. Lee.

YCBA, *Vauxhall Gardens*, 1983: *Vauxhall Gardens*, Yale Center for British Art, New Haven, 1983, catalogue by T.J. Edelstein and Brian Allen.

YCBA, *Visionary Company*, 1997: *The Visionary Company: Blake's Contemporaries and Followers*, Yale Center for British Art, New Haven, 1997, checklist by Jessica Todd Smith.

YUAG, *Alumni*, 1960: *Paintings, Drawings and Sculpture Collected by Yale Alumni*, Yale University Art Gallery, New Haven, 1960.

Andrews, 1989: Malcolm Andrews, *The Search for the Picturesque: Landscape Aesthetics and Tourism in Britain, 1760-1800*, Aldershot, 1989.

Archer, 1980: Mildred Archer, *Early Views of India: The Picturesque Journeys of Thomas and William Daniell, 1786-1794*, London, 1980.

Aris, 1982: Michael Aris, *Views of Medieval Bhutan: The Diary and Drawings of Samuel Davis, 1783*, London, 1982.

Arts Council, Stubbs, 1958: *George Stubbs: Rediscovered Anatomical Drawings from the Free Public Library, Worcester, Massachusetts*, exh. cat., Arts Council of Great Britain, London, 1958.

Baetjer and Links, 1989: Katharine Baetjer and J.G. Links, *Canaletto*, exh. cat., Metropolitan Museum of Art, New York, 1989.

Barbier, 1963: C.P. Barbier, *William Gilpin: His Drawings, Teaching, and Theory of the Picturesque*, Oxford, 1963.

Baskett and Snelgrove, 1977: John Baskett and Dudley Snelgrove, *The Drawings of Thomas Rowlandson in the Paul Mellon Collection*, New York, 1977.

Bell and Girtin, 1935: C.F. Bell and T. Girtin, "The Drawings and Sketches of John Robert Cozens," *Walpole Society*, vol. 23 (1934-5), 1935.

Bindman, 1977: David Bindman, *Blake as an Artist*, Oxford, 1977.

Bindman, 1997: David Bindman, *Hogarth and his Times: Serious Comedy*, exh. cat., British Museum, London, 1997.

Bolton, 1924. Arthur T. Bolton, *The Works of Sir John Soane*, London, 1924.

Borenius, 1936: Tancred Borenius, *Catalogue of the Pictures and Drawings at Harewood House*, Oxford, 1936.

Brewer, 1997: John Brewer, *The Pleasures of the Imagination: English Culture in the Eighteenth Century*, London, 1997.

Brown, 1994: Frank S. Brown, *A Georgian Comedy of Manners: Humorous Watercolours of Life in Bath, the West Country and London by John Nixon (1750-1818)*, exh. cat., Holburne Museum and Crafts Study Centre, Bath, 1994.

Bryant, 1992: Julius Bryant, *Robert Adam, 1728-1792: Architect of Genius*, London, 1992.

Bull, 1981: Duncan Bull with Linda Cabe and Peter Nisbet, *Classic Ground: British Artists and the Landscape of Italy, 1740-1830*, exh. cat., Yale Center for British Art, New Haven, 1981.

Butlin, 1981: Martin Butlin, *The Paintings and Drawings of William Blake*, New Haven and London, 1981.

Calthorp, 1906: D.C. Calthorp, "Robert and Richard Dighton," *Connoisseur*, vol. 14, 1906, pp. 231-4.

Chamberlain, 1910: Arthur B. Chamberlain, *George Romney*, London, 1910.

Chessex, 1985: Pierre Chessex, *et al.*, *Images of the Grand Tour: Louis Ducros, 1748-1810*, exh. cat., The Iveagh Bequest, Kenwood, London, 1985.

Chippendale, 1754. Thomas Chippendale, *The Gentleman and Cabinet-Maker's Director*, London, 1754.

Chippendale, 1762. Thomas Chippendale, *The Gentleman and Cabinet-Maker's Director*, 3rd edition, London, 1762.

Clay, 1941: Rotha Mary Clay: *Samuel Hieronymous Grimm of Burgdorf in Switzerland*, London, 1941.

Clay, 1948: Rotha Mary Clay, *J.C. Ibbetson*, London, 1948.

Clifford and Legouix, 1976: Timothy Clifford and Susan Legouix, *The Rediscovery of an Artist: the Drawings of James Jefferys*, exh. cat., Victoria & Albert Museum, London, 1976.

Colvin *et al.*, 1980. Howard Colvin, J. Mordaunt Cooke, and Terry Friedman, eds. *Architectural Drawings from Lowther Castle, Westmoreland*, London, 1980.

Conner, 1981: Patrick Conner, *William Alexander: An English Artist in Imperial China*, exh. cat., The Royal Pavilion, Art Gallery and Museums, Brighton, and Nottingham University Art Gallery, 1981.

Conner, 1984: Patrick Conner, *Michael Angelo Rooker, 1746-1801*, London, 1984.

Connor, 1977: T. P. Connor, "The Making of *Vitruvius Britannicus*," *Architectural History*, vol. 20, 1977, pp. 14-30.

Constable, 1953: William G. Constable, *Richard Wilson*, London, 1953.

Constable, 1976: William G. Constable, *Canaletto: Giovanni Antonio Canal, 1697-1768*, 2nd edition, revised by J. G. Links, Oxford, 1976.

Cormack, 1983: Malcolm Cormack, *J.M.W. Turner, A Selection of Paintings and Watercolors in the Yale Center for British Art*, New Haven, 1983.

Croft-Murray, 1939: Edward Croft-Murray, "John Downman's 'Original First Studies of Distinguished Persons'," *Burlington Magazine*, vol. 14, 1939, pp. 60-6.

Croft-Murray, 1962-70: Edward Croft-Murray, *Decorative Painting in England, 1537-1837*, London, 1962-70.

Crookshank, 1978: Anne Crookshank, *The Painters of Ireland c. 1660-1920*, London, 1978.

Crookshank, 1994: Anne Crookshank and the Knight of Glin, *The Watercolours of Ireland: Works on Paper in Pencil, Pastel and Paint, c. 1600-1914*, London, 1994.

Crown, 1988: Patricia Crown, *British Comic Art from the Yale Center for British Art, 1730-1830*, exh. cat., Museum of Art and Archaeology, University of Missouri-Columbia, 1988.

Cullen, 1982: Fintan Cullen, "Hugh Douglas Hamilton in Rome, 1779-1792," Apollo, vol. 115, 1982, pp. 86-91.

Daniels, 1999: Stephen Daniels, *Humphry Repton: Landscape Gardening and the Geography of Georgian England*, New Haven and London, 1999.

Davies, 1924: Randall Davies, *Thomas Girtin's Watercolours*, London, 1924.

Dayes, 1971: Edward Dayes, *The Works of the Late Edward Dayes*, London, 1805, reprinted 1971.

Doherty, 1974: Terence Doherty, *The Anatomical Works of George Stubbs*, London, 1974.

Downes, 1987: Kerry Downes, *Sir John Vanbrugh: A Biography*, London, 1987.

Du Prey, 1972: Pierre de la Ruffinière du Prey, "John Soane's Architectural Education," Ph.D. diss., Princeton, 1972.

Edwards, 1970: Ralph Edwards, *Thomas Jones (1742-1803)*, exh. cat., Iveagh Bequest, Kenwood, London, 1970.

Egerton, 1970: Judy Egerton, "William Day 1764-1807," *The Connoisseur*, vol. 174, July 1970, pp. 176-85.

Egerton, 1974: Judy Egerton, "L.G. Duke and his Collection of Drawings," *The Old Water-Colour Society's Club*, vol. 49, 1974, pp.11-28.

Egerton, 1984: Judy Egerton, *George Stubbs, 1724-1806*, exh. cat., Tate Gallery, London, 1984.

Egerton, 1990: *Wright of Derby*, exh. cat., Tate Gallery, London, 1990.

Erffa and Staley, 1986. Helmut von Erffa and Allen Staley, *The Paintings of Benjamin West*, New Haven, 1986.

Esdaile, 1928: Katharine A. Esdaile, *The Life and Works of Louis-François Roubiliac*, London, 1928.

Essick and Belle, 1977: R.N. Essick and J. La Belle, eds., *Flaxman's Illustrations to Homer*, New York, 1977.

Eustace, 1982: Katharine Eustace, *Michael Rysbrack: Sculptor, 1694–1770*, exh. cat., Bristol Museum and Art Gallery, 1982.

Falk, 1949: Bernard Falk, *Thomas Rowlandson*, London, 1949.

Fleming, 1962: John Fleming, *Robert Adam and his Circle in Edinburgh and Rome*, London, 1962.

Fleming-Williams, 1968: Ian Fleming-Williams, "Drawing Masters," in Martin Hardie, ed., *Water-Colour Painting in Britain*, vol. 3, London, 1968, pp. 212-15.

Ford, 1948: Brinsley Ford, "The Dartmouth Collection of Drawings by Richard Wilson," *Burlington Magazine*, vol. 90, December 1948, pp. 337-45.

Ford, 1951: Brinsley Ford, *The Drawings of Richard Wilson*, London, 1951.

Ford, 1960: Brinsley Ford, "The Letters of Jonathan Skelton Written from Rome and Tivoli in 1758," *Walpole Society*, vol. 36 (1956-8), 1960, pp. 23-84.

Foskett, 1963: Daphne Foskett, *British Portrait Miniatures*, London, 1963.

Foskett, 1964: Daphne Foskett, *John Smart: the Man and his Miniatures*, London, 1964.

Friedman, 1976: W. Friedman, *Boydell's Shakespeare Gallery*, New York, 1976.

Friedman, 1984: Terry Friedman, *James Gibbs*, New Haven and London, 1984.

Gage, 1987: John Gage, *J.M.W. Turner: "A Wonderful Range of Mind,"* New Haven and London, 1987.

Garlick, 1964: Kenneth Garlick, "A Catalogue of the Paintings, Drawings and Pastels of Sir Thomas Lawrence," *Walpole Society*, vol. 39, 1964.

Garlick, 1968: Kenneth Garlick, "Lawrence's Portraits of the Locks, the Angersteins and the Boucherettes," *Burlington Magazine*, vol. 110, no. 789, December 1968, pp. 669-73.

Garlick, 1989: Kenneth Garlick, *Sir Thomas Lawrence: A Complete Catalogue of the Oil Paintings*, Oxford, 1989.

Garlick, 1993: Kenneth Garlick, *Sir Thomas Lawrence: Portraits of an Age*, exh. cat., Yale Center for British Art, New Haven, tour, 1993.

Geffrye Museum, 1972: *George Dance, the Elder 1695-1768, the Younger 1741-1825*, exh. cat., Geffrye Museum, London, 1972.

Gere, 1958: John A. Gere, "William Young Ottley as a Collector of Drawings," *The British Museum Quarterly*, June 1958, pp. 44-53.

Gibson-Wood, 1994: Carol Gibson-Wood, "Jonathan Richardson as a Draughtsman," *Master Drawings*, vol. 32, no.3, 1994, pp. 203-29.

Gibson-Wood, 2000: Carol Gibson-Wood, *Jonathan Richardson: Art Theorist of the English Enlightenment*, New Haven and London, 2000.

Gilbert, 1978: Christopher Gilbert, *The Life and Work of Thomas Chippendale*, 2 vols., London, 1978.

Gilchrist, 1863: Alexander Gilchrist, *The Life of William Blake*, London, 1863.

Girtin and Loshak, 1954: Thomas Girtin and David Loshak, *The Art of Thomas Girtin*, London, 1954.

Gowing, 1986: Lawrence Gowing, *The Originality of Thomas Jones*, New York, 1986.

Grundy, 1921: C. Reginald Grundy, "Documents Relating to an Action Brought Against Joseph Goupy in 1738," *Walpole Society*, vol. 4, 1921, pp. 77-87.

Grundy, 1933-8: C. Reginald Grundy, *A Catalogue of the Pictures and Drawings in the Collection of Frederick John Nettlefold*, 4 vols., London and Derby, 1933-8.

Guinness, 1982: Desmond Guinness, "Robert Healy, and Eighteenth-century Irish Sporting Artists," *Apollo*, vol. 115, February 1982, pp. 80-5.

Hammelmann and Boase, 1975: H. Hammelmann and T.S.R. Boase, *Book Illustrators in Eighteenth-Century England*, New Haven and London, 1975.

Hamlyn and Phillips, 2000: Robin Hamlyn and Michael Phillips, *William Blake*, exh. cat., Tate Britain, London, 2000.

Hardie, 1967-8: Martin Hardie, *Water-colour Painting in Britain*, Dudley Snelgrove, ed., with Jonathan Mayne and Basil Taylor, 3 vols., London, 1967-8.

Harris, 1970: John Harris, *Sir William Chambers: Knight of the Polar Star*, with J. Mordaunt Cooke and Eileen Harris, College Park, PA, 1970.

Harris, 1973: John Harris, *Headfort House and Robert Adam: Drawings from the Collection of Mr. and Mrs. Paul Mellon*, exh. cat., Royal Institute of British Architects, London, 1973.

Harris, 1985: John Harris, *The Architect and the British Country House, 1620-1920*, exh. cat., American Institute of Architects, Washington DC, 1985.

Harris, 1986. John Harris, "William Kent's Drawings at Yale and Some Imperfect Ideas upon the Subject of His Drawing Style," in *Essays in Honor of Paul Mellon, Collector and Benefactor*, ed. John Wilmerding, Washington DC, 1986.

Harris, 1990: Eileen Harris, *British Architectural Books and Writers 1556-1785*, Cambridge, 1990.

Harris, 1991: John Harris, "A Carlton House Miscellany: William Kent and Carlton House Garden," *Apollo*, October 1991, pp. 251-3.

Harris and Snodin, 1996: John Harris and Michael Snodin, eds., *Sir William Chambers: Architect to George III*, New Haven and London, 1996.

Hauptman, 1996: William Hauptman, *John Webber, 1751-1793, Pacific Voyager and Landscape Artist*, exh. cat., Kunstmuseum, Bern, and Whitworth Art Gallery, Manchester, 1996.

Hawcroft, 1971: Francis Hawcroft, *Watercolors by John Robert Cozens*, exh. cat., Whitworth Art Gallery, Manchester, and Victoria & Albert Museum, London, 1971.

Hawcroft, 1988: Francis Hawcroft, *Travels in Italy, 1776-1783, Based on the "Memoirs" of Thomas Jones*, exh. cat., Whitworth Art Gallery, Manchester, 1988.

Hayes, 1971: John Hayes, *The Drawings of Thomas Gainsborough*, New Haven and London, 1971.

Hayes, 1972: John Hayes, *Rowlandson Watercolours and Drawings*, London, 1972.

Hayes, 1983: John Hayes, *Gainsborough Drawings*, exh. cat., National Gallery of Art, Washington DC, 1983.

Hayes, 1990: John Hayes, *The Art of Thomas Rowlandson*, exh. cat., Frick Collection, New York; Frick Collection, Pittsburgh, and Baltimore Museum of Art, 1990.

Herrmann, 1986: Luke Herrmann, *Paul and Thomas Sandby*, London, 1986.

Hill, 1999: David Hill, *Thomas Girtin: Genius in the North*, exh. cat., Harewood House, Leeds, 1999.

Holbrook, 1973: M. Holbrook, "Painters in Bath in the Eighteenth Century," *Apollo*, vol. 98, November 1973, pp. 375-84.

Howgego, 1956: James L. Howgego, *William Marlow*, exh. cat., Guildhall Art Gallery, London, 1956.

Hulton, Hepper and Friis, 1991: Paul Hulton, F. Nigel Hepper and Ib Friis, *Luigi Balugani's Drawings of African Plants*, New Haven and Rotterdam, 1991.

Hyde, 1994: Ralph Hyde, *A Prospect of Britain: The Town Panoramas of Samuel and Nathaniel Buck*, London, 1994.

Ingamells, 1997: John Ingamells, *A Dictionary of British and Irish Travellers in Italy, 1701-1800 compiled from the Brinsley Ford Archive*, London and New Haven, 1997.

Irwin, 1962: David Irwin, "Gavin Hamilton: Archaelogist, Painter, and Dealer," *Art Bulletin*, vol. 64, 1962, pp. 87-102.

Irwin, 1975: David and Francina Irwin, *Scottish Painters at Home and Abroad, 1700-1910*, London, 1975.

Irwin, 1979: David Irwin, *John Flaxman, 1755-1826, Sculptor, Illustrator, Designer*, New York, 1979.

Jacobus, 1988. Laura Jacobus, "On 'Whether a man could see before him and behind him both at once': The role of drawing in the design of interior space in England c. 1600-1800," *Architectural History*, vol. 31, 1998, pp. 148-59.

Johnson, 1976: Edward Johnson, *Francis Cotes*, Oxford, 1976.

Joppien, 1973: Rüdiger Joppien, *Philippe Jacques de Loutherbourg, RA, 1740-1812*, exh. cat., Iveagh Bequest, Kenwood, London, 1973.

Joppien and Smith, 1985-8: Rüdiger Joppien and Bernard Smith, *The Art of Captain Cook's Voyages*, New Haven and London, 1985-8.

Kapp, 1972: Helen Kapp, *Daniel Gardner, 1750-1805*, exh. cat., Iveagh Bequest, Kenwood, London, 1972.

Kerslake, 1977: John F. Kerslake, *Early Georgian Portraits*, National Portrait Gallery, London, 1977.

Keynes, 1971: Geoffrey Keynes, *William Blake's Water-Colour Designs for the Poems of Thomas Gray*, London, 1971.

Kraemer, 1975. Ruth Kraemer, *Drawings by Benjamin West and his Son, Raphael Lamar West*, New York, 1975.

Legouix, 1980: Susan Legouix, *Image of China: William Alexander*, London, 1980.

Legouix and Conner, 1981: Susan Legouix and Patrick Conner, *William Alexander: An English Artist in Imperial China*, exh. cat., The Royal Pavilion, Art Gallery and Museums, Brighton, and Nottingham University Art Gallery, 1981.

Lennox-Boyd, Dixon and Clayton, 1989: Christopher Lennox-Boyd, Rob Dixon and Tim Clayton, *George Stubbs: The Complete Engraved Works*, London, 1989.

Levey, 1979: Michael Levey, *Thomas Lawrence, 1769–1830*, exh. cat., National Portrait Gallery, London, 1979.

Little, 1955: Bryan Little, *The Life and Work of James Gibbs*, London, 1955.

Liversidge and Farrington, 1993: Michael Liversidge and Jane Farrington, *Canaletto and England*, exh. cat., Birmingham Museums and Art Gallery, 1993.

Lloyd, 1995: Stephen Lloyd, *Richard and Maria Cosway: Regency Artists of Taste and Fashion*, exh. cat., Scottish National Portrait Gallery, Edinburgh, 1995.

Logan, 1986: Anne-Marie Logan, "Bernard Lens the Younger and the Marlborough Collection," in *Essays in Honor of Paul Mellon, Collector and Benefactor*, ed. John Wilmerding, Washington DC, 1986, pp. 203-15.

Long, 1929: Basil S. Long, *British Miniaturists*, London, 1929.

McParland, 1985: Edward McParland, *James Gandon: Vitruvius Hibernicus*, London, 1985.

Malton, 1792. Thomas Malton, *A Picturesque Tour through the Cities of London and Westminster*, London, 1792.

Mayne, 1949: Jonathan Mayne, *Thomas Girtin*, Leigh-on-Sea, 1949.

Mitchell, 1999: James Mitchell, *Julius Caesar Ibbetson, 1759-1817, "The Berchem of England,"* London, 1999.

Morris, 1986: Susan Morris, *Thomas Girtin, 1775-1802*, exh. cat., Yale Center for British Art, New Haven, 1986.

Morris, 1989: David Morris, Thomas Hearne and His Landscape, London, 1989.

Morris and Milner, 1985: David Morris and Barbara Milner, *Thomas Hearne, 1744-1817: Watercolours and Drawings*, exh. cat., Bolton Museum and Art Gallery, 1985.

Murdoch, 1983: Tessa Murdoch, "Louis François Roubiliac and his Huguenot Connections," *Proceedings of the Huguenot Society of London*, 1983, pp. 26-45.

Murdoch, 1985: Tessa Murdoch, *The Quiet Conquest: The Huguenots, 1685 to 1985*, exh. cat., Museum of London, 1985.

Murdoch, Murrell and Noon, 1981: John Murdoch, Jim Murrell, and Patrick Noon, *The English Miniature*, London, 1981.

Neff, 1995: E.B. Neff, *John Singleton Copley in England*, exh. cat., Museum of Fine Arts, Houston, TX, 1995.

Newby, 1990: Evelyn Newby, *William Hoare of Bath, 1707-1792*, exh. cat., Victoria Art Gallery, Bath, 1990.

Nicolson, 1968 (1): Benedict Nicholson, *John Hamilton Mortimer, ARA: 1740-1779*, exh. cat., Paul Mellon Foundation for British Art, 1968.

Nicolson, 1968 (2): Benedict Nicolson, *Joseph Wright of Derby: Painter of Light*, 2 vols., London, 1968.

Noon, 1979: Patrick Noon, *English Portrait Drawings and Miniatures*, exh. cat., Yale Center for British Art, New Haven, 1979.

Noon, 1997: Patrick Noon, *The Human Form Divine*, exh. cat., Yale Center for British Art, New Haven, 1997.

Olsen and Pasachoff, 1998: Roberta J.M. Olsen and Jay M. Pasachoff, *Fire in the Sky: Comets and Meteors, the Decisive Centuries, in British Art and Science*, Cambridge, 1998.

Oppé, 1920: A. P. Oppé, "Francis Towne, Landscape Painter," *Walpole Society*, vol. 8 (1919-20), 1920, pp. 95-126.

Oppé, 1924: A. P. Oppé, "The Fourth Earl of Aylesford," *Print Collector's Quarterly*, vol. 2, 1924, pp. 262-92.

Oppé, 1928: A. P. Oppé, "A Roman Sketch-book by Alexander Cozens," *Walpole Society*, vol. 16 (1927-8), 1928, pp. 81-93.

Oppé, 1946: A. P. Oppé, *Drawings and Paintings by Alexander Cozens*, exh. cat., Tate Gallery, London, 1946.

Oppé, 1947: A. P. Oppé, *The Drawings of Paul and Thomas Sandby in the Collection of His Majesty the King at Windsor Castle*, London, 1947.

Oppé, 1948: A.P. Oppé, *The Drawings of William Hogarth*, London, 1948.

Oppé, 1951: A.P. Oppé, "Memoirs of Thomas Jones," *Walpole Society*, vol. 32 (1946-8), 1951.
Oppé, 1952: A. P. Oppé, *Alexander and John Robert Cozens*, 1952.

Osmun, 1950: William Raymond Osmun, *A Study of the Work of Sir James Thornhill*, London, 1950.

Parissien, 1992: Steven Parissien, *Adam Style*, Washington DC, 1992.

Paulson, 1972: Ronald Paulson, *Rowlandson: A New Interpretation*, New York, 1972.

Paulson, 1992-3: Ronald Paulson, *Hogarth*, 3 vols., New Brunswick and Cambridge, 1992-3.

Pierce, 1960: S. Rowland Pierce, "Jonathan Skelton and His Watercolours," *Walpole Society*, vol. 36 (1956-8), 1960, pp. 10-22.

Plumb, 1975: J.H. Plumb, *The First Four Georges*, London, 1975.

Praz, 1971: Mario Praz, *Conversation Pieces*, University Park, PA, 1971.

Pressly, 1979: Nancy L. Pressly, *The Fuseli Circle in Rome: Early Romantic Art of the 1770s*, exh. cat., Yale Center for British Art, New Haven, 1979.

Prown, 1966. Jules Prown, *John Singleton Copley in England*, Washington DC, 1966.

Rebora, 1995: Carrie Rebora, *John Singleton Copley in America*, exh. cat., Metropolitan Museum of Art, New York, 1995.

Reynolds, 1952: Graham Reynolds, *English Portrait Miniatures*, London, 1952.

Ribeiro, 1984: Aileen Ribeiro, *A Visual History of Costume: The Eighteenth Century*, London, 1984.

Richardson and Stevens, 1999: Margaret Richardson and MaryAnne Stevens, eds., *John Soane, Architect: Master of Space and Light*, exh. cat., Royal Academy of Arts, London, 1999.

Riely, 1978: John Riely, *Rowlandson Drawings from the Paul Mellon Collection*, exh. cat., Yale Center for British Art, New Haven, 1978.

Roberts, 1995: Jane Roberts, *Views of Windsor: Watercolours by Thomas and Paul Sandby from the Collection of Her Majesty Queen Elizabeth II*, London, 1995.

Robertson, 1985: Bruce Robertson, *The Art of Paul Sandby*, exh. cat., Yale Center for British Art, New Haven, 1985.

Rogers, 1993: Malcolm Rogers, *Master Drawings from the National Portrait Gallery*, exh. cat., National Portrait Gallery, London, 1993.

Rohr, 1998: Alheidis von Rohr, *Johann Heinrich Ramberg*, exh. cat., Historisches Museum, Hannover, 1998.

Rose, 1981: Dennis Rose, *The Life, Times and Recorded Works of Robert Dighton (1752-1814): Actor, Artist and Printseller*, Salisbury, 1981.

Ryan, 1966: W. F. Ryan, "John Russell, R.A., and Early Lunar Mapping," *The Smithsonian Journal of History*, vol. 1, 1966, pp. 27-48.

Salomons, 1911: V. Salomons, Gravelot, London, 1911.

Sidey, 1980: Tessa Sidey, *Amelia Long, Lady Farnborough, 1772–1837*, exh. cat., Dundee Art Gallery, 1980.

Simon, 1985: Jacob Simon, ed., *Handel: A Celebration of his Life and Times, 1685-1759*, exh. cat., National Portrait Gallery, London, 1985.

Sloan, 1986: Kim Sloan, *Alexander and John Robert Cozens: The Poetry of Landscape*, New Haven, 1986.

Sloan, 2000: Kim Sloan, *"A Noble Art": Amateur Artists and Drawings Masters, c. 1600-1800*, exh. cat., British Museum, London, 2000.

Smart, 1992 (1): Alastair Smart, *Allan Ramsay, 1713-1784*, exh. cat., Scottish National Portrait Gallery, Edinburgh, 1992.

Smart, 1992 (2): *Allan Ramsay: Painter, Essayist, and Man of the Enlightenment*, New Haven and London, 1992.

Smart, 1999: Alastair Smart, *Allan Ramsay: A Complete Catalogue of his Paintings*, ed. John Ingamells, New Haven and London, 1999.

Solkin, 1982: David Solkin, *Richard Wilson: The Landscape of Reaction*, exh. cat., Tate Gallery, London, 1982.

Spadafora, 1990. David Spadafora, *The Idea of Progress in Eighteenth Century Britain*, New Haven, 1990.

Stainton, 1975: Lindsay Stainton, *British Artists in Rome*, exh. cat., Iveagh Bequest, Kenwood, London, 1975.

Stainton and White, 1987: Lindsay Stainton and Christopher White, *Drawing in England: from Hilliard to Hogarth*, exh. cat., British Museum, London, 1987.

Staley, 1989: Allen Staley, *Benjamin West: American Painter at the English Court*, exh. cat., Baltimore Museum of Art, MD, 1989.

Steegman, 1958: John Steegman, "Some Reynolds Problems," *Art Quarterly*, vol. 21, 1958, pp. 246-56.

Stewart, 1989: Philip Stewart, "On the 'Iconology' of Literary Illustration," in *Dilemmes du roman: Essays in Honor of Georges May*, ed. Catherine Lafarge, Stanford French and Italian Studies, no. 65, Saratoga, CA, 1989, pp. 251-67.

Stroud, 1961: Dorothy Stroud, *The Architecture of Sir John Soane*, London, 1961.

Stroud, 1966: Dorothy Stroud, *Henry Holland: His Life and Architecture*, London, 1966.

Stroud, 1971: Dorothy Stroud, *George Dance, Architect, 1741-1825*, London, 1971.

Stroud, 1984: Dorothy Stroud, *Sir John Soane: Architect*, London, 1984.

Stutchbury, 1967: Howard E. Stutchbury, *The Architecture of Colen Campbell*, Manchester, 1967.

Stuttmann, 1929: F. Stuttmann, *Johann Heinrich Ramberg*, Hannover, 1929.

Sunderland, 1970: John Sunderland, "John Hamilton Mortimer and Salvator Rosa," *Burlington Magazine*, vol. 112, August 1970, pp. 520-30.

Sunderland, 1977: John Sunderland, "Two self-portraits by James Jeffreys?," *Burlington Magazine*, vol. 119, April 1977, pp. 279-80.

Sunderland, 1988: John Sunderland, "John Hamilton Mortimer: His Life and Works," *Walpole Society* (1986), 1988, vol. 52.

Sutton, 1954: Thomas Sutton, *The Daniells: Artists and Travellers*, London, 1954.

Sutton, 1968: Denys Sutton, ed., *An Italian Sketchbook by Richard Wilson, RA*, London, 1968.

Sutton, 1977: Denys Sutton, "The Cunning Eye of Thomas Rowlandson," *Apollo*, vol. 105, April 1977, pp. 277-85.

Symmons, 1984: Sarah Symmons, *Flaxman and Europe: The Outline Illustrators and their Influence*, New York, 1984.

Tait, 1993: A.A. Tait, *Robert Adam: Drawings and Imagination*, New York, 1993.

Tayler, 1971: Irene Tayler, *Blake's Illustrations to the Poems of Gray*, Princeton, 1971.

Taylor, 1965: Basil Taylor, "Portraits of George Stubbs," *Apollo*, vol. 81, May 1965, supplement between pp. 422 and 423.

Townsend, 1996: Joyce Townsend, *Turner's Painting Techniques*, 2nd edition, exh. cat., Tate Gallery, London, 1996.

Uglow, 1997: Jenny Uglow, *Hogarth: A Life and a World*, London and New York, 1997.

Vaughan, 1996: Frank A. Vaughan, *Again to the Life of Eternity: William Blake's Illustrations to the Poems of Thomas Gray*, Selinsgrove and London, 1996.

Vertue, 1740: George Vertue, *Description of Four Ancient Paintings, Being Historical Portraitures of Royal Branches of the Crown of England*, 1740.

Victoria & Albert Museum, 1984: *Rococo: Art and Design in Hogarth's England*, exh. cat., Victoria & Albert Museum, London, 1984.

Ward and Roberts, 1904: Humphrey Ward and W. Roberts: *Romney: A Biographical and Critical Essay, with a Catalogue Raisonné of his Works*, 2 vols., London, 1904.

Wark, 1970: Robert Wark, *The Drawings of George Romney*, Alhambra, CA, 1970.

Wark, 1975: Robert Wark, *Drawings by Thomas Rowlandson in the Huntington Collection*, San Marino, 1975.

Warner, 1979-80: M. Warner, "Queen Victoria as an Artist," *Royal Society of Arts Journal*, vol. 128, no. 5287, 1979-80, pp. 421-36.

Waterhouse, 1958: Ellis K. Waterhouse, *Gainsborough*, London, 1958.

Waterhouse, 1962: Ellis K. Waterhouse, "Some Notes on William Young Ottley's Collection of Italian Primitives," *Italian Studies*, vol. 1962, pp. 272-80.

Watkin, 1996: David Watkin, *Sir John Soane: Enlightenment, Thought, and the Royal Academy Lectures*, Cambridge, 1996.

Watson, 1940: F. J. B. Watson, "Thomas Patch (1725-1782): Notes on his Life," *Walpole Society*, vol. 28 (1939-40), 1940, pp. 16-50.

Watson, 1967: F. J. B. Watson, "Thomas Patch: Some New Light on his Work," *Apollo*, vol. 85, 1967, pp. 348-53.

Webb, 1954: Marjorie Isabel Webb, *Michael Rysbrack: Sculptor*, London, 1954.

Webster, 1970: Mary Webster, *Francis Wheatley*, London, 1970.

Westall, 1984: Richard J. Westall, "The Westall Brothers," *Turner Studies*, vol. 4, no. 1, 1984, pp. 23-38.

Williamson, 1894: G.C. Williamson, *John Russell, R.A.*, London, 1894.

Williamson, 1903: G.C. Williamson, *Andrew and Nathaniel Plimer, Miniature Painters, Their Lives and Their Works*, London, 1903.

Williamson, 1905: G.C. Williamson, *Richard Cosway, R.A.*, London, 1905.

Williamson, 1907: G.C. Williamson, *John Downman, A.R.A.*, London, 1907.

Williamson, 1918: G.C. Williamson, *The Life and Works of Ozias Humphry, R.A.*, London, 1918.

Williamson, 1921: G.C. Williamson, *Daniel Gardner, Painter in Pastel and Gouache: A Brief Account of His Life and Works*, London and New York, 1921.

Williamson and Engleheart, 1902: G.C. Williamson and Henry L. D. Engleheart, *George Engleheart*, London, 1902.

Wilson, 1984: Michael I. Wilson, *William Kent: Architect, Designer, Painter, Gardener*, London, 1984.

Wilton, 1977: Andrew Wilton, *British Watercolours 1750-1850*, Oxford, 1977.

Wilton, 1979: Andrew Wilton, *J.M.W. Turner, His Art and Life*, New York, 1979.

Wilton, 1980: Andrew Wilton, *The Art of Alexander and John Robert Cozens*, exh. cat., Yale Center for British Art, New Haven, 1980.

Wilton-Ely, 1985: John Wilton-Ely, ed., *A Tercentenary Tribute to William Kent*, exh. cat., Ferens Art Gallery, Hull, 1985.

Woodall, 1939: Mary Woodall, *Gainsborough's Landscape Drawings*, London, 1939.

Ziff, 1970: Norman D. Ziff, "Mortimer's 'Death on a Pale Horse'," *Burlington Magazine*, vol. 112 , August 1970, pp. 531-5.

Zoller, 1996: Olga Zoller, *Der Architekt und der Ingenieur Giovanni Battista Borra (1713-1770)*, Bamberg, 1996.

ARCHITECTURE

Ayres, James, *Building the Georgian City*, New Haven and London, 1998.

Crinson, Mark and Jules Lubbock, *Architecture: Art or Profession? Three Hundred Years of Architectural Education in Britain*, Manchester, 1995.

Harris, John, *The Architect and the British Country House, 1620-1920*, exh. cat., American Institute of Architects, Washington, DC, 1985.

Harris, John, *The Palladians*, London, 1981.

Jackson-Stops, Gervase, ed. *The Fashioning and Functioning of the British Country House*, Washington, DC, 1989.

Lever, Jill, and Margaret Richardson, *Great Drawings from the Collection of the Royal Institute of British Architects*, exh. cat, Drawing Center, New York, 1983.

Lever, Jill and Margaret Richardson, *The Art of the Architect: Treasures of the RIBA's Collections*, London, 1984.

Parissien, Steven, *Adam Style*, Washington DC, 1992.

Parissien, Steven, *Palladian Style*, London, 1994.

Worsley, Giles, *Classical Architecture in Britain: the Heroic Age*, New Haven and London, 1995.

ART, LIFE AND CULTURE IN EIGHTEENTH-CENTURY BRITAIN

Allen, Brian, ed., *Towards a Modern Art World*, Studies in British Art, vol. 1, New Haven and London, 1995.

Brewer, John, *The Pleasures of the Imagination: English Culture in the Eighteenth Century*, Chicago, 1997.

Brewer, John, and Roy Porter, eds, *The Consumption of Culture 1600-1800: Image, Object, Text*, London and New York, 1995.

Lipking, Lawrence, *The Ordering of the Arts in Eighteenth-Century England*, Princeton, 1970.

Lippincott, Louise, *Selling Art in Georgian England: The Rise of Arthur Pond*, New Haven and London, 1983.

McKendrick, Neil, John Brewer and J.H. Plumb, *The Birth of a Consumer Society: The Commercialization of Eighteenth-Century England*, London, 1982.

Pears, Iain, *The Discovery of Painting: The Growth in the Interest in the Arts in England, 1680-1768*, New Haven and London, 1988.

Plumb, J.H., *The Pursuit of Happiness: A View of Life in Georgian England*, exh. cat., Yale Center for British Art, New Haven, 1977.

Porter, Roy, *Enlightenment: Britain and the Creation of the Modern World*, London, 2000.

Solkin, David H., *Painting for Money: The Visual Arts and the Public Sphere in Eighteenth-Century England*, New Haven and London, 1993.

BRITISH DRAWINGS AND WATERCOLORS

Baskett, John and Dudley Snelgrove, *English Drawings and Watercolours, 1550-1850, in the Collection of Mr. and Mrs Paul Mellon*, exh. cat., Pierpont Morgan Library, New York and Royal Academy of Arts, London, 1972.

Bayard, Jane, *Works of Splendor and Imagination: The Exhibition Watercolor, 1770-1870*, exh. cat., Yale Center for British Art, New Haven, 1981.

Hardie, Martin, *Watercolour Painting in Britain*, 3 vols., ed. Dudley Snelgrove with Jonathan Mayne and Basil Taylor, London, 1966-8.

Lyles, Anne, and Robin Hamlyn, *British Watercolours from the Oppé Collection*, exh. cat., Tate Gallery, London, 1997.

Quarm, Roger, and Scott Wilcox, *Masters of the Sea: British Marine Watercolours*, exh. cat., National Maritime Museum, Greenwich, and Yale Center for British Art, New Haven, 1987.

Stainton, Lindsay, and Christopher White, *Drawing in England from Hilliard to Hogarth*, exh. cat., British Museum, London, and Yale Center for British Art, New Haven, 1987.

White, Christopher, *English Landscape, 1630-1850: Drawings, Prints and Books from the Paul Mellon Collection*, exh. cat., Yale Center for British Art, New Haven, 1977.

Wilcox, Scott, *British Watercolors: Drawings of the 18th and 19th Centuries from the Yale Center for British Art*, exh. cat., Yale Center for British Art, New Haven, 1985.

Wilton, Andrew, and Anne Lyles, *The Great Age of British Watercolours, 1750-1880*, exh. cat., Royal Academy, London, 1993.

DRAWING TECHNIQUES AND MATERIALS

Cohn, Marjorie B., *Wash and Gouache: A Study of the Development of the Materials of Watercolor*, exh. cat., Fogg Art Museum, Cambridge, MA, 1977.

Goldman, Paul, *Looking at Prints and Watercolors: A Guide to Technical Terms*, Malibu, CA and London, 1988.

Hambly, Maya, *Drawing Instruments 1580-1980*, London, 1988.

Hunter, Herbert, *Drawing: History and Technique*, New York, 1968.

Krill, John, *English Artists Paper: Renaissance to Regency*, London, 1987.

Lambert, Susan, *Drawing Technique and Purpose: An Introduction to Looking at Drawings*, London, 1984.

Petroski, Henry, *The Pencil*, New York, 1990.

Rawson, Philip, *Drawing*, 2nd edn, Philadelphia, 1987.

THE GRAND TOUR

Black, Jeremy, *The British Abroad: The Grand Tour in the Eighteenth Century*, Gloucester and New York, 1992.

Bull, Duncan, *Classic Ground: British Artists and the Landscape of Italy, 1740-1830*, exh. cat., Yale Center for British Art, New Haven, 1981.

Ingamells, John, *A Dictionary of British Travellers in Italy, 1701-1800*, New Haven and London, 1997.

Wilton, Andrew, and Ilaria Bignamini, eds, *Grand Tour: The Lure of Italy in the Eighteenth Century*, exh. cat., Tate Gallery, London, 1996.

LANDSCAPE AND AESTHETIC THEORY

Andrews, Malcolm, *The Search for the Picturesque: Landscape Aesthetics and Tourism in Britain 1760-1800*, Aldershot, 1989.

Barrell, John, *The Dark Side of the Landscape: The Rural Poor in English Painting, 1730-1840*, Cambridge, 1980.

Bermingham, Ann, *Landscape and Ideology*, Berkeley, 1986.

Cosgrove, Denis, and Stephen Daniels, *The Iconography of Landscape*, Cambridge, England, 1988.

Parris, Leslie, *Landscape in Britain, c. 1750-1850*, exh. cat., Tate Gallery, London, 1974.

METROPOLITAN LIFE

Byrd, Max, *London Transformed: Images of the City in the Eighteenth Century*, New Haven, 1978.

Porter, Roy, *London: A Social History*, London, 1994.

PORTRAITURE

Murdoch, John, *The English Miniature*, New Haven and London, 1981.

Noon, Patrick J., *English Portrait Drawings and Miniatures*, exh. cat., Yale Center for British Art, New Haven, 1979.

Pointon, Marcia, *Hanging the Head: Portraiture and Social Formation in Eighteenth-Century England*, New Haven and London, 1993.

Pointon, Marcia, "'Surrounded with Brilliants:' Miniature Portraits in Eighteenth-Century England," *Art Bulletin,* vol. 83, no. 1, March 2001, pp. 48-71.

Shawe-Taylor, Desmond, *The Georgians: Eighteenth-Century Portraiture and Society*, London, 1990.

Shawe-Taylor, Desmond, *Dramatic Art: Theatrical Paintings from the Garrick Club*, exh. cat., Dulwich Picture Gallery, London, 1997.

Wendorf, Richard, *The Elements of Life: Biography and Portrait-Painting in Stuart and Georgian England*, Oxford, 1990.

THE PRACTICE OF DRAWING IN THE EIGHTEENTH CENTURY

Bermingham, Ann, *Learning to Draw: Studies in the Cultural History of a Polite and Useful Art*, New Haven and London, 2000.

Bicknell, Peter and Jane Munro, *Gilpin to Ruskin: Drawing Masters and their Manuals, 1800-1860*, exh. cat., Fitzwilliam Museum, Cambridge, and Dove Cottage and Wordsworth Museum, Grasmere, 1987.

Sloan, Kim, *"A Noble Art": Amateur Artists and Drawing Masters, c. 1600-1800*, exh. cat., British Museum, London, 2000.

References are to catalogue numbers.